CONVERSION AND DISCIPLESHIP

STEPHEN HAPPEL & JAMES J. WALTER

CONVERSION AND DISCIPLESHIP

A CHRISTIAN FOUNDATION FOR ETHICS AND DOCTRINE

Fortress Press   Philadelphia

Library of Congress Cataloging-in-Publication Data

Happel, Stephen, 1944–
  Conversion and discipleship.

  1. Christian ethics—Catholic authors. 2. Theology.
3. Conversion. 4. Christian life—Catholic authors.
I. Walter, James J. II. Title.
BJ1249.H355 1985   241   85–45499
ISBN 0–8006–1908–0

1820L85   Printed in the United States of America   1–1908

CONTENTS

Part Four:
Dialogical Structures of Conversion:
A Constructive Future

ACKNOWLEDGMENTS

We thank *Eglise et Théologie* for publishing "The Foundations of Christian Moral Experience," an earlier and partial version of chapter 2. Gratitude is owed to MaryAnne Walter for her encouragement throughout the research and writing of this book and for her culinary talents, which provided many occasions for the sharing of friendship and ideas. We thank Mark O'Keefe, O.S.B., for carefully preparing the index.

All thoughtful projects have a prior intellectual history, and by remembering that past we can participate anew in the opportunities given to us. Nearly a decade and a half ago, one man gave both of us our first chance to dare to teach others about Christian faith and morality. What then began separately and in different classrooms we now attempt together. It is with thanksgiving that we dedicate this project to Walter J. Schmitz, S.S., our former Dean and now Professor Emeritus at The Catholic University of America.

Thanksgiving, 1984

INTRODUCTION. WHAT IS FOUNDATIONAL THEOLOGY?

To examine the nature of foundational theology, we begin with stories and sayings. A tragedy in the life of a young couple, a modern parable, and one of the sayings of Jesus focus for us the kind of theology we propose to investigate.

A young couple had two children both of whom were precocious, but the elder daughter was everyone's special child. This three-year-old girl became ill, and the local doctor diagnosed the problem as flu. When the child's temperature had not significantly decreased, alternately higher then lower than normal, a specialist was called. As the child began to slip into coma, the medical personnel diagnosed Rocky Mountain spotted fever, a disease that is normally fatal in only five percent of cases. The girl's brain died before her heart. At the wake, the young couple were asked to give some memory of what they held especially dear about the child. They did so, haltingly. At the end, they thanked everyone for coming to share their grief. They could only say, "I guess God loved her more than we could."

A parable is told about the resistance movement of an occupied country in time of war. One evening, a member of the resistance meets a stranger who deeply impresses him. During a night of conversation, the stranger confides that he is on the same side as the partisan. He announces that he is in charge of the resistance even if it does not always look that way, and he requests the trust of the partisan. And though they never meet again in a situation like the one that night, the partisan believes the stranger. Sometimes he sees the man on the side of the resistance, and he tells his friends that they have a strong leader on their side; but at other times, he sees him acting in the uniform of the police, handing over patriots to the occupying power. When this happens, his friends complain that he is being duped, but the partisan insists, "He is on our side." Finally in exasperation, his friends ask, "Well, what would he

1

have to do for you to admit that you were wrong and that he is not on our side?" But the partisan will not put the stranger to the test.[1]

Finally, there are sayings of Jesus of Nazareth recorded in the Gospel According to Matthew (5:43–47 NEB): "You have learned that they were told: 'Love your neighbor, hate your enemy.' But what I tell you is this: Love your enemies and pray for your persecutors; only so can you be children of your heavenly Father, who makes his sun rise on the good and bad alike and sends the rain on the just and the unjust. If you love only those who love you, what reward can you expect? Surely the tax-gatherers do as much as that. And if you greet only your brothers, what is there extraordinary about that? Even the heathen do as much. There must be no limit to your goodness, as your heavenly Father's goodness knows no bounds."

These three passages, particularly when juxtaposed, put various questions to us. The first story places us, along with the couple, in a simple existential predicament, the death of someone deeply loved. Despite an enormous hole driven into their lives, the couple continues to offer love. Why would anyone continue to love from within the pain and suffering of the innocent? Are there signals of meaning in our world that permit us to be generous and loving despite the negative experiences? The modern parable records a similar experience of trust and love, but it gives prominence to the skeptical friends who want to know the grounds of the trust. They raise a question about the truth or falsity of the assurances the partisan has received. What evidence would the partisan accept as a devaluation of the currency of his trust? What are the "real" patterns of the world?

The sayings of Jesus raise the stakes of the discussion still higher. The experience of trust and generous love for one's neighbor is elevated to a disclosure of God in our world. Instead of a moralizing (and demoralizing) announcement that here is an unfulfillable ideal, we have the outrageous statement that God does not place much stock in someone's "good deeds," that God's love is not a reward but a prior condition for knowing God at all. God offers love to the just and the unjust alike. We cannot prove our worth before the divine presence, only accept the love offered and love both our neighbors and our enemies. Who is this God who permits such unequal distribution of rewards?

Foundational theology tries to answer the most fundamental questions that emerge from our experience of ourselves, our world, and our sense of God. What are the human conditions that permit faith in one another and trust in God? What are the rational principles that permit us to believe? In whom do we believe? Foundational theology reflects upon the basic conditions that make the experience of faith, moral action, and their expression possible.[2]

As a result, this theology must oscillate between a number of constants. On the one hand, it cannot merely repeat cultural values, biblical narratives, or prayerful, sacramental experiences. It must have some distance, since it addresses the questions at the very foot of faith. Those engaged in foundational theology are not alienated from the believing assembly, but they are sympathetic to the problems raised by nonbelievers as well. Thinking critically must not cease when people become believers.

Foundational theologians are interpreters of both their societies and their specific confessional traditions. Knowing that simple repetition of past formulations will only petrify Christianity, they hunt for the symbols, stories, and concepts that will appropriately translate the mystery they sense in both culture and religion into a new experience of God for their contemporaries. They journey with excitement since the mystery they seek is not a conclusion based on a series of clues, like the work done in a mystery novel. Rather, the God who loves the good and the bad alike is one who is radically unknowable, constantly escaping our formulations — and yet available to us only within the forms given to us.

Anselm of Canterbury (1033–1109) said that theology is "faith seeking understanding." It is neither a mindless fideism mistaking our own confusions for the mystery of God nor an exhaustive rationalism that pigeonholes the divine. Foundational theology will let go of neither faith nor reason. That is what makes it a difficult discipline, but that is also why it constitutes the proper entry into all the specific topics theologians discuss.

In what follows, we believe we have outlined an intelligent approach for these initial theological labors. The book begins by attending to the individual's religious experience and traditions and moves toward the intellectual or cognitive dimensions in ethics and doctrine. Finally, it foresees the possibility of ascertaining norms that might govern the way we communicate our religious and moral experience.

Although both authors are Catholic by confessional adherence, we do not believe that the movement described here is limited to our own Christian traditions. We believe that many of the positions taken on specific issues (on the good, on doctrines) are commonly held by contemporary Protestant and Catholic theologians. Where appropriate, we have placed these opinions into a coherent, consistent framework that permits appropriation and application. We think that a systematic, even paradigmatic approach provides a useful entry to foundational theology as a collaborative ecumenical discipline. Never a series of rules to be learned by rote, foundational theology must become a reflection on one's own reasonable movements of the Spirit. Appropriate bibliography should support that conviction. The contemporary concerns of theology must be a common effort to bring the gospel toward the world and vice versa. This is a modest beginning that we hope will provide the introductory design necessary to understand how this is possible — indeed, how essential it is in our times if we are to have a world in which to live.

NOTES

1. See Basil Mitchell, "Theology and Falsification," in *New Essays in Philosophical Theology*, ed. Antony Flew and Alasdair MacIntyre (New York: Macmillan Co., 1964), 103–5.

2. See B. J. F. Lonergan, *Method in Theology* (London: Darton, Longman & Todd, 1972), esp. 235–93; Gerald O'Collins, *Fundamental Theology* (New York: Paulist Press, 1981), 5–31; and Hans Urs von Balthasar, *The Glory of the Lord: A Theological Aesthetics*, vol. 1, *Seeing the Form*, trans. Erasmo Leiva-Merikakis, ed. Joseph Fessio and John Riches (New York: Crossroad, 1982), esp. 17–127. For criticisms of the metaphor of "foundations" and a response, see Francis Schüssler Fiorenza, *Foundational Theology: Jesus and the Church* (New York: Crossroad, 1984), esp. 285–89.

PART 1

ECCLESIAL PRAXIS:
THE EXPERIENCES AND SYMBOLS
OF CHRISTIAN
CONVERSION AND DISCIPLESHIP

CHAPTER 1

CONVERSION AND DISCIPLESHIP WITHIN THE CHRISTIAN TRADITION

And God, that center Who is everywhere, and whose circumference is nowhere, finding me, through incorporation with Christ, incorporated into this immense and tremendous gravitational movement which is love, which is the Holy Spirit, loved me. And He called out to me from His own immense depths.
Thomas Merton (1915–68), *The Seven Storey Mountain*, 1948

Caravaggio's painting of the conversion of Saint Paul stuns us by its seemingly off-center focus. Harsh diagonal light strikes the center of the painting where a horse's right flank is exposed. The large front hoof thrusts powerfully toward the body of a vigorous man sprawled on the ground, his muscular arms stretched upward toward the light. His slightly lifted head becomes the corner of a triangle, of which his arms and the ribbed back of the horse become the sides. He cannot see. To the upper right, caught in the shadows, a groom, ignorant of the drama played out before him, holds the horse's head. The absolutely vulnerable Paul, frozen at the moment of his change, tells us only that power has been turned into weakness, sight into blindness. We do not yet know the future of his story.

The value of this masterpiece is, of course, complex, but the painting shows us a number of things about religious change as found in the New Testament. The life, death, and resurrection of Jesus did not leave people unaffected. We will outline the classic patterns into which the New Testament developed — first, by looking at the effect of the death and resurrection of Jesus upon the disciples; then, by describing the challenge to conversion and discipleship that was inscribed in Jesus' teaching. The community that emerged from this experience of the risen Christ gave birth to paradigms for Christians who followed the call. Later, we will outline one of the most famous instances of religious change, that of Saint Augustine (354–430). From certain elements of his experience and those in the New Testament, we can study conversion as the foundation for theological questions. We all begin in the vulnerable position of Paul, certain that our past will not suffice to sustain us, not knowing where the future will lead.

THE DEATH OF JESUS AND
CHRISTIAN CONVERSION

The death of Jesus provoked a crisis for his followers.[1] They were scandalized by his arrest and trial, traumatized during his execution. In the Markan account of Jesus' Passion, we find a continuing lack of recognition by the disciples. Peter's recognition of messiahship (Mark 8:27–33), as misplaced as it was, turned into his denial and the apostasy of everyone but the women (Mark 14:10ff.). Peter, James, and John, the mainstays of the Jerusalem community, were precisely the ones who fell asleep during Jesus' prayer in the garden (Mark 14:31). The teacher's death seemed to put an end to the common life of discipleship. Yet it was not that he left them but that they betrayed him. What needs explanation in the New Testament descriptions is how this betrayal and isolation turned into a boldness to preach and a willingness to gather together. What changed the disciples so that this experience of guilty fear became an assertion that they were once more in a living communion with the same Jesus?

The explanation that the New Testament gives for this strange shift in the disciples is the resurrection of Jesus: "He has been raised" (Mark 16:1–8 NEB). The place where there was death now held life, and this was accomplished by God's Word. The Gospels of Matthew and Luke develop this bare announcement of God's action in Christ by stressing the spectacular aspects of resurrection — but never by describing the event itself. The only witness to the moment of Jesus' transformation is Jesus himself. For Matthew, the empty tomb supports the faith in Jesus' continued presence (Matt. 28:15). In the Gospel of Luke, the emptiness of the tomb signifies being caught up into the fascinating and awesome mystery of God.

In this entire story, we should notice that Jesus continues as a personal agent. The one whom the disciples knew before death and with whom they ate and drank continued in their presence. This is particularly obvious in the earliest Pauline texts about the resurrection. In 1 Cor. 15:3–8, Christ has been raised by God, producing in the disciples positive effects, especially a boldness of speech and the gifts of the Spirit. And when Paul describes that Jesus appeared to Peter, the Twelve, more than five hundred, James, and finally Paul himself, he is pointing to the appearances not as a proof of the resurrection but as evidence for unity of belief among all Christians. Each person to whom Christ showed himself helped to found a community of faith and shared in the kingdom that Christ had preached while in the flesh.

Jesus' manifestation of himself therefore signifies a great reversal in human experience. The crucified one is now living; what is ordinarily experienced as absence through death is now known as presence; what should be felt as silence and guilt for betrayal is sensed as comfort, forgiveness, and a mission to convey the gift of mercy to others. And wherever these changes occur, Christ himself initiates the movement. He is the one who turns others from living in despair toward facing life through suffering and death.

The same paradoxical changes can be seen in the accounts of Saint Paul's conversion that are the classic descriptions of religious change in the New Testament (Acts 9:1–27, 22:1–21, 26:9–23; 1 Cor. 9:1, 15:8–11; Gal. 1:15–17), In the simplest account in the Acts of the Apostles (chap. 9), Saul gives himself to the vision he receives without knowing what it means. God simultaneously acts on Ananias, the one who will educate Saul in the faith. Jesus addresses Saul personally, even though Saul does not know who is speaking to him. A vision of light blinds him by its excess; Saul hears only a voice calling him. In Acts (chaps. 22 and 26), the accounts end with the baptism of Paul and his missionary commission. He is chosen for an authentic apostolate by the Risen One whom he has been persecuting.

What happens in the process of conversion? There are (1) a disorientation, (2) an experience of gathering together the fragments of the exploded past, and (3) a forgiveness for failures and a sense of mercy (4) originating in some Other who is not oneself. The participant feels grasped by God who has shown himself in Jesus the crucified one. For Paul, this Christ comes as the light shown to the world, learned within the life of a community. Paul's conversion to Jesus is not an isolated moment. Ananias teaches him; the communities of Christians welcome him though somewhat fearfully. The whole experience is one of overwhelming life, a recognition of the past as given to death and sin, and a release of entirely new energies for the future. What has been his grace should be given to others.

Thus the classic pattern is set. Just as Jesus' death is experienced as freedom rather than the burden of betrayal, so Paul's past persecutions are left behind as sin, transformed into the apostolate to the Gentiles. Reversal of sin into forgiveness, of suffering and pain into generous love, of death into life—all these shifts shape the way in which Christians have undergone the law of the cross. The death and resurrection of Jesus is the pivotal possibility for Christians;

it marks the way they look at their past and the way they anticipate the future.

CHALLENGE IN THE TEACHINGS OF JESUS

Death and resurrection colored the manner in which the authors of the New Testament understood the preaching of Jesus. What they recognized through the event of Jesus' transformation was that during his life he had been awakening the very same experience in those who heard his words. Within the gestures, parables, and sayings of Jesus, the same explosive person appeared who was now in glory with God. The religious change that had come over the disciples was available in the words Jesus offered to those who could hear.

There had been a long history of repentance and conversion in the Hebrew Scriptures.[2] In some emergencies (e.g., 1 Kings 8:33ff.), penitential observances were expected of everyone; but in individual cases as well (e.g., when Ahab had Naboth murdered to steal his vineyard, 1 Kings 21:1–29), fasting and prayer were believed to avert divine anger. In the great temple prayer of Solomon (1 Kings 8:33ff.), days of atonement were named. When the prophets criticized Israel's practice of repentance, it was not a rejection of external expression of sorrow but a challenge to turn from sinful acts definitively and to make interior dispositions coincide with ritual (Joel 2:12; Amos 4:6; Hos. 2:8–9, 3:5, 5:4, 14:2; Isa. 6:10, 10:20–21, 30:15; Jer. 4:1, 26:3, 36:3, 7).

John the Baptist's basic message of repentance and baptism (Mark 1:4; Matt. 3:2, 8:11) occurred therefore within a tradition. The arrival of the kingdom was imminent; judgment was close at hand; the only task left to human beings was conversion. This change and the ritual purification in the river that he required were demanded of all, even of righteous Jews (Matt. 3:7ff.). Like the prophets before him, the Baptizer called for a conversion, a *metanoia* from within, so that all one's life might correspond to God's demands. Baptism was the action that externalized the difference; it was one's own and the community's way of knowing that a shift had occurred.

With Jesus we hear a similar message—"The time is fulfilled, and the kingdom of God is at hand; repent, and believe in the gospel" (Mark 1:15) — but the accent has moved.[3] The *metanoia* Jesus required was due to the fact that the reign of God had arrived. Conversion was not so much a duty born of sin and guilt as a joy at being able to relinquish one's now ridiculous past. Jesus' ministry was a call to conversion (Luke 5:32), but it surpassed the prophets (Matt. 12:39ff.). Because God had chosen to show himself here and now, some unconditional decision was demanded (Mark 1:15; Matt. 4:17, 18:3). We must totally surrender (Luke 18:13) to a God who has chosen to seek out sinners (Luke 15:7, 10). But it is not so much hard work on our part, as letting God operate within us (Matt. 18:3).

The same call to change and the power for conversion can be overheard in the stories, parables, and proverbs that Jesus tells. There are all sorts of "easy" readings of Jesus' preaching that make them moralizing tales or things we must do. Some would think of them primarily as conceptual information: we should have this or that idea of God. Although it is permissible, even necessary, as we shall see, to draw intellectual data and moral principles from these stories, their original form is more ambiguous. As Paul Ricoeur has said:

> The Parable surprises, astonishes, shocks, provokes: exposing such and such a prejudgment (an opinion or belief imposed by the milieu, one's education or the epoch), it obliges one to reconsider things, to come to a new decision.[4]

The first object of these stories is not to teach concepts but to point the way through our lives, often indirectly. A drama or plot unfolds that is close to the daily life of the original audience in first-century Hellenized Judaism. A crisis erupts in the tale, provoking a change in the hearer. Disoriented, the listener must make some reversal to see the world whole.

Let us look at the parable of the Good Samaritan (Luke 10:30–35).[5] The story is clearly not a utilitarian narrative, as though its primary message were, Keep out of harm's way on the Jerusalem-to-Jericho road. It is also not just a story to make us laugh or to make us feel comfortable. Rather, the story pits several important actors against one another: a victimized Jew, a Levite, a priest, and a detested Samaritan.

In the initial action, we commiserate with the robbed traveler, but quickly we are given the option of identifying with a helper, perhaps a priest or a Levite. Yet they pass by, perhaps fulfilling our latent anticlerical prejudices. Then, however, we are left with a particularly ugly option: either we must become like the Samaritan who is generous or we must return to thinking of ourselves as the victim to be helped by him. Both options are distasteful, but lying as a victim in the ditch is a good deal better than thinking oneself inside the gentleness of a Samaritan! Entering the kingdom is like being a victim who is helped by his or her own worst enemy.

The ordinary Jewish world was radically confronted by this story. The priest and Levite may have had good ritual reasons not to defile themselves with what, after all, might have been a corpse. The notoriously dangerous road to Jericho was an easy place to be robbed — but suddenly it had become the place in which God was encountered. At the place where the traveler had no other choices, help came to him. God is like that; in the most tragic of circumstances, when there seem no other options, God chooses to disclose the power of divine presence. But to be helped, we must realign our priorities, for it means being cared for by our enemies and, of course, ultimately, loving them.

Such parabolic language has a general structure of encounter, reversal, and the opening up of a new future. We (1) encounter in the world of the parable a new way of looking at things, but only on the condition that we are willing to shift our attitudes. The many-sided meaning of such tales releases all kinds of responses. By (2) reversing the ordinary world of our experience (where, e.g., fathers do not always seek out their erring sons, Luke 15:11ff.), the teller of these stories steadily anticipates (3) new worlds where something different can occur.

If we focus upon the responsibilities that appear amid these expanded horizons, we turn toward ethics. If we search out the intellectual claims within these stories, we move toward doctrines. By focusing upon the teller of the stories, we can see the emergence of the early Christologies of the New Testament. Turning to the audience, we note how these narratives founded communities of believers or churches. In each case, the overwhelming power of Jesus' words was enough to start the process of religious change. No doubt there were those who went away puzzled or angry, but there were also a minority who returned for further stories, those who found that the events Jesus proclaimed made them different people.

DISCIPLESHIP: THE CALL TO HOLINESS

Jesus did not act like an ordinary rabbinic teacher.[6] Usually students searched out their own elder, proving to him their qualifications for study. The center of the relationship was an investigation into the interpretation of the law. But Jesus called his own "students" together without regard for their educational background. Not only Levi the tax collector but the women who served him and who remained with him until the end do not fit the norm.

The authority of Jesus himself was enough to command discipleship (Mark 2:14; Matt. 4:19–20; Luke 5:1–11). The disciples attached themselves to Jesus, not just to his teaching. Unlike the prophets, unlike other teachers, he provoked a question: "Who do you say that I am?" (Mark 8:27ff.). He was the bond uniting his followers.

Being a disciple of Jesus, having given up one's own past life, was fulfillment in itself. One needed to look no further—but the way of being "with" this teacher was not so much to memorize his words as to live his life. And his story included suffering. To be a witness to Jesus was not to repeat his language but to become someone like him.

The call to the reign of God requests holiness from those who follow. The witness disciples must give is centered on the person of Christ; it simultaneously identifies with him and actively wills to live his way in the ordinary world. The absolute trust he had in the Father, even through death, was Jesus' own faithful response to God. Our discipleship must mirror his way.

Jesus' various teachings on reversal of our usual priorities (that the last shall be first, Matthew 19:30; that humility raises us up, Matthew 23:12; Luke 14:11, 18:14; or that the rich and the poor change places in the kingdom, Luke 16:19–31) pattern early Christian discipleship. In this new experience of the reign of God, the lowly have the primary place. So for Saint Paul, there is an eschatological equality of believers, neither Jew nor Greek, slave nor free, male nor female. Women held particularly conspicuous places in the community, despite their social status at the time.[7]

The language of the New Testament teaches us that the paradigm for all conversion is found in the death and resurrection of Jesus.[8] The Christ is experienced both as a story for us to follow and as the power enabling us to follow that example. The words of the New Testament "work upon us" because they continue to present his person; the witness of discipleship mirrors in its very action the life he offers. The prayerful existence of the community is dependent upon its continued insertion into the life of Christ himself. We can describe (for that is all we are doing at this point in our study) conversion in the Christian experience as a reversal in which the self, the world, and God are reshaped. The self leaves behind the baggage of sin and self-inflicted suffering; the world becomes a place in which God dwells; and God turns toward humanity with a renewed sense of care. This translates the whole affair into somewhat pedestrian vocabulary, of course, since the originating experience is the explosive transformation of the dead Jesus into the living Lord for others.

CONVERSION IN THE TRADITIONS
OF THE CHURCH

A classic in literature is a text to which we feel obliged to return again and again. Tolstoy's *War and Peace*, Joyce's *Ulysses*, and Shakespeare's *Hamlet* continue to provoke our interpretive skills. Certain classics determine an entire tradition of works, as the first impressionist paintings reshaped the way artists understood their craft, or as Martha Graham redefined contemporary dance by her early choreography. The same is true in theology. The *Confessions* of Saint Augustine began a whole genre of literature, the autobiographic confession. His work continues to be reread because it overturns our understanding of ourselves and refuses to be overlooked when we think about what it means to be human and religious.[9]

The prayerful context of Augustine's work establishes the fundamental dialogue between God and the self. Augustine's search for intimacy during his entire life refused to be satisfied. Born into a house of two allegiances, to pagan and Christian desires, Augustine sought personal autonomy through rejection of the religious attitudes of his mother and through an attachment to a mistress to whom he was faithful for fifteen years and by whom he fathered a child. In his quest for independence, he was looking for some companionship, a family of equals, who pursued the same earnest desire for truth and goodness. But in every experience, whether in sexual expression as affection and rebellion, in Manichean dualism as an explanation for the fatedness toward evil in humanity, or in Neoplatonic philosophy, his desires were disillusioned: "Our hearts are restless until they find rest in thee" (*Confessions* I.1).

Augustine gradually sensed that the only way his own and his friends' conflicts would be transformed was through dissolution of the old bonds of friendship and the establishment of a new social pattern. Through his readings in the Latin translations of Greek Neoplatonic philosophy, he understood that in the quest for the good and the true, the good itself was operative in the human spirit. Though he was trained as a rhetorician, capable of arguing for any position with or without personal conviction, he refused to remain skeptical about the possibility of attaining ultimate truth. And he established links of friendship, constantly based upon the common quest for the good. In this context, he heard a story, the biography of Antony of the Desert, who left everything he owned upon hearing the words of the gospel. Augustine asked, These men had power; why can't we?

The flashpoint of decision and resolution occurred in August 386, when Augustine recognized that religious change, couched in his desire to be moral, would not happen through his own work. Overhearing some children shouting "Take and read" across a garden wall, Augustine read the following: "Let us conduct ourselves becomingly as in the day, not in reveling and drunkenness, not in debauchery and licentiousness, not in quarreling and jealousy. But put on the Lord Jesus Christ, and make no provision for the flesh, to gratify its desires" (Rom. 13:13–14). Here was Augustine's divine call. His will was released from the bondage of an emotionally divisive conflict; the scales were tipped by something beyond human agency. Augustine confirmed the dismissal of his mistress and rejected an arranged engagement for marriage. He was baptized and left for Africa where he established a religious community of scholars and pastors. His time was spent preaching, caring as a pastor for the needy, and writing for thinkers in the church. His shift in life had released a new power.

Augustine tells his own story through memory. Doubling back upon himself, he mirrors his own past as a discovery of the self. Authentically autonomous people are not those who can "make" themselves out of nothing but those who discover in their self-reflection that there is another agent, God, upon whom they are dependent. For Augustine, the struggle to put into language before a divine audience the evolution of his religious self became a paradigm for later self-discoveries. It demonstrated the classic pattern: conflict over fundamental issues of self-identification with regard to truth and goodness, the information and power of some enabling other (Antony and the gospel in the case of Augustine), and re-formation into a supportive community that can sustain the envisioned change. The authenticity of the change was warranted existentially through a genuine release of new personal authority. Surrender to God permits a genuine discovery of the self.

CHANGE OF HORIZON

What happened to Augustine can be described as a shift in horizons.[10] Horizon can be understood literally as the line where earth meets sky and where it limits our field of vision. When we are standing in one place, we can see particular figures against the background; when we move, some figures may be obscured, and the horizon changes. There are also horizons to our knowledge and desires. Our understanding and interests change, determined by the horizons within which we know and love. In this sense what lies beyond one's horizon is simply outside the range of one's knowledge and interest: one neither knows nor cares. The figures that might appear will be interpreted at best as exceptions; more often they will not even be registered.

So lawyers, doctors, engineers, elevator operators, laborers, and house cleaners will all have different interests and live in somewhat different worlds. These horizons can be complementary. Yet occasionally horizons are opposed to each other. What is understood in one world is not attended to, not understood, in another. What one person finds a good, another calls an evil. Horizons, therefore, provide us with the necessary traditions, questions, and options to understand our world and to live within it, but they also establish the boundaries of what we will know.

One way we can move from one horizon to another is by changing jobs. To a certain extent, we all do this by becoming weekend "do-it-yourselfers"; we shift horizontal patterns of experience and enter another world. But these changes are largely within our already settled behavior and identity. Sometimes, however, we enter a situation that requires a vertical shift. We find it necessary to leave behind the past and to take up unfamiliar actions and norms.

The most common example of a vertical transformation in horizons is falling in love. What made no sense before, one's older brother or sister languishing beside the telephone, waiting for it to ring, suddenly takes on new meaning when one grows up and one's own special friend is supposed to call. Falling in love creates simultaneously a new subject and a new horizon. Lovers find themselves humming tunes in public, smiling at odd moments, crying at others. Alternately generous and possessive, they cannot imagine how society can have been so dull before they found the one they love. A clearing has emerged in one's personal history, a universe that was unavailable before one's changed way of being. The new self and the new world emerge together.

The change that Paul, the early disciples, and Augustine experienced should be understood as such a vertical shift in horizons. What seemed ridiculous and perverse (that the dead criminal Jesus was the Messiah) now emerged as of paramount importance to Paul. (I am Jesus whom you are persecuting!) What seemed difficult and impossible to Augustine (living according to a moral norm) now appeared a joyful release of power. Religious conversion established a new self who could act authentically in the world and created a new world where the self could choose to be good. The patterns of emotional, political, and social conflict, then of a period of dislocation and fear, a flash point, a moment of decisive intervention, permit freedom and a "new" spirit.[11] Within each individual's conversion, a new and loving God discloses the world of generosity from which everything originates. Suddenly even what was evil in the past is seen as having led toward a God who forgives. Betrayals are disclosed as wounded trusts; modest faith in the Other is refined into a greater freedom to embrace God and neighbor. Such is the transforming power of conversion.

THE SYMBOLIC EXPRESSIONS
OF CONVERSION

The reversals in Christian conversion are never purely personal or private. Only when lovers tell their beloved how much they love do they discover, even for themselves, just how serious their affective attachment is. Only then do they know how much of themselves they are willing to give over to the other in order to form a common bond. The call to holiness requires some outer word even to formulate the experienced conversion.

The prime spontaneous expression of our turning toward God is the individual that we are, the whole person directing his or her life toward the One who loves us. The death and resurrection of Jesus enables us to know God in a new way, such that our old fearful aversions, hatreds, and flights from understanding can become attachment, union within love, and the seeking of truth for its own sake. We risk ourselves no matter what the cost, no matter what the required shifts in horizon.

Symbol is the external expression of these inner changes.[12] Actually, symbol is the enactment of the knowledge, attraction, and morality of those inner changes. Symbolic expressions are a complex of gestures, words, and/or images that evoke, invite, and/or persuade us into participation with what they describe. Without symbols, we would not know what we are about. So even our bodies are the symbolic emergence of the self, such that nonverbal gestures tell us, our friends, and our enemies what we know and feel. Gifts that we give to others provide a symbolic articulation of our attachments and aversions. If photographic portraits were not a symbolic presence of the beloved, we would not worry so much about the possibility of their destruction. If certain birthdays and anniversaries were not so symbolic, we would not spend so much time searching for gifts.

In the New Testament communities, symbols of Christian conversion were equally important. Falling in love with God in Christ required some gestures, words, or images so that it could appear. The first language of Christian expression was prayer: a deliberate turning toward the Father in wonder at the love God bears us, a thankful direction of one's life toward that love and the constant request for the support and assurance of divine assistance. The model for such prayer was Christ's own obedient loving attention to his Father. The public expression in the early community for this experience was common prayer and what Christians later called the sacraments of the church, especially Baptism and the Eucharist.

Eucharist and Baptism are first Christ's own symbolic self-expression. According to the accounts of the final supper with his disciples, Jesus offered his own life and death for the sake of those whom he loved. Entrusting his memory to the fragile elements of bread and wine, he turned his own self-sacrifice into an embodied presence of that love. In the final meal of friendship with the Twelve (Mark 14:17ff.), celebrated in the context of Jewish Passover, Jesus poured out his own reality into the cup of the covenant and the bread of affliction. The same affective self-expression occurred in Jesus' baptism by John in the Jordan River (Matt. 3:13ff.). In this symbol, Jesus assumed responsibility for his own mission. Tested in the desert (Mark 1:12ff.), he anticipated the journey toward Jerusalem and the demands for absolute self-denial that it would require of him.

The Christian community took up the two symbols of the Eucharist and Baptism for their own process of self-identification. In the series of directives that Paul issued to the church at Corinth (1 Cor. 11:17ff.), he pointed out how the sharing of the Lord's Supper required the community's commitment to self-sacrifice. Eating the body and blood of the Lord at Eucharist required a willingness to share oneself with others, just as the betrayed Christ continued to offer himself to his friends and enemies. The links within the community experience must participate in the bonds Jesus himself established.

This was also true of Baptism (Rom. 6:1ff.). Entry into the life of Christ was accomplished through ritual immersion. Just as Christ assumed his mission from the Father in his baptism, so Christians shared the life, death, and resurrection of Christ. The journey through baptism walked the way of Christ by anticipation. Paul stressed that our old life was left behind, and the new life of the Spirit took over. Death no longer has dominion over us, so that it has become possible to live as Christ himself did, without sin and within righteousness. No longer slaves of sin but servants and friends of love itself, we become capable of entering the coming presence of God's kingdom. Conversion, discipleship, and sacramental or symbolic expression interweave in the New Testament; they have continued interwoven in the history of the Christian community.

PSYCHOLOGICAL ANALYSIS AND
THEOLOGICAL SYNTHESIS: CONVERSION
AS THE BASIS FOR THEOLOGY

To complete our overview of conversion, we turn to the important interpretations of the American philosopher and psychologist William James (1842–1910) and the Canadian theologian Bernard Lonergan (1904–84). They provide us with a contemporary grammar for the experiences outlined in the New Testament.

In *Varieties of Religious Experience*,[13] James describes two kinds of personalities, the healthy-minded and the sick souls. The former are aware of themselves and their world as being in development toward what is good and true, and they are largely unpreoccupied by the negative problems that might bring them up short. To the healthy-minded, things are as they appear to be, so they are basically unsuspicious. They enjoy the world in which they live.

The second set of people feel a need to be "twice born." For them, personal peace cannot be attained by simply adding or subtracting from the finite goods that are part of their world. Nature is insufficient in itself; some intervention is required from outside to reorient things, especially human beings. "Natural good is not simply insufficient in amount and transient, there lurks a falsity in its very being." These people feel a need for the harmonious resolution of the discordances in the universe, a requirement of justice for the oppressed and love for the unloved.

The abrupt shift in horizons we have described in the New Testament, Augustine, and Paul occurs in the second group of individuals. Some, perhaps on their way to conversion, alternate between ways of life, oscillating in their uncertainty about where life makes sense to them. Others, by carefully insulating portions of their experience, allow two levels of their life to coexist in conflict: their religious experience with one aim and their moral life undercutting it with other goals and actions.

But at certain moments, what James calls the "hot place of consciousness" takes over so that there is a shift in the center of one's personal energy. A major group of feelings, ideas, and goals is confronted with new devotions, attachments, and convictions. What occurs is an emotional shock, an intellectual and affective disorientation. Entering a period of incompleteness, imperfection, brooding over the past, depression about the future, even a morbid introspection about one's life, one begins to turn toward the new set of values. The pain of separation from the old self is often excruciating; the ambiguity of taking up the new self is frightening. The divided self lives in two worlds, insecure in any realm of language, isolated from all communities.

The bifurcated self exits this tormented middle ground through self-surrender. The "subconscious" takes over, so that some undercurrent leads the person beyond division into unity. One simply "lets go" into the other self one hopes to become. Perhaps it is a temporary exhaustion from the struggle to maintain the two selves, perhaps it is the agency of some catalyst; in either case, a new person emerges. The release of a new level of spiritual vitality first evidences the newness. The converted see new possibilities, even heroic energies available; a higher control of the self and the world appears, such that they cease worrying, have a certain assurance about their beloved's presence (for example) even if there is absence, and discover truths that could not be perceived before. The horizon of the world expands and the subjects and objects within that new dramatic stage seem freshly minted.

In a recent sociological and psychological study of converts to and from Catholicism, Dean Hoge and his assistants[14] found much the same patterns. The search for a deeper level of interior peace leads many people to the rejection of most finite solutions to their problem. Once they recognize that their quest is for God, they actively hunt for the transcendent symbols that will close the gaps within their personal and familial experience. Finding that they need to remove themselves from their previous social contacts, they come upon some catalyst (a story, a book, a mentor, a friend or spouse) that helps them across the threshold of decision. Having emerged into a new world, they integrate what they can of the old life they knew and reject what no longer makes sense. They often feel compelled to witness to their newfound freedom and pleasure at being a new individual before God.

Bernard Lonergan has described religious conversion as an "other-worldly falling in love."[15] It is a total and permanent self-surrender without conditions, qualifications, or reservations. As a dynamic acceptance of our vocation to holiness, it precedes all our individual actions. Using the language of conversion, he describes three other shifts in fundamental horizons: an intellectual, a moral, and an affective conversion. What does he mean, and does it help us to distinguish the meaning of religious change?

We might think of the world in which we live as actually three realms of interrelated concern: common sense, theory, and the poetic.[16] The language of common sense relates items in our horizon to us. Through it we are able to meet concrete situations as they arise; and though common sense does not aim for precision or clarity, through it we focus what we require to "get along" in the world. A great deal of common sense is transmitted through proverbs, folk customs, and the skills and habits that are passed down from parent to child, teacher to student.

Theory, on the other hand, tries to introduce some formal system into the world of common sense. It aims for consistency, coherence, and congruent definitions. When proverbs conflict (e.g., "A stitch in time saves nine" and "Haste makes waste"), theory tries to define terms. Its ideal would be to understand things in relationship one to another rather than as a world in relationship to us. So instead of saying, "It is hot", when asked a question about the temperature, we respond with "Eighty-four degrees Fahrenheit." The measure is some standard outside us, something neutral as it were, prescinding from our status as observers.

The poetic world distorts the speech and gestures of common sense to evoke what seems beyond speech or logical demonstration. It operates in the realm of feelings, expressing and inviting participation in possible enactments of value. So dance is movement, but not quite like the gestures of walking or running. Music produces sounds, but not simply by recording the random noise of the streets. Poetry has a meaning for us more deeply engraved than casual conversation.

How do we learn to distinguish these worlds of human meaning? In reductionist views, when common sense prevails, theory seems ideal and abstract, with little usefulness. After all, the theory of relativity will not fix the refrigerator. Poetry records lies, distorting the plain world with romantic nonsense. In some few minds where theory dominates, the expressions of common sense seem vulgar and foolish, and poetry an illusion. And occasionally, in artists, when the poetic sensibility governs life, common sense skills appear mundane, plodding and ugly; theory, often satanic and destructive technique. So what permits us to value the theoretic and poetic aspects of life while still being able to eat, sleep, and raise children?

Lonergan argues that there is a real conversion that is necessary, a transformation of our intellectual horizon permitting us to differentiate and interrelate these worlds without reducing one to the other.[17] This requires attending to the fact that there is an interiority that notices all expressions, whether those of the everyday world, of theory, or artistic symbols. To turn to one's own subjectivity is to attend to one's own operations, structures, norms, and potentialities. It is not just having a theory about what it means to know, but paying attention to the one who makes theories. Such a shift in horizons permits differentiation without reduction, the possibility of interrelating the worlds without confusion, and even the ability to shift back and forth from one to the other without false application or delusion. This is a first descriptive approximation of what Lonergan means by intellectual conversion, though we will return to it later to clarify some aspects of moral life. A similar transformative movement occurs in affective, moral, and religious life.

Affective conversion occurs in the appropriation of our images and symbols. Each of us has an internal language by which we communicate to ourselves; it primarily emerges in dreams. We can be unconsciously governed by these symbols or we can learn how to make them our own. Under one aspect of the about-face that occurs in this realm, we move away from images that express our narcissism, our self-interested feelings, and our affective impotence to attach ourselves to valuable persons, places, or things within a network of relationships, loyalty to a community, and faith in our capacity to change human destinies. Affective change, therefore, involves three aspects of attachment and detachment: (1) a recentering in the patterns of the subject from detached scrutiny or irony to attachment; (2) a shift in the object toward which the subject's affections are drawn (from self-interest to concern for others—family, society, nation, world); and (3) the location of the appropriate aesthetic symbol to express one's affective meanings. Like all conversions, it can occur gradually or rapidly, in a single place or piecemeal in many situations.

Moral conversion recognizes that knowing, even knowing how we are knowers, is insufficient for doing the correct thing. Most of us understand the conflicts that come from searching for the proper value in a difficult situation, knowing the right thing and doing something else, or opting for a genuine value that goes against our own inclinations or emotions. The sharp about-face that occurs in the New Testament for Paul or that occurs later for Augustine invariably involves a moral element. The old order has passed away; a new way of acting occurs, built upon the gifts of the Holy Spirit.

Religious conversion is a permanent self-surrender to God without conditions or qualifications. It entails absolute trust despite all negative experiences. It shifts from self-love or love of any finite object to the love of the Absolute Other. The love of this God is not an abstract love; it trusts that truth will be achieved in that all our questions will be answered, that love will conquer all evil despite the experience of death, and that our commitments to justice and peace will actually transform people and their world even though we all know the painful undertow of sin. Grasped by the Other, we recognize that our desire for God turns into joy that we have been with God before we knew it. Eventually, we learn to love the Other in and for the sake of the Other—and not for what that God can do for sorry lovers like ourselves. This religious falling in love may occur in any one of the worlds of our expression: in common sense, theory and science, or poetry, though it is probably more usual in the language of common sense and the poetic.

The specifically Christian element within conversion is the person of Jesus the Christ. Christians believe that in their turning toward God, God has graciously turned toward them. Not only are we present to God, but in our prayerful attitude of wonder, God is present to us. This mutual presence may occur for the believer day after day in the kitchen, the workshop, the education and correction of children, and the difficult task of loving one's spouse. It may appear in the theoretic language of philosophic mysticism. But perhaps most often, it occurs within the world of the poetic, where symbols seduce us into God's presence before we are aware of the pull of love. Drawn from the everyday busy experience of accomplishing human tasks, symbolic chariots of fire slow down near us so that we can take our place in them. Giving ourselves to the poetic expression of Christian experience, we anticipate the life of God that we will one day share in glory.

WHERE HAVE WE COME?

The work of this chapter is crucial to understanding the journey in the remaining chapters. By beginning with conversion and discipleship, we maintain that Christians originate their theology empirically, by trying to understand their own experiences of God. These experiences may not prove sanctity, nor are they necessarily rapturous, but they are distinctive. We have located the experience in the language of conversion, or in the Greek, *metanoia*.

The about-face that the Christian Scriptures ascribe to Paul and other disciples is rooted in the death and resurrection of Jesus and in the disciples' reflections upon his life with them. Without that experience, there would have been no Christian tradition. Each conversion is a reenactment of that originating event. Conversions may occur slowly, laboriously, and crudely; sometimes, they happen abruptly, painfully, and without recourse to one's former way of life. Augustine is in a way an example of both; over thirty years, he slowly but surely moved toward Christian life, but he needed that sudden voice calling to him to make it happen.

One of the advantages, methodologically, of beginning with the language of conversion is that it permits us to take as our basic data the symbols, stories, and images of the New Testament as well as those from the history of the Christian community. The language of religious writers (e.g., the mystics) has often been taken to be excessive and uncognitive. But it seems important to take such speech seriously as a basis for theological discussion. We have appropriated elements of this religious change and given them labels: shift in horizon, symbolic expression, structures of change, and so on. This vocabulary will enable us to develop some important aspects of Christian life. Though Christian life begins with experience, it is not determined by the simple amassing of more or bigger experiences of change. From within conversion itself, there arise the demands for conceptual clarification and normative reflection.

The global, all-encompassing shift we call religious conversion frames many important further elements that are intellectual, institutional, and evaluative. For the religiously converted have also been fanatics, uncritical destroyers of cultural and personal identities, rigid ideologues for what could be seen afterward as private opinions and perverse speculations. Religious people have occasionally been moral hypocrites, intellectual imbeciles, and affective isolates. So the appeal to experience as the foundation of theology is not without its perils. As we move toward more sharply defined positions, it will become clear that Christian conversion is in every case an ecclesially developing experience in which intellectual, moral, and affective elements must be included. Christian conversion does not occur in a narrow corridor where fearful, self-protective people live. When Jesus disclosed the Father, it was not as a God of the heart who excluded the mind, or as a divinity resident in dematerialized values devoid of the body. When the Word of God became flesh, he assumed all of humanity, thereby transforming it completely. We Christians believe this because we see the transformation taking place in the New Testament and in those holy men and women who continue the story that Jesus preached. Foundational theology reflects upon such stories of conversion.

NOTES

1. For a summary and interpretation of recent biblical work on this material, see Edward Schillebeeckx, *Jesus: An Experiment in Christology*, trans. Hubert Hoskins (London: William Collins & Co., 1979), esp. 320–97.

2. See "*metanoia*," in *Theological Dictionary of the New Testament*, ed. Gerhard Kittel, trans. Geoffrey W. Bromiley (Grand Rapids: Wm. B. Eerdmans, 1967), 4:975–1008.

3. For our general approach, see Robert Funk, *Language, Hermeneutic, and the Word of God* (New York: Harper and Row, 1968); Norman Perrin, *The New Testament: An Introduction* (New York: Harcourt Brace Jovanovich, 1974); and idem, *Jesus and the Language of the Kingdom: Symbol and Metaphor in New Testament Interpretation* (Philadelphia: Fortress Press, 1976).

4. Paul Ricoeur, "The 'Kingdom' in the Parables of Jesus," *Anglican Theological Review* 63 (1981):166.

5. See Bernard Brandon Scott, *Jesus, Symbol-Maker for the Kingdom* (Philadelphia: Fortress Press, 1981), 25–32. Cf. John Dominic Crossan, *The Dark Interval* (Niles, Ill.: Argus Communications, 1975), 104–8; and Funk, *Language*, 199–222.

6. See "*manthano, mathetes*," in *Theological Dictionary*, ed. Kittel, 4:390–461; L. William Countryman, "Christian Equality and the Early Catholic Episcopate," *Anglican Theological Review* 63 (1981): 115–38; Edward Schillebeeckx, *Christ: The Experience of Jesus as Lord*, trans. John Bowden (New York: Crossroad-Seabury Press, 1980), 237–93; and Elisabeth Schüssler Fiorenza, "The Biblical Roots for the Discipleship of Equals," *Journal of Pastoral Counselling* 14 (1979): 7–15.

7. See Wayne A. Meeks, *The First Urban Christians: The Social World of the Apostle Paul* (New Haven: Yale Univ. Press, 1983), esp. 23–25, 55–63, 70–71, 81; and Elisabeth Schüssler Fiorenza, *In Memory of Her: A Feminist Theological Reconstruction of Christian Origins* (New York: Crossroad, 1983), esp. 160–241.

8. See William Loewe, "Lonergan and the Law of the Cross: A Universalist View of Salvation," *Anglican Theological Review* 59 (1977): 162–74.

9. For the interpretations of Augustine, see David Burrell, *Exercises in Religious Understanding* (Notre Dame, Ind.: Univ. of Notre Dame Press, 1974), 11–41; Peter Brown, *Augustine of Hippo* (Berkeley and Los Angeles: Univ. of Calif. Press, 1969); Eugene TeSelle, *Augustine the Theologian* (London: Burns & Oates, 1970); and Frederich van der Meer, *Augustine the Bishop: Religion and Society at the Dawn of of the Middle Ages*, trans. Brian Battershaw and G. R. Lamb (New York: Harper & Row, 1961).

10. Bernard Lonergan, *Method in Theology* (New York: Herder & Herder, 1972), 235–37.

11. The vocabulary employed follows Rosemary Haughton, *The Transformation of Man: The Study of Conversion and Community* (Springfield, Ill.: Templegate Pubs., 1967).

12. See S. Happel, "Sacrament: Symbol of Conversion," in *Creativity and Method: Essays in Honor of Bernard Lonergan*, ed. Matthew L. Lamb (Milwaukee: Marquette Univ. Press, 1981), 275–90.

13. William James, *Varieties of Religious Experience: A Study in Human Nature* (New York: Collier, 1961), 114–260.

14. Dean R. Hoge et al., *Converts, Dropouts, and Returnees: A Study of Religious Change Among Catholics* (New York: Pilgrim Press, 1981), esp. 47–52.

15. Lonergan, *Method*, 240–44.

16. For the language used here, see H. L. Dreyfus and S. J. Todes, "Discussion: The Three Worlds of Merleau-Ponty," *Philosophical and Phenomenological Research* 22 (1961–62): 559–65.

17. Lonergan, *Method*, 237–40.

FURTHER READINGS

Reginald Fuller. *The Formation of the Resurrection Narratives*. London: SPCK, 1972.

John Baptist Metz. *Followers of Christ*. New York: Paulist Press, 1978.

Francis J. Moloney. *Disciples and Prophets*. New York: Crossroad, 1981.

Edward Schweizer. "Dying and Rising with Christ." In *New Testament Issues*, ed. Richard Batey, 173–90. London: SCM Press, 1970.

David Tracy. *The Analogical Imagination: Christian Theology and the Culture of Pluralism*, 154–229. New York: Crossroad, 1981.

CHAPTER 2

THE FAITHFUL FOUNDATIONS OF
ETHICS AND DOCTRINE

Experience is the child of Thought,
and Thought is the child of Action.
Benjamin Disraeli (1804–81)
Vivian Grey

THE HUMAN SITUATION:
A REFLECTIVE ANALYSIS

We began with the experience of conversion to indicate that all reflection originates in an act of interpretation on experience. In other words, there is no conscious awareness without our interpreting the significance of experience. We could say, then, that experience of significance and interpretation are simply two sides of one coin that condition each other.

At one level, we understand the world in terms of survival, pleasure, pain, and death, and conduct ourselves prudently in relation to the material world. The world is familiar to us, and so we inhabit it and act in a common-sense fashion according to its necessary laws and patterns. We select, relate, and synthesize the data of our everyday world in terms of its "natural" significance. Common sense is our habitual way of interpreting the natural significance of our environment.

Moral and religious events, and their interpretations, are always dependent on our ordinary natural world, but never identified with it. Thus, there are three levels of human consciousness and interpretation by which we know and relate ourselves to the world: natural, moral, and religious. Our argument is that the movement from one level to another requires distinct symbols, concepts, forms of reasoning, and reference points. New symbols and concepts need to be introduced at higher levels of consciousness that are capable of including data not accounted for by the symbols and concepts employed at a previous level. Because the interpretations and interrelationships of experience are more complex at the higher levels, new frames of reference and new forms of reasoning of a distinctively moral or religious nature become necessary. Each level surpasses the one before it without denying or negating its contents, and each represents a unique and qualitatively different way of being in the world.[1]

What are the phenomena of our ordinary awareness of the world which serve as the background or springboard for entering into the moral and religious dimensions of experience? The data we will isolate concern the "limit" experiences we encounter in our everyday lives.

We all experience elements of finiteness and contingency. We know ourselves as temporally and spatially located, and so it is not long before we realize that we cannot do more than one thing at a time, and the things we do must be done in the context of space. Most often, limitedness is not so disconcerting that our lives are called into question. There are, however, other more profound moments of finiteness and contingency, like a serious illness or the realization of our own mortality, which provoke an anxiety that calls forth a search for meaning that transcends our ordinary understandings of the world.

We experience not only the facts and laws of the natural world but also our capacity to go beyond that world through deliberate acts; we know freedom of choice and self-determination. We act consciously and deliberately, and in this we experience ourselves as controlling, manipulating, and directing the natural world. In our freedom we know that we can fashion ourselves by determining not only the kind of people we want to be but also the acts we will perform. Yet we never have unlimited freedom in our dealings with the natural world, ourselves, and our acts. Finiteness, characterized by time and space and the possibilities of our culture, all limit and define our exercise of freedom.

Furthermore, we are an existence embodied with others in the world. Our bodies remain part of the material world and are affected by the physical and chemical laws of nature. Our free acts, as acts of incarnate beings, always entail an element of submission or obedience to the structure, nature, and laws of material things. Our control over material reality is partial and incomplete, and there will always be side effects to our acts—such as pollution in the manufacture and operation of automobiles—that we do not want but that are causally linked to our acts.

In addition, we exist as beings with others in the human world. There are others around us from whom we come and with whom we live on some intimate level (e.g., parents and family), upon whom we rely for general services and with whom we must cooperate. We are social beings living within cultural communities that both enhance and limit the possibilities of what we can become and do. We can interpret the other as a source of joy and happiness, security, and friendship, or we can look on the other as threat and always think of ourselves as vulnerable to the other's intentions and acts.

Evil is also part of our everyday world. Nonmoral evil comprises any lack of a perfection at which we aim or any lack of fulfillment that thwarts our human needs and desires and makes us suffer.[2] So, for example, we have the natural desire to live, yet death looms on the horizon; we desire to determine the self, yet our experience of living with others naturally shapes these desires either by law or by custom; we desire knowledge, but ignorance remains within us; we desire to be safe, but the natural world can be hostile to human welfare in disasters like earthquakes and tornadoes.

There is another kind of evil, called moral evil, and we experience this primarily within ourselves and in others, but also as a power within our social institutions. We encounter this kind of evil when we do things we know we should not do and when we become people we know we should not be. In other words, we assume a guilt for which we take some personal responsibility, and this limits our awareness of our own goodness, the goodness of others, and that of our institutions. In the face of both kinds of evil, nonmoral and moral, we seek meaning that transcends our ordinary understandings of the world.

Finally, we all have what might be called "peak" or "ecstatic" experiences.[3] These are occasions of true joy, harmony, and profound reassurance, and they, like the other phenomena, challenge our ordinary understandings of the world. In response to all these experiences, and to the challenges they present, the human eros seeks to make sense out of the human situation by discovering meanings that transcend natural significances and by relating us to the world, to others, and to God in terms of these meanings. At the level of moral experience and interpretation we seek to relate ourselves to the world and others through justice, truth telling, and the like. In religious experience and interpretation we seek to relate ourselves to the source and ground of all reality, who transcends yet is immanent in our everyday world of experience.

MORAL EXPERIENCE AS AN ATTEMPT
TO INTERPRET THE WORLD

The phenomena we have just described make up some of our most ordinary experiences. These natural realities serve as the signals of transcendence—or as "rumors of angels," as Peter Berger once described them. As an experience of an unknown within the known, the experience of them provokes us to ask moral and religious questions. We must inquire now into the specific foundations of moral experience — the basic conditions that allow it to arise.

It is a fact that nonreligious people are capable of interpreting their lives and actions morally, and the reason for this is that those conditions which make possible moral experience hold for all human beings. Stated simply, people do not need to be explicitly religious to be moral. Yet this fact does not negate the possibility of a distinctively Christian morality. Belief in Jesus as Lord and a commitment to discipleship in his name have a direct bearing on Christian moral experience and interpretations, even though these beliefs and commitments do not fundamentally alter all the specific foundations of morality itself.

We might begin by describing what the foundations for moral experience are not. The moral life cannot be reduced either to our ordinary experience of the world or to religious experience. Moral experience and its interpretations are unique and thus they differ qualitatively from these other two realms. Contrary to the claims of many fundamentalists, moral experience does not necessarily find its foundation in revelation or Scripture. Nor does moral experience originate in some inner moral sense or sentiment or "mental taste" as David Hume (1711–76) argued. To believe, as we do, that moral experience is always related to our awareness of the sensible world is also to deny the assertion of Immanuel Kant (1724–1804) that the starting point of morality is a priori pure practical reason. Finally, the views of cultural relativists and of some psychological thinkers, for example, Sigmund Freud (1856–1939), must be rejected: moral experience is not an appropriation of cultural mores or merely the development of the superego.

Moral consciousness is essentially the experience and interpretation of value and thus of a world that is not yet, but that is capable of coming into being. The experience of value always calls forth our commitment and action to bring into existence a world and a set of human relations that might be, ought to be, but are not yet. Thus, moral consciousness is an attempt to interpret the world and then to relate ourselves to the world and others (human and nonhuman) in terms of these interpretations.

To interpret our lives morally means to imagine and to propose a world and a set of human relations that should govern our existence with one another and with nonhuman life. In the act of interpretation we intend meaning or significance, and thus to interpret the world in this sense denotes that we intend moral meaning or value. When we ask questions about what we are to be or to do, we are intending moral meanings. The values we intend in questions of moral meaning are neither logically derived from some other human experience nor reducible to something other than themselves.[4] Unlike the understanding of empirical data, moral interpretations always involve evaluative knowledge that is at once affective and cognitive, and the interpretations have as their object the making of being.[5]

We are essentially self-transcending subjects in personal freedom. We are self-transcending in two different ways: we can go beyond ourselves from what we were yesterday (e.g., we can get taller or stronger), and we can go beyond ourselves in a more radical way by exercising our personal freedom in intending meaning. With regard to the latter possibility, we can seek to understand intelligently, judge reasonably, and act responsibly. In each case, what we are doing is transcending ourselves in our personal freedom. When we confront the natural world but then ask questions about the values (moral meanings) that are at stake for ourselves and others with whom we live, we are intending values that are implicit in experience.

So far, this is only a very cursory sketch of moral consciousness. We have not yet delineated the precise conditions of the possibility of moral experience and its interpretation. Very briefly, there are four *general* conditions or foundations for moral experience, one *structural* condition, and a *Christian* condition that ground the possibility of authentic moral experience in a Christian mode. It is only the last condition, namely, the Christian condition, that qualifies moral experience as specifically Christian. The other two kinds of conditions, namely, general and structural, are constitutive of human moral experience as such.

THE GENERAL CONDITIONS: BIPOLAR
SOURCES OF MORAL EXPERIENCE

The conditions that establish the general foundations for moral experience can be divided into two groups: those that *drive* us to value-meanings and those which *draw* us into moral consciousness. Metaphorically we call these two sets of conditions bipolar sources because the "drive" and "draw" poles condition each other. Thus, moral consciousness arises in the interplay between an inner dynamic search for moral meaning (drive) and an attraction or lure to discover and participate in value (draw) not grounded solely in our own desiring or choosing.

There are two conditions that make up the drive pole in moral experience: intentional consciousness, and human inclinations and needs. And there are two conditions that constitute the draw pole: the social world as value-laden, and grace as God's life calling us to authentic humanity.

Drive to Moral Meaning

Intentional Consciousness. Our consciousness of the world comprises a series of operations that are all intentional. For example, human consciousness involves the operations of seeing, hearing, smelling; inquiring, imagining, understanding; reflecting, judging; deliberating, deciding; etc. All these operations are transitive; that is, they have objects not merely in a grammatical sense as denoted by transitive verbs but also in a psychological sense.[6] In other words, each of the operations is intentional in the psychological sense that by the operation we become aware of the object. An example may be helpful in making concrete the operations of human consciousness. When we read a book, we are involved in seeing, inquiring, understanding, reflecting, evaluating, and so on. The object or content of what is seen, understood, etc., becomes present to us through the respective operation itself. As we shall see more clearly later in this volume, the cumulative effect of the operations of human consciousness is objective knowledge of human reality that is mediated by meanings.

Whenever any of the operations are performed, they not only intend objects but also have the further psychological dimension of occurring consciously. Simply stated, by performing the various operations we can become aware of ourselves operating. So when I read a book, not only am I aware of what is being read, but I can also become aware that it is I who am reading the book. The awareness that it is I who am reading is awareness of myself as subject and not as object. Now, I can make myself the object of my own consciousness through introspection, but this is a different matter from being aware of myself as subject. In summary, then, operations of a subject not only intend objects but also have the further psychological dimension of occurring consciously, whereby the subject is made present to the self as subject.

As self-transcending subjects, we move beyond ourselves by asking questions, and then by giving intelligent answers that not only are judged to be truthful but are also answers on which we act responsibly. The crucial question is, What grounds our questioning which moves us beyond ourselves in being intelligent, reasonable, and responsible? The answer to this question is what are called transcendental notions.[7] The transcendental notions (intelligibility, truth, beauty, and value) are the dynamic ground of our questioning that moves us from ignorance to knowledge. In our questions for understanding and judgment we intend transcendental objects (the intelligible and the real/true, respectively), but the conditions that make possible this intending are already present in the self. Thus, the "real" and the "good" are present in our questioning and are what *drive* us to seek what we do not know yet.

One of the transcendental notions is value. When we attempt to interpret the world, we ask questions about value: What I am about to do, is it valuable? Worthwhile? Stated in other words, What I am about to do, does it have meaning (moral meaning)? When we ask such questions we are seeking to know about how the world and human relations might be, ought to be, but are not yet. We are also driven to ask comparative questions, that is, not only about whether something is valuable and worthwhile but also about whether some value is more worthwhile than another value. So we can ask questions about whether it is more valuable to help others than to satisfy our own needs.

In sum, the transcendental notion of value, which grounds all our questions in moral consciousness, constitutes one of our capacities for self-transcendence into the moral life. In giving intelligent and reasonable answers to these questions, we become aware of ourselves as agents who must act responsibly in the world. Moral consciousness is indeed an attempt to interpret our experience and relate us to the world, a world that is not yet but that is capable of coming into being through our moral dispositions, decisions, and actions.

Human Inclinations and Needs. The second condition that constitutes the drive pole in moral consciousness is human inclination and need. We all have certain basic human desires that drive us out of ourselves to be fulfilled. These are called rational needs because they are real and genuine, as opposed to alleged or apparent. As such, they exist universally but formally in every person prior to any acculturation within society, and they are constitutive of being human. The basic needs drive us to certain kinds of values and relations that complete or fulfill our natural desires.

We should not get the impression that because these inclinations are constitutive of being human, they will lead us automatically to the corresponding values and relations—the values and relations that fulfill them. This certainly is not the case. Whereas needs do exist in all of us formally before we are acculturated, they are always subject to acculturation within a concrete society, which itself can either advance or thwart the securing of the values or relations. Human history, which is constituted by our personal and social exercises of freedom, has much to do with whether our basic desires are fulfilled properly.

Though it may be impossible to specify with accuracy all the rational needs, a partial list of the universal human inclinations would surely include the following: the need to preserve life, the need to mate and raise children, the need to seek out other persons and attain their approval (friendship), the need to use intelligence in guiding our actions, the need to establish good relations with unknown higher powers (gods or God), and the need to develop skills and exercise them in play and the fine arts.[8] As we can see, though, some of these natural desires drive us to certain values (e.g., life) and others drive us to certain kinds of relations (e.g., friendship).

We have an interest in these fundamental values and relations before being attracted by them, and so we are not neutral with regard to attaining them in our own lives and in the lives of others. In fact, these fundamental needs are the foundation of our basic commitments to the underived values and relations that are necessary for human opportunity and flourishing. When we ask questions about value, that is, when we attempt to interpret the world morally, we are asking questions at least in part about these fundamental human desires and how to fulfill them in our own lives and in others' lives. Though questions about morality are often broader than concrete questions about human needs—for example, about our proper relations to the non-human world—our inclinations become the data, so to speak, that precede many of our questions for moral understandings, judgments, and deliberations.[9] As we can see, then, there is an intrinsic interplay between our intentional consciousness and our basic human needs.

Draw in Moral Consciousness

The Social World as Value-laden. It is probably less fashionable today to speak about being drawn to value in moral experience. One reason is certainly the contemporary emphases, which derive from the Enlightenment, on individual freedom and the desire to determine for ourselves what is valuable. Although there is certainly some validity in emphasizing our freedom and responsibility to determine for ourselves what is valuable, a distorted view can lead to several problems. One such problem is a radical individualism with its attendant emphasis on the absolute autonomy of the person. Another problem lies in the trap of voluntarism, in which one maintains that all value determinations are made by the person through the will alone. In this case, something *becomes* valuable simply because someone *willed* it to be so.[10] Voluntarism as a moral stance, and every moral theory that places too much emphasis on our freedom to determine value, ignores or denies the fundamental insight into the nature of persons that we are drawn to value.

The human world is a social world that is already value-laden. None of us is born into "value neutrality." We are born into concrete societies that already have shared meanings, and we are socialized into these meanings and values from the day we are born. This obviously does not imply that the moral interpretations of our society are the best, or even humane; it is simply to make the point that our culture is not value-neutral. In addition, we are born into ecclesial societies, which themselves are constituted by shared meanings and values into which we are socialized. Unless we all want to reinvent the moral wheel, we appropriate at least some of the shared values of our societies. Our life with others, which makes up part of our ordinary experience of the world, demands some participation in these moral interpretations for cooperation to take place.

Furthermore, the relational nature of value itself suggests that the subject is not the sole referent for value determinations. Value resides neither totally in the subject desiring nor totally in the object desired. Our rational needs drive us to value, but we are also attracted by the objects and relations that fulfill these needs. Value is always a relational notion. It is the harmonious relation between what is intended and desired, on the one hand, and what can properly fulfill these intentions and desires, on the other hand. Some object or relation is denoted good because it possesses the intrinsic properties to fulfill what is intended by questions for meaning and what is desired by the rational needs. Value is a primary notion, and that of good is derivative from it. In other words, something is good because it is valued, and not vice versa. In sum, moral consciousness arises in the interplay between the drive to value and the draw of a value-laden world.

God's Grace Calling Us to Authentic Humanity. In the fifth century there was a great debate between Saint Augustine, the formidable bishop of Hippo, and Pelagius (ca. 355–ca. 425), a lay monk from the British Isles, concerning whether grace was necessary for people to perform their moral duties. Pelagius argued that grace is given by God but that it is given only that we may do the good *more easily*. He maintained, against Augustine, that we can perform morally good acts without grace, although it would be more difficult than with grace. Saint Augustine, in his famous book *The Problem of Free Choice*,[11] recoiled from such a position and argued vigorously for the necessity of grace if we are to be moral and to act rightly.

Prescinding from the polemics of the debate, it seems that Augustine's position was closer to the mark. Grace, or God's sharing divine life with us, is offered to all people whether they are consciously aware of it or not. The inner and even mysterious participation in God's life enables, and calls us to, authentic humanity in our moral lives. Such a call requires a response on our part, and it is the argument of this volume that conversion constitutes the most adequate response to the divine enablement.

One need not be an explicit believer to share and participate in God's life-giving love. In fact, the nonbeliever's experience is not impervious to what Christians call grace. Moments of true joy, relations characterized as self-giving friendship, and occasions of undeserved benefaction are all symbols of God's grace that are open to the nonreligious person's experience but not named as coming from God. These are truly redemptive moments mediated by other interpretations that have no explicit reference to the divine. Nevertheless, these occasions are grace-filled because they truly represent the divine gift of life flooding the hearts of those who have no rightful claim to such joy, friendship, and benefaction.

For the disciple of Jesus the grace of God is explicitly looked on as one of the general conditions for the possibility of moral experience to arise. God's life draws us to himself, who is the origin and end of all values. Our authentic response to value is always also a response to God's call. This is so because the very condition of the possibility of our authentic response is a sharing in God's life already freely given and received. Thus, for the disciple of Jesus all values are looked on as gifts from God, and our authentic responses to these values are ways of truly participating in the life of God.

MORAL CONVERSION: THE STRUCTURAL
CONDITION OF MORAL EXPERIENCE

So far we have spoken of the four general foundations of moral experience. We must now attend to the structural condition, or moral conversion, that makes possible authentic moral consciousness. Within the context of moral conversion we must also speak of the foundational moral experience that thrusts us into a truly human moral life.

Though the biblical understandings of conversion are important and instructive for the disciples of Jesus, nonreligious people can also undergo a moral conversion without explicit reference to the person of Jesus. Whether one can adequately sustain such a conversion without religious affections and beliefs is, of course, another question. In any case, it is our position that moral conversion is possible even outside an explicitly religious context.

Conversion can be understood in one of two ways: either as a change in the *content* of our fundamental orientation or, following the structural theories of development suggested by Jean Piaget (1896–1980), Lawrence Kohlberg (b. 1927), and James Fowler (b. 1940), as a *structural* change in our fundamental horizon.[12] In the former case, the conversion is horizontal; in the latter case, it is vertical. Although content is fundamentally linked to structure, we argue that moral conversion, like all the other conversions about which we will speak, is more basically a structural reality.

We need to draw a distinction between a horizontal and vertical exercise of freedom.[13] A horizontal exercise of personal freedom is a decision or choice that occurs within an already established field of vision or horizon. The field of vision is controlled by the kinds of existential questions and relevant data that we are interested in and that are available to us. In this case, we could undergo a horizontal conversion, that is, a change of *content*, by giving new answers (content) to old questions within an established horizon. For example, we could ask the same question about what we ought to do in a particular situation and find that the old answer was no longer sufficient and that a new answer is more appropriate. The new answer could arise because of a better perception of the relevant data or of the values at stake in the situation.

To be more concrete, we might ask how much money we should give out of our surplus to aid the poor. On the basis of our perceptions at one moment, we might find that fifty dollars is sufficient. But on the basis of new information about the plight of the poor, we might find that a new answer is necessary (e.g., one hundred dollars) to meet the needs of the poor. As we can see, the existential question remains the same, but the answer (content) changes.

On the other hand, a vertical exercise of personal freedom (structural change) can be described as "the set of judgments and decisions by which we move from one horizon to another."[14] In this case, we could undergo a vertical conversion by asking "radically new questions which creatively restructure the content (old and new) into a totally new horizon."[15] Fundamentally, then, moral conversion entails the asking of radically new existential questions about the world and the persons with whom we live.

To take the example above about the poor, we could ask a radically new question not about how much to give from our surplus but about the meaning of persons as our neighbors and their value. No doubt such an existential question would restructure our entire way of perceiving the world and relating to the poor of the earth.

Simply defined, moral conversion is a modality of self-transcendence in which we change the criterion of moral decisions and choices from personal satisfaction to values including the satisfaction of persons' needs. The first thing to be noted in the definition is that moral conversion is a modality of self-transcendence. A modality of self-transcendence is the personal engaging in a vertical exercise of our freedom toward value which has heretofore not occurred. In other words, before moral conversion we have lived at the level of premoral consciousness, where the satisfaction of our own needs of whatever kind has held sway in all or most decision making. Once converted, though, we transcend ourselves by adopting a new criterion of decision and choice for action. This new criterion is value including the satisfaction of persons' needs. The new criterion arises because of a structural change in our consciousness that has resulted from asking radically new existential questions about the meaning of persons. No longer do the converted ask which kind of selfishness is appropriate in a given situation, now we ask which kind of value will satisfy persons' (including our own) true needs.

We have argued that moral experience is concerned with value (moral meaning). Meaning is what is intended in questioning, and moral meaning is what is intended by questions of value. When we begin to ask questions of value, we ask questions about the meaning of persons and their well-being. Indeed, the foundational moral experience that thrusts us into authentic moral life is essentially the experience of the value of persons and what befits their well-being. This experience is bipolar in that the questions that drive us to self-transcendence and the objects that draw us in moral consciousness are persons and the values that fulfill their basic human needs. In other words, that to which we are driven in our questions of value and to which we are drawn in moral experience is primarily the fundamental symbolic value of persons.

Moral conversion as a change in criterion of decision and choice occurs once the foundational moral experience has taken place in our lives. Until we come face to face with the irreducible value of persons and the necessity to satisfy their basic human needs, moral conversion as a modality of self-transcendence is an impossibility. In this way, we could consider the foundational moral experience and moral conversion as two sides of the one structural condition of authentic moral experience.

THE ORDER OF CHARITY AND THE ORDER
OF GOODS FOR PERSONS' NEEDS

In one way, what we have been speaking about in moral conversion and the foundational moral experience relates to the traditional Christian categories of the order of charity (*ordo caritatis*) and the order of goods for persons' needs (*ordo bonorum*). The question of the order of charity has been long-standing in the Christian traditions, and it reached its classical formulations in the writings of Saint Augustine and Saint Thomas Aquinas (ca. 1225–74).[16] In both classical formulations we see that, after love of God, persons are the primary value to be loved. What we have called the foundational moral experience of persons as value and the corresponding moral conversion that places persons and their needs as the criterion of decision and choice is similar to what Augustine and Aquinas referred to in their writings. Yet there are also differences, and for our two classical authors the differences concern the necessities to love and not only to appreciate persons, on the one hand, and to develop priorities (an order) of love of neighbor, on the other.

The Order of Charity

Although moral conversion and the foundational moral experience call us to transcend ourselves to the value of persons, it is more a challenge than an achievement. Moral conversion only discloses the gap existing between the self we are and the self we should be. Besides moral conversion there is the necessity to move beyond ourselves with regularity and not by fits and starts. We do this only insofar as we fall in love. One author has put the matter appropriately: "For only in such falling-in-love do our full persons escape the centripetal force of our persistent egocentric gravity."[17] Such falling in love requires a further conversion, an affective conversion.

Affective conversion is a modality of self-transcendence in which we move away from narcissistic love to a self-giving love of others. New existential questions about the meaning of persons call for a new horizon, and now the criterion for love is no longer self-love but other-love on a regular basis. Affective conversion transcends moral conversion in that we not only *appreciate* the irreducible value of persons but also *love* persons for who they are (neighbors) and look on them as gifts. It gives us the stability to love regularly and consistently no matter in what condition we might find the person-neighbor.

Affective conversion is a progression from moral conversion, in that it presupposes its existence, yet it must be considered distinct from moral conversion. To make persons and their needs the criterion for decision and choice is not the same as loving persons as our neighbors. Not only does the reason for choosing the fulfillment of human needs as the criterion for decision differ in the two conversions, but also the degree and depth of the psychological and moral force for regularly choosing on the basis of this criterion differ. In other words, our moral impotence to choose regularly and consistently on the basis of human needs is overcome when we truly love, and not only appreciate, the neighbor. When we undergo an affective conversion, the end we seek is different; that is, we choose on the basis of human needs in order that a community of love might result, although the actual attainment of such an end is not a prior condition for adopting the criterion. Thus, the end for which we choose and act in affective conversion is based on hope. The kind of hope about which we are speaking is a distinctive characteristic of all falling in love, and it enables us to expand again our horizons and to reenvision the world and its possibilities for human well-being and fulfillment.

It is certainly possible for nonreligious people to undergo an affective conversion, but for the disciple of Jesus such a conversion is the central dimension of the Christian call. What it means to be a disciple of Jesus is to love the neighbor without restrictions, and for Jesus that includes even love of our enemies (Matt. 5:43–48; Luke 6:27–28, 32–36). We are certainly called to love all persons, but for Jesus there is a definite priority or order that should inform our love. It is clear from the gospel accounts of Jesus' life and message, especially in Luke's Gospel, that the poor and disadvantaged in society are to be preferred to the rich and powerful. Their needs are to be satisfied first, in preference to the needs and desires of those who have benefited the most from society's goods. To love as Jesus did is to love preferentially, and this requires a Christian order of charity.

A belief in the person of Jesus and an abiding hope that what he did and taught will ultimately be brought to completion, along with participation in the shared meanings and values of the Christian story and community, are rich resources that both enable and sustain affective conversion. Indeed, moral and affective conversions become Christian to the extent that they come into being by reference to the religious experience and shared meanings of the Christian community. This suggests that Christian religious conversion, about which we will speak later, becomes the *Christian condition* for the possibility of Christian moral experience and interpretations. By permeating and reinterpreting moral experience according to Christian meanings, Christian religious conversion distinguishes the moral experience of the disciple from all other forms of moral consciousness.[18] The same is no less true for the affective experience of the disciple who has undergone religious conversion. The disciple now loves the neighbor without restriction or qualification, as a sign of the inbreaking reign of God. The specific motive for such love becomes discipleship to Jesus, and this motive is nourished and sustained by a hope for the final realization of God's reign.

The Order of Goods for Persons' Needs

The disciple of Jesus who emerges from the long and difficult struggle in moral conversion is one who not only values persons but also seeks to fulfill persons' (including the disciple's) true needs. For to experience the value of persons is also to experience the necessity of satisfying human needs in a way that enables people to flourish. Human needs have corresponding values that fulfill them, and it is precisely these values the converted person now adopts as the criterion of choice and decision.

Not all human needs are of the same kind. Just as these needs can be placed into some form of hierarchy, so also can the values and relations that fulfill them. Thus we can speak of an order of values or goods (*ordo bonorum*). The proper fulfillment of human needs according to a hierarchy is the subject matter of justice. When we speak of the order of goods and its achievement for human opportunity and flourishing, we are at the same time speaking of the virtue of justice that becomes characteristic of the converted person. Once again, though, we are enabled to be just and perform just acts consistently and regularly when we undergo an affective conversion whereby we fall in love. In somewhat traditional language, we can say that charity really is the form or dynamism behind the consistent performance of justice.

Natural desires, which drive us to certain values, can be placed in some form of hierarchy. First, there are *vital* needs that include such things as the desire for life, health, vigor, etc. Then there are *social* needs, such as the desire for the order that makes possible cooperation for common goals. Although vital needs are more fundamental, we should not take the view that the vital needs of individuals always are to be preferred to the needs of the general community. *Cultural* needs, such as artistic expression, are also basic, and they rank higher than the others. Next, there are *personal* needs, and they concern our desires for love, justice, and truth. Finally, there are the *religious* needs that drive us to seek out higher powers (God) and establish good relations with them.

We can see from this partial list of human desires, placed within an ascending order of importance, that there are corresponding values and relations — for example, health, social order, play, friendship — that fulfill our needs. Our participation in the *summum bonum*, which the disciple of Jesus calls life with God, depends on our capacity to be just, that is, our capacity to seek the well-being of the neighbor by fulfilling his or her human needs within the hierarchy. Our questions about value, which constitute our self-transcendence into moral consciousness, are in fact questions about the meaning of persons and the fulfillment of their needs. Stated simply, these questions are about a world and set of human relations that can be and ought to be for the well-being and fulfillment of people.

In part at least, the determination of objective morality is made on the basis of whether we choose and whether we act on values higher in the hierarchy when we can as well as not. Stated another way, other things being equal, if we can fulfill either a cultural need or a personal need but not both, then our choice ought to be for the satisfaction of our neighbor's personal need.

The problem we all face on a regular basis is that "other things are *not* equal," and so we must make hard choices between values that are not of the same kind.

There are even times when justice will require that we satisfy a value lower in the hierarchy because of some extreme situation. For example, it seems just that a ruler of a very poor country should prefer the securing of vital needs like food, shelter, and education over the vigorous development of cultural values when both cannot be realized. Such a situation would not preclude development of cultural values, but it certainly would be unjust for the ruler to prefer these values over those vital to human well-being.

For the disciple of Jesus, the fulfillment of needs is neither avowedly impartial and abstract (blindfolded) nor dispassionate and minimalistic. Informed and sustained by the biblical witness, the converted disciple is called to be biased in favor of preferring the needs of the poor and disinherited over the wants of the powerful and rich.[19] As such, Christian moral consciousness itself is biased in its realization of justice in a world not yet fully redeemed. As we struggle in our moral conversion to prefer the needs of the poor and to join in solidarity with their causes, we are sustained by a hope in the eschatological fullness of the new heaven and earth (Rev. 21:1-4). In fact, our moral and affective conversions themselves can become mediations of our solidarity with all victims of unjust situations as we await the fulfillment of God's reign.[20]

CONVERSION AND THE ETHICS OF VIRTUE

Recently, Christian ethicists have been reclaiming a longstanding tradition that emphasizes the importance of virtue in the moral life.[21] An ethics of virtue is concerned with the character or style of our moral living. A discussion of character, then, attempts to highlight the kind of people we are or should be (e.g., just, kind, loving, chaste) rather than the kind of actions we should perform. There is no opposition, however, between character/virtue and doing, because certainly there is interaction between the kind of people we are and the kind of actions we perform.

As we have seen, moral and affective conversions are modalities of self-transcendence. A discussion of these conversions is properly a discussion of the ethics of virtue. Our moral character or style of life is determined, at least in part, by the kind of existential questions and answers present within our horizon. For the morally unconverted person, the horizon of consciousness is bounded by questions about personal satisfaction, and the answers are controlled by realizations of individual selfishness. However, for the converted person the horizon of consciousness is expanded in vertical exercises of freedom to appreciate (moral conversion) and love (affective conversion) persons and the values fulfilling their needs. Here the virtues can be looked on as concrete qualities of the converted person predisposing him or her to kinds of value. The virtues of the converted person are actually concrete manifestations of the conversion process lived out on a regular and sustained basis. Thus the virtuous person is properly the one who has emerged after a long struggle to be predisposed regularly to decide on the basis of the value of persons and to choose values fulfilling persons' true needs.

When moral and affective conversions take place within a Christian ecclesial context, the relation between the conversions and the ethics of virtue takes on a further significance. The conversions are now understood as transformations of the disciple in response to the gospel message mediated through the Scriptures and the shared meanings and values of the ecclesial community. They are concrete realizations both in the subject and in his or her acts of the fundamental orientation to life in response to God's call to perfection. In turn, the conversions enhance and deepen this fundamental orientation to live a life of holiness and discipleship. The virtues are understood as qualities predisposing the disciple regularly to prefer the values that fulfill the needs of the poor and disinherited over those of the rich and powerful. Virtues, which both come into being through the conversions and are realizations of them, are lasting dispositions that direct the disciple to the realization of the Christian orders of charity and goods (*ordines caritatis et bonorum*).

Virtues aim not only at perfecting people, they aim also at creating just conditions and relations for a just society. In other words, the virtues aim at bringing into existence structural relationships that fulfill human needs. So, for example, our lasting dispositions of love and justice seek to create humane policies for welfare programs that provide for the poor and those who cannot care for themselves. What nurtures and sustains both the conversions and the virtues is the Christian story mediated through the daily life of the ecclesial community past and present. The lives of the saints, the liturgical celebrations of the community, and prayer all continue to nourish the style of life and social existence that have now come into being.

CHRISTIAN WITNESS AND
CHRISTIAN FAITH

Christian foundational theology requires attention both to the experience of our "natural" or common-sense world and to the traditions that come from Christian texts and experience. The limit situations we have described remain abstractions, of course; yet critical distance does not mean estrangement from the stories, symbols, and poetry of full-bodied existence. Even though there are only specific religious traditions (Hinduism, Buddhism, Islam, Christianity), abstracting their common characteristics and conditions can be enriching. The general structures permit dialogical comparison of specific positions and an understanding of differences as well as identities.

Having distinguished moral from religious understanding, we need to answer questions like, What are the origins of religion? What is faith? How is religious experience different from other kinds of experience? Is it universal? Do beliefs come from religious conversion? If they claim to be knowledge, in what sense are they so? Do they differ from the beliefs of scientific investigation? These are all much controverted, difficult questions. Although some of the subtleties in these problems cannot appear, our positions account for these discussions by providing an intelligent introduction to the theological and anthropological foundations for Christian thought.

The Bipolar Sources of Religious Experience

Just as the origin of our moral judgments is in a dual experience, that of thrusting toward what we ought to be and that of being drawn toward the good, so the experience of being religious is twofold. On the one hand, there is our thirst for, our desire for God, and on the other hand, the discovery that God has preceded this drive with an antecedent gift of love. Both aspects are integral to our experience of God; both are operative throughout our entire lifetime, though we do not always attend to both. Let us look first at the drive toward ultimate Transcendence, and then at the experience of gift.[22]

Our natural world is full of questions. We ask who, what, when, where, and especially why things are as they are. People who question never seem to be satisfied, always sorting out further contexts and shapes, understanding new ways of conceptualizing data, judging the truth or falsity of their own and others' observations, and deciding whether any of the judgments are worthwhile. We seem to be an open-ended system of unrestricted intending. There remains a constantly expanding horizon of interest, conceptualization, reason, and evaluation. Without this openness, human beings would simply not be who they are. Rocks are aggregates, insensitive and unconscious; animals are sensitive but instinctual; human beings actually construct worlds beyond the ones they know and love, by asking questions and imagining the ways in which the world is not—at least for now.

The questioning that moves us, however, presupposes that there is something to be known, an intentional object, but also presupposes an underlying evaluative strategy that tacitly assumes that objects are worth knowing or loving. Why is it worth experiencing things or people? Why do we assume that our life in the common-sense world is worth living? Is the world actually intelligible? Such value-oriented questions point to the fact that as human beings we do not operate wholly through carefully reasoned ideas or clear and distinct concepts.

We have a faith in the fact that life is worthwhile, that ultimately there will be comfort and justice.[23] There are days that we can exit the humdrum daily experience through playing a game, becoming part of the third quarter or the second inning. By entering a work of art such as a painting, we allow our own time to be defined by its frame, its color and texture, instead of our own. Heroic activity is another example. Courage in defiance of death, whether our own or that of those we love, cannot be completely justified on rational grounds; yet we occasionally live that way and habitually trust that it is a possibility for all. The sociologist Peter Berger has called these critical moments (questions about value, faith in the order of the world, the suspension of temporal suffering in play or art, courage and the need for justice) signals of transcendence. They do not necessarily prove that ultimate value exists, but they show us that we operate with some assumption that the world is finally understandable and that friendship rather than malice grounds and governs the universe.

The questions describing the origins of morality query the limit experiences that provoke us toward an anticipation that ultimate value, a final ground supports, sustains, and even cares for our world. They are boundaries or thresholds we cross, only to discover that the empirical world as we ordinarily know it remains incomplete, contingent upon the possibility that there is One who envelops it.

The origin of our religious experience is not so much a matter of the answers we give, the names we use, but of the questions that rise from our attempts to know and love. We reach toward an unconditioned whole that may provide the ultimate horizon for all our questions and answers. These are questions about God. God is not the specific formulation we offer to fill our judging and deciding; rather, God is the fulfillment of the basic intentionality of the human questioner.[24]

The pursuit of an ultimate concern, however, opens into a sense of being grasped by God. Letting our questions take over, our values take root, our loves take charge permits us to experience our lives as gift. Suddenly the wonder of knowing that our contingency is not a threat, that we need not operate in paranoid competition with others, that our small increment of understanding is some portion of the truth becomes more telling than all the skeptics' doubts. We sense a power in experience not of our own making.[25]

The classic description in this century for this reality is that of Rudolf Otto in *The Idea of the Holy*.[26] He described the gifted quality of existence as an irreducibly sui generis experience of the sacred. Our dependent creatureliness meets an incalculable, majestic vitality, wholly other than we are. The mystery we experience in the divine exceeds all our understanding, falling outside the limits we set for human knowing and loving, and yet this reality fascinates, draws us toward itself. We are seduced into a kind of rapturous transport or into the unity and solemnity of eternal order. He called this experience of the Holy, the *mysterium tremendum et fascinans*.

The uniquely differentiated experience of the divine is not, as Thomas Merton has said,[27] to be identified with a regressive immersion into nature, an erotic peak experience, an aesthetic experience like seeing a painting, or even the generosity of one's self-gift to another. It is rather a radical decentering of the subject into an Other over whom he or she has no control. Falling in love with God is not simply a better version of being in love with our friends, lovers, or neighbors. The mysterious Other appears in our experience as "nothing," One whom we cannot name but whom we know as operative in the world's affairs and in our own lives.

The mystics regularly speak about an experience of God in which their entire persons are stretched toward the Other in interior prayer. Fixed upon One whom they love who surpasses all finite reality, they are willing to leave creation behind, since in God they will recover everything as a joy. Knowing their own limited status in the world, they experience this humility as exuberant gift. Finally, progressively detaching themselves from specific loves, they center upon the Other in a vital union of intersubjective love in which they can truly say that they and God are one without erasure of their own identity. One could take many texts to exemplify these assertions, but let us quote Thomas Aquinas, whose work will never be said to scant rationality: "The ultimate in human cognition of God is to know that one does not know God."[28]

This paradoxical statement fits with our descriptions of religious conversion. The about-face that can occur in an individual through turning to God in Christ does not mean that we have ready-made, hand-me-down information about God. Indeed, the object of religious change remains as mysterious as the process in which that Other operates. Our transformation has the character of a response to the gift of God's love, but the way in which we "know" that God is actively pursuing us is through the symbols of conversion.

Christian Religious Experience:
The Witness of Faith

Many people have described themselves as religious without being Christian. The experience of religious change, of God as a mysterious Other drawing us, of knowing God in various limit situations, can be documented in many traditions. What specifies the wonder inherent in Christian experience? How would we qualify Christian love? Who is the God of the Christians? All these questions are of foundational import, but they also extend into specific topics in systematic theology.[29]

Before clarifying the Christian dimension of religious conversion, we should indicate two conditions that function structurally as a support for the larger architecture of theology: witness and faith.[30]

Witness may be defined as the words, works, actions, or lives that (1) attest to an intention, an inspiration, or idea, (2) which is absent to the hearers, (3) to which, despite the fact that it transcends their present experience and past memory, (4) they assent.[31] Witness is like a report with which we agree on the basis of the testimony of others. Report can be distinguished from an empirically based registration of an event in which we knew something by virtue of our immediate participation in its presence.[32]

Much in our lives is based upon report. Some reports, like the language of the courtroom, we take seriously; about others, such as newspaper accounts, we are skeptical. What is intrinsic to testimony itself, that we choose to depend upon some remarks and reject others? To understand the criteria for belief, we must examine the nature of witness.

When we listen to a story told by an eyewitness, what counts for its truth is not just the intrinsic coherence or realism of the narrative but the veracity of the storyteller. For example, in a courtroom, false testimony is not the product of a witness misseeing an event, for many witnesses may register an incident differently; rather, false witness is the perverse intention to deceive the hearer. The authentic witness is one whose oath or promise provides personal backing for the report we hear or read. Crucial witnesses are those who are so convinced of their story that they are willing to die for it.

There are, of course, fanatics, quite misguided individuals who have died for stories even patently false. So the sole criterion for truth cannot be the authority of the speaker. The story itself requires other validations, either as prediction of a future possible state or as confirmation of a past event. We can see that scientific investigation functions by an analogous process, with an emphasis upon the empirical warrants for truth.

None of us generates all the information, judgments, and values that occupy our common history. To achieve some advance in knowing, we must depend upon the communications of others. Engineers depend upon the mathematically generated tables of other thinkers; actors assume that the texts they use to memorize their lines are accurate reports of Shakespeare's words. In each case, there are both a judgment that it is worth believing the report and a decision to assent. In each case, we assume that the communication that we have received is correct and that the one who is speaking is not attempting to deceive us. In the case of a scientific experiment, analysts assume that they could duplicate the results they are accepting, if they had time, money, patience, and so on; so too actors believe that if they were textual critics and paleographers, they could determine the authenticity of the text they are using. But they will not. They trust the work of others, the witness of scholarship enshrined in the material they receive. In the end, the nonscientific basis for their assent is laid at the shrine of the truthful witness.

Testimony in the case of religious events operates no differently. Not all religious knowledge is immanently generated. It is transmitted by others to whom we accord the status of privileged holiness; it is overheard in the remarks of those to whom we grant legitimate authority; it is told in stories to which we give credence because they found communities that continue to give sense to our lives. And yet part of the truth of authentic religious witness is that we are enabled to enact its basic message in our existential situations. Granting the witness a prior authority, we try out the experiment for ourselves.

There is a basic human faith by which we all function in that we assume the worthwhile character of human existence. We trust that it is valuable to ask questions, to live within language, and to share some structured society. This is neither completely demonstrable, nor conclusive in its formulation. We assume that it is worth striving for truth, justice, and love. Indeed, without completely empirical warrants in our ordinary world, we offer love, promises of fairness and equity, and declarations of truth. We call this faith, dependent upon the witness of humanity's struggle for a survival beyond the most rudimentary goods.

Religious faith chooses to believe an oral, visual, or textual tradition about the ground of the world. It assumes that it is worthwhile to ask the question, Why is there something rather than nothing? It expresses itself in prayer and ritual, prophecy, story, law, doctrine, and apocalypse. It knows that it is worth encountering a Thou who speaks through the universe.

Christian faith, however, requires a "leap" beyond the witness of natural or even traditional events. It is the act of surrendering to God in Christ, who is the one faithful witness to the way the world can be. In one sense, it is analogous to ordinary human and religious faith in that the human processes of knowing and loving continue on the other side of faith. But Christian experience also confronts all the ordinary attitudes of knowing and loving with a radical announcement: that they are incapable of sustaining their own development toward what is good, true, and beautiful.[33] All our intersubjective experience is unable to overcome the malice that marks human competition and betrayals; none of our technical skills can erase the finite end of death.

The Christian Word announces this radical insufficiency of human experience only within the total sufficiency of God's willingness to take on human evil and death as a personal project, to encompass human problems without displacing genuine human power.[34] Jesus is one who could give himself completely to the Father without losing his own authentic humanity. Our faith, imitating his complete trust in God, becomes the assent to cooperate with God in the divine activity of overcoming pain, suffering, and evil in the world.

Faith is the knowledge born of religious love. We discern the value present in the one we love, here an incarnate One who fulfills the very desire to desire love itself. Hearing that God has loved us first (1 John 4.10), the witness of a particular life and death to the Father's care, puts before us a question for decision: Will we return this love or not? It is only after we make such a decision that questions of fact, definitions, doctrines, and systems are articulated.[35] These are beliefs of which we shall speak later. Christian faith is first of all a way of being, that by which God turns us toward himself; only then is it that to which we adhere.

The specifically Christian dimension of faith, therefore, is not an appeal to experience, since many religions are convinced of the truth of their union with the divine. It is not the appeal to a book, since at least both Judaism and Islam depend upon Scriptures. Nor does its veracity turn upon an appeal to ecclesiastical authority. Rather, the unique character of Christian faith is the trust that God has spoken and continues to speak through one individual, Jesus of Nazareth, and the community that was founded in his name.[36] Modifying Walter Kasper's definition somewhat, we may say that faith is a fundamental decision on the part of individuals in which they find themselves, their way of life, others, and the whole of reality by discovering God in Christ.[37] Our primary identity, found in Christ, is such that we hope to witness to this experience for others.[38]

Christian conversion therefore is not necessarily different from the way in which other religious change occurs. The process of being drawn by God and driving oneself toward transcendence can be paralleled in other religious traditions. What specifies Christian conversion is adherence to the person of Christ and the way in which he turned toward the Father in his life of preaching and in his death on a cross. Faith is, in this sense, absolutely concrete, dependent upon the historical particularity of Jesus of Nazareth. Faith declares its experience of a mutuality between God and believers and Christ, such that believers share in the life of God.

Christians do not fall in love with an abstract divinity unavailable to understanding; rather, the change that occurs in Christians becomes scandalously particular, opening to others in the strenuous responsibility for neighbors that Jesus demands. The gift of God's love that we discover as having preceded all our striving enables us to be free for justice, truth, and love without worrying about the cost to ourselves. As it grows and develops, such faith empowers us to transform the world. The test of our conviction, of our witness, becomes the price of our own lives.

NOTES

1. B. V. Johnstone, C.Ss.R., "A Proposal for a Method in Moral Theology," *Studia Moralia* 22 (1984): 203.

2. Louis Janssens, "Ontic Evil and Moral Evil," *Louvain Studies* 4 (1972): 134.

3. David Tracy, *Blessed Rage for Order: The New Pluralism in Theology* (New York: Seabury Press, 1975), 105.

4. Howard Harrod, *The Human Center: Moral Agency in the Social World* (Philadelphia: Fortress Press, 1981), 35.

5. Bernard J. F. Lonergan, *Insight: A Study of Human Understanding* (New York: Harper & Row, 1978), 609.

6. Bernard Lonergan, *Method in Theology* (New York: Herder & Herder, 1972), 6–7.

7. Ibid., 11–12.

8. Richard A. McCormick, "Bioethics and Method: Where Do We Start?" *Theology Digest* 29 (1981): 305.

9. Lonergan, *Insight*, 597.

10. See Joseph Fletcher, *Situation Ethics: The New Morality* (Philadelphia: Westminster Press, 1966), esp. 40–68.

11. Saint Augustine, *The Problem of Free Choice*, trans. Dom Mark Pontifex (Westminster, Md.: Newman Press, 1955). For a more complete comparison between Augustine and Pelagius on the relationship between grace and morality, see Saint Augustine, *The Retractations*, trans. S. Mary Inez Bogan (Washington, D.C.: Catholic Univ. of America Press, 1968), 32–40 (I.8).

12. Walter E. Conn, "Conversion: A Developmental Perspective," *Cross Currents* 32 (1982): 324.

13. See Lonergan, *Method*, 237–38.

14. Ibid., 237.

15. Conn, "Conversion: A Developmental Perspective," 324.

16. Saint Augustine, *On Christian Doctrine*, trans. J. F. Shaw (Chicago: Great Books, Encyclopaedia Britannica, 1952), chaps. 27–33. Saint Thomas Aquinas, *Summa Theologica*, trans. fathers of the English Dominican Province (New York: Benzinger Brothers, 1947), IIa–IIae, q. 26, aa. 1–13.

17. Conn, "Conversion: A Developmental Perspective," 325.

18. For a helpful discussion of the distinctiveness of Christian moral experience, see

Charles E. Curran and Richard A. McCormick, eds., *Readings in Moral Theology*, no. 2, *The Distinctiveness of Christian Ethics* (New York: Paulist Press, 1980).

19. Daniel C. Maguire, "The Primacy of Justice in Moral Theology," *Horizons* 10 (1983): 75.

20. See Matthew L. Lamb, *Solidarity With Victims: Toward a Theology of Social Transformation* (New York: Crossroad, 1982), esp. 1–12.

21. E.g., see Stanley Hauerwas, *Character and the Christian Life: A Study in Theological Ethics* (San Antonio: Trinity Univ. Press, 1975), and Bernard Häring, *Free and Faithful in Christ: Moral Theology for Clergy and Laity*, vol. 1 (New York: Seabury Press, 1978).

22. See Lonergan, *Method*, 104–24; and David Tracy, *Blessed Rage for Order*, 91–118.

23. Peter Berger, *A Rumor of Angels: Modern Society and The Rediscovery of the Supernatural* (Garden City, N.Y.: Doubleday & Co., 1969), esp. 61–94.

24. Karl Rahner, "An Investigation of the Incomprehensibility of God in St. Thomas Aquinas," in his *Theological Investigations*, vol. 16, trans. David Morland (New York: Crossroad, 1979), 244–54.

25. James Robertson Price, "Lonergan and the Foundation of a Contemporary Mystical Theology," in *Lonergan Workshop V*, ed. Fred Lawrence (Chico, Calif.: Scholars Press, 1985), 163–95; and idem, "The Objectivity of Mystical Truth Claims," *Thomist* 49 (1985):81–98.

26. Rudolf Otto, *The Idea of The Holy: An Inquiry Into the Non-Rational Factor in the Idea of the Divine and Its Relation to the Rational*, trans. John W. Harvey (New York and London: Oxford Univ. Press, 1969), esp. 12–40; see also Robert Sokolowski, *The God of Faith and Reason* (Notre Dame, Ind.: Univ. of Notre Dame Press, 1983).

27. Thomas Merton, "Transcendent Experience," in Thomas Merton and D. T. Suzuki, *Zen and the Birds of Appetite* (New York: New Directions, 1968), 71–78.

28. Thomas Aquinas, *De Potentia* 7, 5, ad. 14, in *Opera Omnia* (Paris: Vives, 1889), 23: 229.

29. See below, chap. 7, 155–58.

30. Paul Ricoeur, "The Hermeneutics of Testimony," *Anglican Theological Review* 61 (1979):435–61; and Josef Pieper, *Belief and Faith*, trans. Richard and Clara Winston (Chicago: Henry Regnery Co., 1965), 3–91.

31. Lonergan, *Insight*, 703–18; and idem, *Method*, 41–47.

32. For an elaboration of this distinction through the phenomenology of Edmund Husserl, see Robert Sokolowski, *Husserlian Meditations: How Words Present Things* (Evanston, Ill.: Northwestern Univ. Press, 1974), esp. 34–42.

33. Lonergan, *Insight*, 666ff.

34. Hans Urs von Balthasar, *Love Alone*, trans. Alexander Dru (New York: Herder & Herder, 1969), 68–86.

35. Lonergan, *Method*, 115–16.

36. See Bernard Lonergan, *Philosophy of God, and Theology* (London: Darton, Longman & Todd, 1973), 20, 67.

37. Walter Kasper, *An Introduction to Christian Faith*, trans. V. Green (Ramsey, N.J.: Paulist Press, 1980), 82.

38. John Baptist Metz, *Followers of Christ*, trans. Thomas Linton (Ramsey, N.J.:

Paulist Press, 1978), 42–44; and idem, *Faith in History and Society: Toward A Practical Fundamental Theology*, trans. David Smith (New York: Crossroad, 1980), 163–66. See the important remarks on religious identity and social praxis in Francis Schüssler Fiorenza, *Foundational Theology: Jesus and the Church* (New York: Crossroad, 1984), 213–45.

FURTHER READINGS

Dietrich Bonhoeffer. *The Cost of Discipleship*. London: SCM Press, 1969.

Walter Conn, ed. *Conversion: Perspectives on Personal and Social Transformation*. New York: Alba House, 1978.

Avery Dulles. *Models of Revelation*. Garden City, N.Y.: Doubleday & Co., 1983.

Ray L. Hart. *Unfinished Man and the Imagination*. New York: Seabury Press, 1979.

Enda McDonagh. *Gift and Call: Towards a Christian Theology of Morality*. St. Meinrad, Ind.: Abbey Press, 1975.

Daniel C. Maguire. *The Moral Choice*, esp. chap. 3. Garden City, N.Y.: Doubleday & Co., 1978.

Stephen Charles Mott. *Biblical Ethics and Social Change*. New York: Oxford Univ. Press, 1982.

H. Richard Niebuhr. "The Center of Value." In his *Radical Monotheism and Western Culture: With Supplementary Essays*, 100–113. New York: Harper & Row, 1970.

Gene Outka. *Agape: An Ethical Analysis*. New Haven: Yale Univ. Press, 1972.

Robert Sokolowski. *The God of Faith and Reason: Foundations of Christian Theology*, esp. 1–52. Notre Dame, Ind.: Univ. of Notre Dame Press, 1982.

CHAPTER 3

THE JOURNEY OF A PILGRIM PEOPLE
IN FAITH AND MORAL DEVELOPMENT

What is all knowledge too but recorded experience, and a product of history; of which, therefore, reasoning and belief, no less than action and passion, are essential materials?

Thomas Carlyle (1795–1881), *On History*

Moral, affective, and religious conversions are by no means once-and-for-all momentary transformations of the self. The journey of the conversion experiences is indeed long and, on many occasions, quite arduous. The tendency at this point might be to believe that the conversions occur instantaneously, have little or no background for their development, and are complete at their inception. Nothing is further from the truth, though. Many times we experience the conversions more as beginnings than as established achievements, and there are two fundamental explanations of why this is the case.

First, we are beings who come to authenticity and maturity over a period of time through various developmental stages. Our past achievements only become beginnings for advancement to further stages of development. At times, we even need to remain at a certain stage, whether that stage is psychic, moral, religious, or affective, to consolidate and integrate what has gone before.

On the other hand, our journey in the natural developmental processes is not at all guaranteed. We are not prepackaged beings who inevitably and inexorably develop in some kind of sterile environment. We are beings in history, and our own histories constitute who we are. Our histories are narratives of how we have come to be the kinds of persons we are in light of our personal exercises of freedom within specific cultures and communities. Unfortunately, one factor that conditions our freedom is sin, personal and social. Our own personal sinfulness and the sin that makes its way into our social structures impede us from advancing steadily and easily toward further development. Conversion is always a turning away from sin and selfishness, but as we all know too well, this is no easy task. Thus the second explanation of our experience of difficulty in the conversion processes lies in the history of human sinfulness.

KOHLBERG AND FOWLER: COGNITIVE AND AFFECTIVE DEVELOPMENT

Conversions are always developmental processes, and these processes are intimately related to, but *not* identifiable with, the natural stages of development in the human person. In this century, developmental psychologists, for example, Jean Piaget, have uncovered the structural characteristics of natural human development. Piaget's[1] research into the cognitive development of children has been influential in the recent work of Lawrence Kohlberg and James Fowler. There are surely many difficulties when Christian categories of conversion draw on the insights of these authors.[2] Our aim is not, however, to establish the validity of Kohlberg's and Fowler's theories, though they are helpful in illustrating how and why the conversion experience is a process of transformation, but to show that our moral and religious lives grow to maturity over a considerable period of time.

Both Kohlberg and Fowler belong to the structural school of human development. Unlike the psychoanalytic and social-learning schools of development, the structural school attempts to go "under" the content of cognitive-moral judgments and affective-faith experiences to discover the deeper operations of knowing and valuing that underlie, ground, and organize the thematic content of these judgments and experiences. In other words, Kohlberg and Fowler have been interested in articulating the "operational rules or laws which the mind follows in reasoning or making judgments."[3] These rules are implicit, and they underlie consciousness in such a way that they are the patterned processes which constitute our thought.

Kohlberg and Cognitive-Moral Development

Kohlberg has discovered that there are six distinct stages of cognitive-moral development, and he has organized these stages on three levels: (1) preconventional, (2) conventional, and (3) postconventional. Each stage is defined not in terms of content but rather according to the formal character of moral judgment, that is, how we resolve conflicting claims. The criteria for the for-

mal character of moral judgment are cognitive, and so the criteria are concerned with how we think about moral problems and give reasons for
decisions. The structure of each stage is defined in a formal way according
to our social-perspective taking in making judgments and decisions.[4] For
Kohlberg, the normative criterion against which judgments are measured and
the stages are developed is distributive justice.

It is important to note that Kohlberg argues that the sequence of the stages
is universal and invariant, and each stage is progressively more comprehensive, differentiated, and integrated (equilibrated) than the one before it.[5]
Kohlberg's stages of cognitive-moral development can be described briefly in
the following way.[6]

Preconventional Level. In the two stages that constitute this level, children are
responsive to the cultural rules and labels of good and bad, right and wrong,
but they interpret these labels either in terms of physical and hedonistic consequences (punishment, reward, exchange of favors) or in terms of the physical power of those who pronounce the rules or labels.

Stage 1. The Punishment and Obedience Orientation. What determines an
action's goodness or badness are the physical consequences regardless of the
human meaning or value of these consequences. For example, a child at this
stage will judge the breaking of a cup to be bad even though he or she was
really trying to be careful. Avoidance of punishment and unquestioning
deference to power are valued in their own right. The social perspective of
this stage is egocentric.

Stage 2. The Instrumental-Relativist Orientation. The rightness of action
consists of that which instrumentally satisfies one's needs and occasionally the
needs of others. Human relationships are understood to be much like relationships found in the marketplace. Elements of fairness, reciprocity, and equal
sharing are present in this stage, but they are understood in a physical, pragmatic way. Reciprocity is a matter of "You scratch my back and I'll scratch
yours." This stage takes a concrete individualistic perspective.

Conventional Level. At this level, which includes two stages, what is perceived as valuable in its own right, regardless of the immediate and obvious
consequences, is maintaining the expectations of the individual's family,
group, or nation. Not only is the attitude one of conformity to personal expectations and social order, but also of loyalty to it, of actively maintaining, sup-

porting, and justifying the order, and of identifying with the people or group involved in it.

Stage 3. The Interpersonal-Concordance or "Good Boy–Nice Girl" Orientation. Good behavior is interpreted as that which pleases or helps others and is approved by them. There is a good deal of conformity to stereotypical images of what is the majority or the "natural" behavior. Behavior is frequently judged by intention, and one earns approval by being "nice." This stage takes the social perspective of the individual in relation to other individuals.

Stage 4. Society-Maintaining Orientation. The person's orientation at this stage is toward authority, fixed rules, and the maintenance of the social order. Right behavior consists of doing one's duty, showing respect for authority, and maintaining the given social order for its own sake. This stage differentiates the societal point of view from interpersonal agreement or motives.

Postconventional Level. In the following two stages there is a clear effort to define moral values and principles that have validity and application apart from the authority of the groups or people holding these principles and apart from the individual's own identification with these groups. For Kohlberg, it is at this level that the person achieves an autonomous or principled morality based on his normative criterion of distributive justice.

Stage 5. The Social-Contract Orientation. Actions are considered right by reference to general individual rights and to standards that have been critically examined and agreed on by the whole society. The person is clearly aware of the relativism of personal values and opinions, and there is a corresponding emphasis on procedural rules for reaching consensus. Apart from what is constitutionally and democratically agreed on, the right is a matter of personal "values" and "opinion." The emphasis here is on the "legal point of view," and outside the legal realm it is free agreement and contract that are the binding elements of obligations. For Kohlberg, this is the "official" morality of the American government and Constitution. Its social perspective is that of an individual aware of values and rights prior to social attachments and contracts.

Stage 6. The Universal-Ethical-Principle Orientation. In this last stage of the unfolding principle of justice, right is defined by the decision of conscience in accord with self-chosen ethical principles appealing to logical comprehensiveness, universality, and consistency. These principles are abstract and ethical (e.g., the Golden Rule); they are not concrete moral rules such as some of the Ten Commandments. For Kohlberg, these principles are the universal principles of justice, of the reciprocity and equality of human rights, and of respect for the dignity of human beings as individuals. This stage takes its social perspective from the "moral point of view" from which social arrangements derive or on which they are grounded.

Fowler and Faith Development

James Fowler has applied some of the insights of Kohlberg's theory to the realm of faith development. Like Kohlberg, Fowler argues that his structural stages of development are hierarchical, sequential, and invariant.[7] But he differs from Kohlberg and Piaget in that he refuses to accept their assessment that natural cognitive structures tend to dominate the affective dynamics of the person. Because he claims he does not adopt Piaget's theoretical separation of cognition and affection, Fowler looks on faith as "a structured set of operations in which cognition and affection are inextricably bound together."[8]

For Fowler, faith may be, but is not necessarily, "religious" in the sense of being informed by a religious tradition. Rather, faith is "a person's or a community's way-of-being-in-relation to an ultimate environment."[9] If translated into Jewish or Christian terms, "ultimate environment" would be called the "Kingdom of God" by Fowler. Furthermore, faith involves acts of knowing, constructing, or composing an apprehension of the ultimate environment. In this way, Fowler maintains that faith is a primary motivating power in the journey of the self and is a core element in our character and personality.[10]

Like Kohlberg, Fowler argues that it is the structural characteristics, not the content, that determine the stages of faith. The characteristics Fowler uses are (1) form of logic (cognitive operations), (2) form of world-coherence (patterns of coherence in our ultimate environment), (3) role taking (social-perspective taking), (4) locus of authority (sources of authoritative insight or "truth" regarding the nature of the ultimate environment), (5) bounds of social awareness (width and inclusivity of the primary identifications by which we determine our community of faith), (6) form of moral judgment (stages that are modifications of Kohlberg's stages of cognitive-moral development), and (7) role of symbols (our symbolic competence).[11]

We now turn to a brief summary of Fowler's six stages of faith development.[12]

Stage 1. Intuitive-Projective. The stage-1 child (ages four to seven or eight) experiences the world as fluid and full of novelty. The capacity for perspective taking is egocentric, and the child's locus of authority are the parents or parentlike adults. The child's understanding of good and bad is not yet "moral," and symbols tend to function as identical with or as part of what they represent.

Stage 2. Mythic-Literal. The child operates in this stage from the ages of six or seven to eleven or twelve. The young boy or girl now becomes an empiricist, separating the real from the unreal on the basis of practical experience. Alongside this empirical world, there is the very private world of speculative fantasy and wonder. Stories or myths, whether of a personal or cultural-religious nature, are used to express the child's sense of an ultimate environment. The boundaries of the social world expand beyond the family, and a new element of reciprocity enters the child's life. At stage 2, a symbol must refer to something specific, and thus the child operates out of a kind of literal-correspondence understanding.

Stage 3. Synthetic-Conventional. The transition to this stage does not occur before ages eleven or twelve, and Fowler believes that a significant number of adults are best described by this stage right through middle age and into their older adulthood. The real achievement of stage 3 is its way of structuring the world and the ultimate environment in interpersonal terms. The person is capable of mutual role taking, that is, the individual constructs an image of the self as seen by others and then takes account of the fact that others are performing the same operations in their relationships.

In this stage the person is a conformist in that he or she is acutely aware of the expectations and judgments of others, yet has not constructed an independent perspective. The person's life is segmented into related and overlapping "theaters" of action and relation, for example, family, intimate groups, work or school, religion, etc. Not all the significant others in these "theaters" are in agreement in their expectations, judgments, and evaluation, and thus faith must find a way of synthesizing these valued expectations and judgments. There are two possible ways of synthesizing: to compartmentalize (i.e., the person meets the expectations of each group when it is present), or to create a hierarchy (i.e., some significant others are considered more important, with other "authorities" being subordinated to them).

Fowler's stage 3 can be correlated with either stage 3 or 4 in Kohlberg's scheme of moral development. Finally, Fowler has found that at stage 3 the person typically is precritical or "naive" in the apprehension of symbol. God is frequently understood as friend, companion, comforter, or guide.

Stage 4. Individuating-Reflexive. At this stage, generally not before the early twenties, the person emerges from his or her dependence on significant others for the construction and maintenance of faith. The sense of self is now reciprocal with a faith outlook that mediates between the self and significant others. Because the person now knows that his or her views are different from those of others, he or she realizes that a justification of its truth and adequacy is required. This stage is not necessarily an individualistic stage, because the person does not always separate from the former interpersonal relations, institutional ties, or religious background. However, the individual no longer fashions identity in terms of these relationships, as at stage 3, but looks on them as expressions of a more autonomous identity and outlook.

The authority for stage 4 is validated by internal processes, and truth must "fit" with the other elements of one's outlook taken as a whole. Fowler has found that people in this stage may use principled judgment similar to Kohlberg's stage 5 at the postconventional level, although the person's morality is still influenced by class or group bias. Finally, the import of a symbol, ritual, or myth is separated from the entity itself and is conveyed in ideas or propositions. The concerns for meaning, internal consistency, and protecting the boundaries of the self drive the person to formulate clear ideas that minimize any emphasis on the symbol's or myth's power to transform the individual.

Stage 5. Paradoxical-Consolidative. Transition to stage 5 is rare before the age of thirty, and most people never advance to this level of faith development. This stage involves the integration of many dimensions that were suppressed or evaded in stage 4. Also, this stage requires a critical coming to terms with one's social unconscious: the myths, norms, ideal images, and prejudices with which one has grown up. To advance to this stage one must know suffering and loss, responsibility and failure, and the grief that is part of having made irrevocable commitments in life.

Individuals at this stage exhibit a dialectical style whereby they embrace polarities and tend to see both sides of an issue simultaneously. Also, faith-knowing involves a more critical self-awareness, and thus thinking and judgment are related to one's own subjectivity. This critical self-awareness enables the individual to internalize many of the authorities that have previously operated in his or her life.

Moral judgment is much less distorted by class or group biases, and so the person consistently judges from the "higher law" perspective which is characteristic of Kohlberg's stages 5 and 6. The individual's relationship with myth and symbol is reclaimed at this stage in that their affective and aesthetic import are rejoined with ideas and propositions to make an impact on the self. The individual is now enabled to see in a new way by the symbol and thus is able to grasp life and reality in a fresh and enlarged way.

Stage 6. Universalizing. The individual at stage 5 remains caught in the paradox of conflicting loyalties, and so a readiness to spend and be spent on behalf of others is limited by concern for oneself, or one's family, or one's group survival. The transition to stage 6 overcomes this paradox through a moral and ascetic thrust to universal apprehensions of love and justice. At this stage, the individual realizes that the fractures and divisions within the human family can be overcome only through a universal commonwealth of being. Very few people ever achieve this stage, and Fowler numbers Martin Luther King, Jr., Mahatma Gandhi, and Mother Teresa of Calcutta among those who have achieved this level of faith development.

Those who do arrive at this stage experience a oneness or unity with the intent of the ultimate environment. Authority inheres in a heart and mind purified of egoistic impulses and attentive to the requirements of Being. The boundaries of social awareness become universal, and loyalty to Being is the fundamental principle of moral reasoning. Although Fowler is unsure whether stage 6 really describes or requires any basic structural advance beyond stage 5, he believes that its radical relativization of the self as center is so dramatic a redirection of the structures of faith that it constitutes a qualitative revolution.

Our intent in summarizing the structural stages of moral and faith development is to underscore the necessity of viewing the life of faith and morality as a gradual and cumulative unfolding of ourselves as we attempt to decenter the self. Human interiority has a history, and the landscape of this history is to become a person-for-others. What Kohlberg and Fowler illustrate for us is that self-transcendence through decentering the self is ontogenetic and developmental; that is, there are inherent structures within us (ontogenetic) that unfold according to universal and invariant developmental stages whereby we move from egocentrism to the possibilities of self-giving love toward others and God. Figure 1 below seeks to correlate the various stages of these two authors as a way of summarizing their structural theories.

Although a conversion typology cannot be modeled simply on the findings of these authors, we should certainly have the sense that conversions away from selfishness to responsible action and faithful witness are hardly once-and-for-all momentary experiences of transformation. The conversions are dependent on the achievements of the natural stages of cognitive and affective development, but they also go beyond them in how they transform us. Conversion always comes into being under the grace of God mediated through our natural structures and others with whom we live. We will return to the theories of Kohlberg and Fowler later in this chapter after we take up the last of the four kinds of conversion, namely, intellectual conversion.

FIGURE 1

STRUCTURAL STAGES OF KOHLBERG AND FOWLER

Kohlberg's Stages	Fowler's Stages
Preconventional Level	
1. Punishment and Obedience	1. Intuitive-Projective
2. Instrumental-Relativist	2. Mythic-Literal
Conventional Level	
3. Interpersonal-Concordance	3. Synthetic-Conventional
4. Society-Maintaining	
Postconventional Level	
5. Social-Contract	4. Individuating-Reflexive
6. Universal-Ethical-Principle	5. Paradoxical-Consolidative
"Religious Stage 7"	6. Universalizing

POETICS IN RELIGIOUS DEVELOPMENT:
REVELATION AND SYMBOL

Fowler outlines rather briefly the various roles symbols play at different stages in our conversion. Generally, the movement can be seen as a shift from fusion with one's social or mythic-cultural symbols, through a period of criticism and distance, to a reintegration by which the individual finds a world disclosed that is somehow deeper and richer than his or her first apprehension.[13] In the final stages of development, symbols seem to comprehend the paradoxical and polar character of life, not by way of escape from thoughtful discrimination of differences but by a wisdom that sees beyond such discrepancies to a unity that underlies self and world.

Because we, with Fowler, do not wish to divorce the affective and cognitive dimensions of symbol, we recognize that the expression of converted faith will have meanings qualified by the different moments of people's lives. Sometimes the modes of apprehension will be due to age, sex, education, affect, or existential concerns. Occasionally, there will be differences due to affective breakdown or cognitive and ethical confusions. The complex interactions of conversion, faith, and symbolic expression are as various as the histories of individuals and communities.

But just as there seem to be certain structural similarities in human cognitive, ethical, and affective development, so too there are patterns in the expressions of religious conversion. Moreover, the patterns seem to have a certain genetic relationship; that is, one emerges from the other with some regularity, not on analogy with the life of plants but in the interrelationships of poetic form.

What follows[14] is an attempt to see how God discloses himself through the gradual development of the symbolic forms that believers use to express their converted development. Although it is more than possible for someone at a primary level of religious and moral development to make use, for example, of prescriptive symbols (laws), those same prescriptions may recur at a higher level with rather different meaning. Narrative images, such as those in the Book of Genesis, may be rejected at one stage only to be recovered at a later level of development. First, we shall describe the notion of revelation that is operative in our description of conversion and faith; then outline in their various stages the symbolic expressions which disclose that revelation. This will be an important prelude to our being able to see the role that intellectual development plays in foundational theology.

Revelation

The way we understand God's presence to us depends greatly upon our understanding of communication in general. Since the vocabulary and syntax of human interaction is an analogue of what it means to say that the indefinable Other turns toward us and initiates dialogue, what we say about the nature of dialogue makes a difference. "How" we conceive of God's conversation with us determines "what" God is saying to us.

Avery Dulles has outlined a number of models of communication through which Christian revelation has been understood.[15] One of the most common until recently was that of the proposition. According to this view, God has spoken through conceptually available, syllogistically analyzable truths that are set out clearly in the Bible and the tradition of the church. This interpretation focuses upon the truth character of God's speech and demands unequivocal Christian assent. But it tends to limit communication to abstract cognition and to divorce itself from wider human experience.

In reaction to this, others have emphasized the outer and inner dimensions of revelation. Some see God's Word as primarily available in the facts of history, not in the interpreters' understanding of history but in God's deeds accessible to all reasonable observers. Here history is God's meaning for the world, and revelatory events are self-interpreting. The problem is that not all historians seem to see the same thing; there is no neutral observational status through which divine presence is accessible.

Those who stress the "inside" of revelation turn to mystics and contemplatives to understand the way in which God communicates. God becomes the inner content of revelation, attained through rapture or mystical excess. All external articulations, whether doctrinal, historical, or institutional are relative to the inner union with God. This understanding emphasizes the nonconceptual and affective dimensions of religion, often permitting a dialogue with other world religions, but it usually appears vague, without particular historical or doctrinal content.

A fourth type of revelation returns to the distance between the divine and the human, stressing not the unity but the paradoxical disparity in revelation. Creatures cannot be vehicles of divine presence unless God wills it so. When God is known through faith, the divine remains hidden, dark and mysterious, confronting humanity with its failure to be its best self found in Christ. God appears as an independent Other, addressing us through the Word; but the lack of intrinsic connection between God and the vehicles of self-communication makes it difficult to understand how God is not arbitrary and capricious. The position can be effective in preaching, but it is systematically weak.

Dulles proposes a definition of symbolic revelation that combines what he believes to be the best aspects of the others and yet goes further. We would like to modify his approach slightly and define revelation as a *gifted religious discovery expressed in symbols.*

Most would agree that a number of elements need to be included in any contemporary definition of revelation. Revelation is an activity through which God discloses himself; revelation is intersubjective communication. This communication is a knowledge or awareness beyond our own abilities: though revelation occurs within human experience, it always exceeds it. God appears only indirectly through it. God is the initiator of the dialogue; divine free love occurs and we are the response, indicating the reciprocity of our faith and God's words. Revelation simultaneously tells us about God and about the value, order, and future of ourselves and the world. Revelation, in this sense, is both a challenge to the world's failures and a confirmation of its authentic virtues. To understand how all this can take place, it is crucial to know how symbols are a communication of the self.

When we communicate with one another at the deepest levels, for example, in love, we share ourselves symbolically. First in our bodies, then in an external, often physical element, we unfold to another what we mean. Without the symbol, we might not even know ourselves what we meant, but certainly no one else would. Symbols express our affective, cognitive, and moral selves in a global fashion, offering to someone the heart of what we are. Symbols discover for us and for others new ways of our identity in the world. Following down the paths opened by a symbol, we are confronted by other people and their worlds, confirmed in our own journeys, and sometimes transformed by sharing in the common horizon created by the symbol itself.[16]

God allows us to discover divine presence through symbols. Like the discovery that takes place in science, there is a coalescence of insights and unexpected patterns of data, in which our search for understanding is satisfied. Then we discover that the new vocabulary accounts for anomalies or difficulties we had not anticipated, illuminating new realms of experience. Finally, we feel the confirmation that comes from knowing that others can share our hypotheses about the world, that future answers can be anticipated and problems solved.[17]

God speaks to us through symbols in much the same way. Our quest for meaning and value is passionate and intelligent; we will not settle for stupidity or anxious hatred. In certain limit situations, patterns coalesce into a whole through which the insight is grasped that a power not our own is operative (whether in stories, events, images, or concepts). There occurs an illumination in which there appears a peace, patience, or quite inexplicable joy that a threshold has been crossed. This discovery is confirmed by sharing our insights with a community and by the release of a new energy for witness to others.

Revelation is *discovery* because there is some new communication about our world now available to us; it is *religious* because the symbol discloses One who addresses us in relationship to the whole of life; and it is *gifted* because we know that we did not initiate the solution to our problem. The symbols that God uses transform us, lifting us from one horizon to another, not unlike certain poems, plays, and dances. Symbols reshape our commitments, persuading us that the world can actually be the way we hope it ought to be. Symbols can show us knowledge that would be inaccessible to discursive or propositional thought. The symbol's multivalent meanings permit us entry into the foreground of a world, making a home among familiar things or people, only to lead us toward a horizon that we barely anticipate.

It should be obvious to readers that the language we have used about revelation records the same grammar as that of Christian conversion. Conversion, whether sudden or slowly evolving, is the personal and communal "place" where God's Word is spoken to us. Just as Jesus was the perfect symbolic disclosure of God's self-presence to us, God's unfolding of himself in an "other," so conversion to Christ becomes our entry into participation with God. Through this one unalterable, unfathomable symbol, we discover God's voice, which overturns our expectations about the betrayals of sin and the limited end we all suffer in death. Taking the Way which Christ is, we discover both truth (cognitive aspects) and life (moral and affective dimensions). The revelation of God in Christ creates the response that is our experience of conversion and our knowledge of faith.

The Unfolding of Revelation

Revelation should not be seen as a univocal notion. The symbols that embody God's voice for us are multiple and complex.[18] What we have in the Hebrew and Christian Scriptures is a library of religious forms that convey to us multivalent aspects of the divine speaker. Nonetheless, there is some advantage in trying to interrelate the various linguistic genres of the Bible, since that shows us something about how faith responded in the past and can be expected to appear in the future. At various times, one or another form of revelation has been the focus of Christian existence. Indeed, it is likely that each of us forms our own primary analogue through which we see the whole of our converting toward God. We shall look at the basic types of revelatory discourse that appear in the Scriptures and offer one way of genetically interrelating them.

Both by virtue of our understanding of converison and through a reading of the oldest Christian texts, we must judge prayer to be the primary Christian symbolic mode of disclosing divine presence.[19] In turning toward God, believers discover that they are addressed by a Thou over whom they have no control. The declarations "Jesus is Lord!" (1 Corinthians 12:3), "Come, Lord Jesus" (Revelation 22:20) and "Maranatha" (1 Corinthians 16:22) are address and invocation to a presence no longer masterable by our manipulation of space and time. The one who was dead is now living. Early christological hymns (Phil. 2:6–11; Col. 1:15–20; 1 Timothy 3:16; 1 Pet. 3:18–22) celebrate divine action in the event of Christ. Supplication for the coming presence of the kingdom becomes recognition of divine achievement for us. The language of prayer forms our sensibilities in the process of expressing the symbol.

From such a rapturous identification with God emerges the witness beyond oneself or one's local community. God has sent us to speak on the divine behalf. Prayer becomes prophecy, the testimony to others of which we spoke earlier. The prophets, for example, Jeremiah (2:1), know the address from an Other as mission to speak in God's name. In the prophet's words, there is the disclosure of the divine Word for the world. This announcement questions, provokes, promises, and liberates the hearer. In the "I" of the prophet, we overhear the "I" of God. The response to the revealed word is faith, an identification with the program of God's care and concern.

These two forms of divine-human interchange liberate the language of story, the narratives told about what God has done for his people, especially in Christ. Witnesses submerge their own role into the story itself. The events become the most important mode of gifted discovery about what God has done. The significant event becomes the node around which the history turns; the remembrance founds a community, delivers it from danger, forgives its sins. Just as telling one's own story to a therapist recovers the hidden memories that may block free activity in the present, so retelling the story of Jesus continues to provoke us toward his way of being a witness to God in the world. Remembering the stories of Jesus, the early Christians, and the deaths of the martyrs and saints is a refusal to forget the message, to represent the same possibilities in the present, and to live by anticipation the story proclaimed.

Other forms of revelation are also important, such as the prescriptive discourse of the law which attempts to sort out the practical demands of the discovered gift of God's love. The memories of deliverance, especially for a Jew, require memorial instructions on how to live that freedom. Obedience to the law is a way of living inside the election and the promise of God. Never mere compliance to outer forms, the Torah is a way of forming one's heart in the way God hopes the world to be (e.g., the Book of the Covenant, Exod. 20:22 – 23:19; and the Holiness code, Leviticus 17 – 26). The will is engaged even when the heart is not always ready to respond. In the letters of Paul, the proclamation of Jesus as Lord begins to take on the form of legal prescription and ethical demand (e.g., 1 Thess. 5:12ff.; 2 Thess. 3:6; Romans 13), simply because the everyday world requires concrete implementation. This became truer in later texts of the New Testament (e.g., 1 Timothy 6; Titus 2 – 3). Prescription focuses the specific embodiment of the originating event, disclosing the sometimes painful ethical requirements that remain inside the global experience of conversion and faith.

Besides prescription, however, there is also the kind of reflection upon the originating religious event that we can group under doctrine and wisdom discourse.[20] Wisdom literature in the Jewish Scriptures attempts to realize the significance of the exodus for the common human limit situations. What does our liberation mean for the constant suffering of humanity, as in the Book of Job? What does salvation mean for those outside the religious tradition who convert, as in the Book of Jonah? How does God's plan for the world include all human beings, however mysteriously? In a strict sense, wisdom literature is the beginning of systematic thinking about religion, an attempt to combine all the elements of one's religious experience in a whole. This kind of reflection can be seen in certain aspects of the Christian Bible in the Letter to the Hebrews and parts of the Letters to the Colossians and Ephesians.

When reflection turns toward the inner organization of religious experience, it appears as doctrine, an attempt to see the meaning of the extraordinary event of Christ and to envision daily existence under its power. Just as there is a drive to sort out the harmonies of the universe in wisdom discourse, so in early Christian doctrines there is the shift toward a measured tone and clear meaning and a stress upon content. Both sapiential theology with its emphasis upon order and doctrinal or ecumenical formulations with their tendency to compromise on nonessentials loosen some of the tension found in the parables and stories of Jesus. Each of these genres, however, is concerned to show how Jesus' story can become part of the patterns of eating, sleeping, knowing, and loving that characterize our ordinary world.

Apocalyptic language will have none of this.[21] This form of early revelation was provoked by political crisis, religious conflict, and rejection by society at large. As in the Book of Revelation, it expects radical change, a final intervention by the divine power to overcome the evil that exists in the world. It challenges all private understandings of religious compromise and confronts any complacency that might lurk in the human heart, asserting that the only real hope for transformation is through God's singular activity. There is a "not yet" to every event of religious change, to every conversion, that makes it incomplete, the not quite fulfilled resurrection of the unity of the universe.

Each of these genres of revelation is distinctive, fixing the expectations of readers or hearers on a certain pathway toward God's presence. Each discloses some differing aspect of who God is, has been, and will be for Christians. In that way, no one form of revelatory discourse is exhaustive or can become the dominant strain in the experience of believers. Learning to read one form of Christian revelation, for example, the difficult visionary genre of apocalypticism, means gaining an imaginative competence, having a particular access to the world, ourselves, and God. Just as some people never learn to read poetry very well, so too some find difficult the way in which God's message appears. This difficulty, however, does not cancel its value. Struggling with the doctrinal exigency within the Christian experience may be much more educative than easy readings of Jesus' parables, because it challenges our preference for self-mystification. The languages of revelation are multiple, just as the voice of God is varied.

INTELLECTUAL CONVERSION AND THE
NATURE OF THEOLOGY

Earlier we pointed to a shift in horizons that, following Lonergan, we called intellectual conversion. We noted different patterns of our experience and the ability we have to differentiate and interrelate them. The important ability to pay attention to our own ability to understand is the beginning of a change within us by which we become conscious of our own patterns of knowing. Certain aspects of foundational thought on ethics and doctrine are dependent upon this shift, making it necessary for us to explain more clearly what we mean.[22]

We have stressed in our investigations thus far the experiential aspects of Christian life: especially conversion and its symbolic expressions. In the sections to follow, we would like to distinguish between piety, religion, and devotion and theology proper. We do not intend to divide them, but we intend to differentiate their operations so that it becomes possible to understand certain kinds of questions that ethical and doctrinal statements answer. Christian theology originates from within conversion, but it asks questions that many believers face rarely if at all. The notion of intellectual change should assist us in understanding why certain kinds of questions emerge.

From Witness Through Criticism to
Witness Including Criticism

The intellectual shift of which we have been speaking begins in the movement toward doctrine in Christian experience. The need to make coherent and congruent the various symbolic interpretations of Christian life promoted the clarification of concepts, the shaping of definitions, and a sometimes trying effort to interrelate them. Finding a consistent set of terms and relations for Christ's teachings, how they apply to new situations, what their relationship is to previous teaching, what counts as authentic teaching—this forced upon believers a shift in perspectives. Instead of looking at the way revelation directed itself toward their salvation, believers began to ask how aspects of conversion were related to each other. Are the things that Christians say true only for them, or are they true within the wider political, social, and economic worlds in which they live?

We can see a drift in the New Testament in the way Jesus himself is understood as related to the Father. Though the hymns we mentioned earlier make it clear that early believers experienced the risen Lord as divine (*theos*) because he was with the Father in a special way, language indicating Christ as the "only" son of God (John 1:14) occurred relatively late in the New Testament period.[23] How is Jesus as the Messiah related to God, in a sense, irrespective of us? This question required some three hundred years and much theological controversy and political maneuvering to answer — and then for a specific classical culture. Though no community will ignore the answers developed at the Councils of Nicaea (325) and Chalcedon (451), the question continued to require new formulations.[24]

These formulations are not and were not in the language of stories, images, and symbols. Believers' minds asked certain kinds of questions, because intellect will not be cut off any more than affect will be. Indeed, if Christ made whole our person, then our thought processes themselves have been healed by redemption. Moral and doctrinal reflection is born in the inquiry into consistency, clarity, and the future consequences of one's beliefs.

The symbolic forms of revelation are irreplaceable and irreducible. Their witness is (1) inexhaustible, always providing a (2) surplus of meaning in the life of believers. By their ability to (3) recommend and promote a way of life, they help us participate in (4) significant actions, confronting us with the fact that (5) we are not on our own the ones who make the universe. Symbols are a rich, multivalent way in which we can become conscious of our roots in the past. In short, without the disclosure of Christian meanings in symbols, we might quickly lose the depth and extent of the proclamation.

Yet symbols also give rise to thought. They provoke us toward interpretation; and interpretations can conflict. Their many-sided richness of meaning can require us to take some distance from them just to see their coherence. Their incompleteness with regard to the ultimate concern they embody can produce a certain ironic or even comic questioning of the matter at stake. One may wonder what is the appropriateness of certain kinds of symbol (e.g., dance, visual art, or types of music) to the religious object.

In Jesus, there remains a claim that his particular life, death, and resurrection are of universal significance, that is, that it applies in all places and at all times to every situation. The symbols associated with this specific figure generate a permanent demand for the interpretation of later history (words, works, actions, and lives). His absence in body exerts pressure upon believers to make sense of their present and his continued presence. They recognize that to hold on to the physical images and symbols is to turn them into idols and to show a passive indifference to their meaning for the present. The symbols of Christ himself require a level of critical conceptualization with a recognition that the believer can never "leave behind" the symbols, indeed must always return to them to enrich reflection.

To appropriate the critical moment that clarifies some of the meanings of symbolic language, we need to make an intellectual shift. The change in horizons that takes place in our thinking processes is twofold: (1) an attending to definitions, conceptualizations, and their clarity, and (2) an understanding of the thinking operations that make such definitions possible. We will call the first *theory* and the second *intellectual conversion*.

Intellectual conversion, therefore, is a shift not only from seeing the world in relationship to our own perspectives but also toward the invariant patterns of knowing that make that understanding possible. It recognizes what counts as evidence at various levels of our knowing, that differing kinds of conditions must be fulfilled for truth in perception, understanding, judgments, and decisions. An intellectual shift in horizons knows that "seeing" is not necessarily "knowing," that the warrants for knowing the truth of language like "already," "now," "the future," "mind," "self," or "God" will not be found by pointing to empirical things or kicking a rock. Just as the types of experiences we have are multiple, so too is the evidence that warrants their truth. One knows, in other words, not just what one knows, but how one knows. One can judge quite legitimately that one is a knower.

If we think back to the role symbols play in the development of faith, we can see that some of the differences between stages 4 and 5 as Fowler understands them are the shift from a conventional attitude toward the symbols of religion, through their critical translation into ideas, to a postcritical appropriation of their meaning. We permit the symbols to form us despite the fact that we know that they are the limited presence of the divine. This is the emergence of a critical religious conversion.

This is an extremely important notion. Many believers assume that it is possible to know the objects of their faith simply by looking at them. Questions that come because one or another image (e.g., of Christ) do not quite fit together are taken to be doubts about faith. Attempts to clarify doctrinal understanding are taken to be accretions to or attacks upon the biblical Word. Applications to complex contemporary moral situations, which require sophisticated knowledge of medicine, philosophical anthropology, or politics, are assumed to be irrelevant. But to have an authentic understanding of one's ability to know encourages an appropriation of oneself such that one's religion or piety is enriched rather than destroyed. One's faith and its expressions become part of a larger world, mediated by human meanings of various sorts. Christian discourse refuses to be a sectarian impulse and focuses an authentic dialogue with many cultures.

Christian witness therefore is not simply a matter of taking an already formulated Christian football and running with it to a clear goal line. Rather, believers in their adherence to the event of Jesus of Nazareth enter a conversation with the thoughtful cultures to which they belong so that Christ may be disclosed more widely. Intellectual conversion is a moment within Christian self-understanding, not an extrinsic philosophical imposition upon the basic testimony that comes from personal identification with Jesus. We can say that just as there is a kind of witness that ministers to our neighbors who are poor, lonely, cold, and unhoused, so too there is an intellectual ministry to a world that asks hard and painful questions about relevance, truth, and goodness. Moreover, this world of difficult intellectual challenges originates not outside Christian faith but within it, because the questioner is the believer him or herself. Religious witness must make use of the sharpest tools available to disclose the sculptural form at the heart of the world.

Let us take the classic example of Thomas Aquinas's interpretation of theology.[25] True knowledge about God was for him the understanding that God has of himself. Since only God knows who he truly is, he must reveal himself to us. All our knowledge is therefore dependent upon God as teacher. Religious knowing, therefore, is unlike geometry, where reason works on its own to generate the first principles; it must wait to hear what God says. Our knowledge is always subordinate to the knowledge God has of himself. There are three ways in which this sacred teaching can be present in the believer: through faith, which is assent to what we hear as the Word of God speaking; through science (i.e., what we would call theology), which is a reflective knowledge of how the Word of God bears on all creation; and through vision, which is a unitive love and contemplation of God. Now, science or reflection upon faith can become a habit or second nature to us if we work at it long enough. But because thought too is weakened by the flaws of sin, especially pride, we need the gifts of the Spirit (wisdom and understanding) to exercise it well, so that we do not keep falling into error. The thinker about God's Word must pray to be maintained in truth. Thoughtful reflection is carried on within personal and communal witness.

As is clear, theology for Aquinas is both a speculative and a practical discipline—not simply because it is assumed that it is from explicit personal faith that theologians reflect, nor because theologians always operate within an ecclesial context, but because theology intends God as an "object" whose knowledge and love are coextensive and cooperative. God's thought and action can never be divided. Theology aims for such a unity, reflecting its divine origin and dependence upon revelation. Yet it is primarily speculative, according to Aquinas, since it concerns the knowledge through which human beings locate, understand, and validate the object of religion and its relationships. It can only be secondarily practical, since practical reason constructs or makes the objects it examines. Theology, however, returns to practice because both God and all reality in relationship to God (nature and the neighbor) must be understood in light of God's own plan of love for the universe.

In this context, Aquinas's interpretation of the shape of theology put together a coherent series of terms and relations that clarified the ways in which Christian piety, thinking, and grace could be understood within the wider context of his own intellectual world. Using the psychology and metaphysics of Aristotle (ca. 384–322 B.C.E.), Aquinas specified clear definitions of what it means to know, what it means to know God, and what knowing God means in relationship to the world as a whole. He developed a theory and a system for theology. By establishing some intellectual techniques for ordering questions to come to a solution, he created an extraordinary medieval systematic synthesis.

The further move of this century is what we call method; it attempts to understand and articulate the conditions under which theory and system can take place validly. Foundational theology is therefore an exercise in method. It makes clear what the various elements of the Christian experience and theological enterprise are, defines them with as much clarity as possible, and studies the bases that give them cogency, coherence, applicability, and truth.

Just as the theologian Origen (ca. 185–254) used middle Platonic philosophy to understand the evangelical images, or Thomas Aquinas used Aristotle's metaphysics, or Rudolf Bultmann (1884–1976) used Martin Heidegger (1889–1976), so contemporary theologians will witness to their faith by understanding it through the questions, categories, and cultural suppositions of the most articulate tools available to them. In essence, they cannot really avoid it. Their witness will already function within a cultural and scientific matrix; their task as theologians is often to explicate this conversation as clearly as possible for the sake of shaping the future of Christian experience.

FROM LAW TO PERSONAL RESPONSIBILITY
INCLUDING LAW

The foundational moral experience, which thrusts us into the authentic moral life, is a symbolic experience. Others affectively awaken in us a call to share in their lives and to fulfill basic human needs. Like all experiences of symbol, the experience of the value of persons and their needs gives rise to thought that can be formulated in concepts and judgments.

Values can be interpreted in about as many ways as there are people doing the interpreting. The result is that there will be inevitable conflicts of interpretation arising from the initial moral experience of the meaning (value) of persons and their needs. Thus there is the necessity to take a critical distance from the symbol (value) to make an intelligent and correct judgment on the available interpretations of the value. In taking a critical moral distance we do not withdraw from the affective appreciation of the value of persons, just as in critical religious judgments we do not depart from and leave behind our piety and devotion. However, we do include within our affective experience a moment of criticism. By transcending to a critical moral point of view whereby we appropriate the conditions of our own knowing and loving, we undergo what is called a critical (intellectual) moral conversion.

Moral conversion is a response to the gospel call to transform ourselves in anticipation of the fullness of the reign of God. It denotes a gradual movement away from self-centeredness and selfishness to a modality of self-transcendence whereby the disciple adopts the value of persons and their needs as the criterion of decision and choice in moral-decision making. Yet, this conversion is incomplete as it stands. Unless we take critical possession of ourselves through intellectual conversion, we never fully recognize the necessity for personal responsibility in the moral life.

The individual who has not undergone a critical moral conversion will inevitably identify the value of persons and their needs with the various conventionally defined values, customs, and laws of a given culture.[26] Thus, whereas the criterion of decision and choice has changed (moral conversion), the *criterion of judgment* about what is valuable has not changed. Only when we can take a critical distance from our own culture and its conventionally defined form of values, customs, and laws by moving into the realm of interiority can we as morally converted people realize the importance of personal responsibility for judging value (critical moral conversion).

In critical moral conversion we do not deny the importance of cultural values and laws. But we no longer defer to the authorities of culture (e.g., civil government, marketing analysts, etc.) and their regular interpretations, as the criterion of judgment for what is truly valuable. This is by no means some form of radical individualism by which moral isolationists seek to protect their freedom to determine for themselves what is or is not valuable. It is a modality of self-transcendence in which the critically converted person shifts the criterion of judgment of value from authorities external to the self (culture and its authorities) to the self as a personal source of value.

If we return to Kohlberg's three levels of moral development, we can see more concretely the implications of critical moral conversion. Kohlberg has described the two stages of the preconventional level as the punishment and obedience orientation (stage 1) and the instrumental-relativist orientation (stage 2). In both stages Kohlberg has found that the criterion of choice and decision is based on personal satisfaction. Young adolescents are self-centered at this level, and thus they have not yet undergone any real foundational moral experience and moral conversion.

In the transition from the preconventional to the conventional level of moral development, the adolescent undergoes a moral conversion. In stage 3 (the interpersonal-concordance of "good boy–nice girl" orientation) the adolescent has expanded the structural capacity for social-perspective taking. Although Kohlberg does not call the results of this stage a moral conversion, he does note that a shift occurs in the criterion of decision and choice. We have called this shift a change in the criterion of decision and choice from personal satisfaction to the value of persons and their needs, or moral conversion. As the converted adolescent advances to Kohlberg's stage 4 (society-maintaining orientation) he or she begins to consolidate the beginnings of the moral conversion from stage 3. Once again, we are not identifying Kohlberg's stages with the conversions. We are attempting, though, to correlate these conversions (figure 2) with the findings Kohlberg (and Fowler) have produced.

In stage 4 the adolescent or adult advances beyond the needs of the social group, for example, family and friends, to the needs of persons in general, society, and the general social order. As we recall, Kohlberg describes the stage-4 person as one who is oriented toward authority, fixed rules, and the maintenance of the social order. To be sure, there is real advancement in the moral life at the conventional level. But the moral conversion remains essentially uncritical. At this level there is no true realization of personal responsibility for the judgment of value, because the individual consistently defers to the authorities of the group (stage 3) or society (stage 4) and their usual interpretations as the criterion of judgment of value. The value of persons and their needs are regularly defined by reference to the conventionally available terms of the group or society, including their biases and prejudices.

The uncritical morally converted individual is really what could be called a naive realist. He or she believes that the knowing and the judging of value are like taking a look at what is available in the group or society. In other words, the individual knows and judges the value of persons and the fulfillment of their needs by looking to the various interpretations of the group or culture. Here, the uncritical person is always vulnerable to exploitation from every side as the result of familial, social, and cultural shifts in the interpretation of value. One becomes like a ship without a captain in stormy seas be-

FIGURE 2

STRUCTURAL STAGES AND THE CONVERSIONS

Kohlberg	Fowler	Conversions
Preconventional		
1. Punishment and Obedience	1. Intuitive-Projective	
2. Instrumental-Relativist	2. Mythic-Literal	
Conventional		Moral
3. Interpersonal-Concordance	3. Synthetic-Conventional	
		Affective
4. Society-Maintaining		
		Religious
Postconventional		Critical-Moral
5. Social-Contract	4. Individuating-Reflexive	
		Critical-Religious
6. Universal-Ethical-Principle	5. Paradoxical-Consolidative	
"Religious Stage 7"	6. Universalizing	

cause one drifts not only with the changing interpretations of value but also with the shifting biases and prejudices of the culture.

Only the critical realist, that is, one who has undergone an intellectual conversion, can survive well in the sea of conflicting interpretations of value. For only the critical realist can acknowledge that the facts of human knowing and judging value are related to the appropriation of our own operations of self-transcendence. The real world is not already out there to be looked at, as the naïve realist believes. The real world is the world mediated by meaning and motivated by value, and it is constituted by reference to the invariant process of experiencing, understanding, judging, and deliberating. The criteria for objectivity are not just the criteria of what regularly happens in the world and what various authorities regularly say. They are the compound criteria of experiencing, of understanding, of judging, and of deliberating.

If we return to Kohlberg's stage theory of moral development we can see more concretely that the transition to the postconventional level marks the move to what we have called a critical moral conversion. At stage 5 (the social-contract orientation), Kohlberg notes that the individual judges actions to be right by reference to standards that have been critically examined and agreed on by the whole society. This shift to interiority is manifested all the more at stage 6 (the universal-ethical-principle orientation). No longer does the morally converted person accept the criterion of judgment of value to be what the cultural authorities say it is. Some critical distance is taken in stage 5 from cultural interpretations with their attendant biases, but it is especially in stage 6 that the individual consults the process of human knowing and judging internal to the self and the intrinsic ordering of values. Prior attachments to social interpretations and laws, which so characterized the stage-4 person, are not necessarily denied or considered null and void.

The stage-5 person, and especially the stage-6 person, does not retreat into an ideal private world in which he or she withdraws from the ordinary experience of life with others to judge value. No doubt such withdrawal is a danger to be avoided. It is particularly at stage 6 that the critically converted person accepts and chooses the self as the criterion of the real and of the truly good in his or her self-transcending judgments of value.

In the acceptance of the self as the personal center of the origin of value, a shift in the criterion for judgment of value occurs. In other words, we recognize that the criterion of judgments of both fact and value is the self-transcendence of the subject. We recognize also that moral meaning (value) is indeed independent of ourselves, and so the judgment of value is really to state what is truly good or better for persons and their needs. Judgments of value, then, always articulate a world and a set of human relations that ought to be in order for us to remain human and to flourish. They state what is the case about humanity in a world that is not yet realized although capable of really coming into being.

We have already made clear that critical moral conversion does not entail the rejection of law which governs social cooperation and the social order. The critically converted individual is no antinomian, and so the taking up of personal responsibility does not replace the necessity for social restraints and avenues of cooperation enacted through law. However, there is the realization that not all laws of a society are just, and thus they do not always distribute fairly the burdens and benefits of culture. Laws must be judged to be just and fair, and the criterion for this judgment is the self-transcendence of the subject made manifest in critical moral conversion.

FROM NATURE TO HISTORY
INCLUDING NATURE

By beginning this book with Christian experience, we have committed the reader to a particular way of doing theology. This path is through personal and communal history. We have shifted from a foundational theology based upon unchanging human nature to one focused through historical change. The journey chosen determines to some extent the knowledge offered and understood. Here we see theology from the viewpoint of a contemporary culture that praises change and sees cultural stasis as at best boring, at worst repressive. Does this not give in to a relativism that absorbs the decisive character of the Christian message? Is not God's authority weakened in this understanding of theology? It would be pretense to say that shifting from static nature to the dynamics of historical change does not make a difference. But what difference does it make?

Aristotle defined nature in a number of ways:[27] (1) as the source or cause of being moved or being at rest; (2) as the immediate material substratum of things that have in themselves a principle of motion or change; (3) as the shape or form that is specified in the definition of a thing; and (4) as the why of a thing. Because "nature" seemed to include both intelligible and material aspects of a thing, it was often easily misunderstood as static and substantial, the primary analogue being natural objects such as rocks. When this was applied to the human being, defined as a rational animal, our nature easily was misconstrued as an ahistorical, material reality, largely subject to necessary laws. In such a framework, history could at best be the becoming that was on its way to a new stasis. History was not understandable on its own merits but was understandable only in terms of metaphysical principles.

The Enlightenment of the seventeenth and eighteenth centuries began to limit the "nature" of things to what could be determined through answering scientific questions. The generalized similarities that emerged in experiments determined what a thing was. At the same time, Immanuel Kant encouraged people to use their own reason in taking responsibility for their understanding of the world. The French Revolution (1789) permitted all classes to think of themselves as in some way in charge of their own history. Since that period, human nature has no longer been seen as static or lumpishly substantial. It has become necessary to understand whether it is possible to "think change," to understand the nature of historical becoming itself. Historical consciousness has supplanted classical categories of explanation.[28]

By focusing upon conversion and the experience of God, we have obviously sided with the post-Enlightenment tradition. History makes us what we are. Becoming is not exemplary narrative, anecdotes that record particular whims or opinions about an unchanging humanity. Rather, human being and human acting cannot be divorced. Without knowing the concrete history of a person, a community, an idea, or an action, we know only the abstract and formal possibilities that may or may not operate in experience. Memory does not simply retain the past, but its retentions are constitutive of the present and anticipate the future. Human beings are involved in their own self-making.

Now, this changes the sense in which we can speak of human nature. Although there are formal possibilities: perception, understanding, judgments about facts, and decisions for or against values, they remain abstract outside the particular histories involved. It is the specific dialectic of positions taken, the conflicts into which people enter, the attractions that fulfill and the repulsions that separate that define the "nature" of human beings. Each historical moment is not just another example of an old law but a genuinely new event. To be human means to be able to choose or reject the past in acceptance or refusal of a future. Since history can never be chosen inside a horizon without particulars, the nature of being human means a situated freedom in which choice encompasses nature.

Why is this an important shift? Because it refocuses the character of religion, Christianity, and theological reflection.

If religion and morals are known as part of the necessities of nature, gift is likely to appear as part of the contingency of natural objects. God is disclosed through theophanies like the burning bush or in hierophanies like the granting of the Torah on Sinai. Morality is determined by the "natural" law, whose primary analogue is not human history but the nature of things with their regularities and patterns. One's personal and communal history is either in conformity or it is not. One becomes a Christian or a Catholic at one time without remainder. One's history is either living inside that configuration or it is not.

But as even Augustine recognized, "the fundamental principle for the pursuit of this religion [i.e., Christianity] is history."[29] Can the contingency of the death-resurrection of Jesus be experienced as the ultimate historical gift, the authentically new possibility actualized in our world in and for us? Can the human self-making that adheres in conversion to this Christ be known as a gift?

If Christian experience is seen through the world of cosmic necessities, a particular sort of Christianity emerges. It is one in which Christ is seen as a cosmic principle, and miraculous overturnings of natural necessities are as-

sumed to be divine disclosure. But if Christianity is seen as primarily historical, as constituted by change, then Christ's death and resurrection did in fact
effect a new world in which we can live. It is through historical events that
we know the care and protection of God. We are not defined as Christians
at some moment; rather, what it means to be a Christian emerges in the developmental history of people and communities. Just as we do not give up
witness for skepticism or moral responsibilities for personal license, so we do
not let go of situated necessities for an unmitigated construction of ourselves.
Personal and communal freedom, in each case—whether of truth, value, or
human identity—is a situated history. We become Christians through our
own histories, but those stories are bounded by the concrete possibilities available at specific moments in time. Historical self-making includes a responsible
attitude toward nature, whether that be our own bodies or our environment.

The standard objection in both Catholic and Protestant theological circles
to our approach is that by beginning with the experience of God and religious
change, we have irremediably caught ourselves in a relativism that destroys
the possibility of objective moral values and objective revealed truths. We
would deny this and believe that both the process and the structure of the
book in hand augment the force of this denial. As we have said, to know the
conditions proper for judging the objectivity of something is a complex knowing process. To have a grasp of those operations and the various interrelated
sufficient conditions for judging truth or falsity of values requires intellectual
conversion. By understanding the invariant operations of what it means to
understand, theologians are capable of avoiding the either/or Scylla and
Charybdis of relativism and objectivism. As will become quite clear, the questions that promote our experience, our understanding, our judgments, and
our decisions are formal imperatives—unfilled intentions that gain specificity
only in the history of our investigations. Our book is written from such a developing viewpoint.

Foundational inquiry will always be a thematization of the horizon of
knowing, evaluating, and loving as operations—thus providing *new* formulations in every culture. The concrete dialogue of positions about what constitutes knowledge, value, and love provides evidence for the dialectic of formal
imperatives as questions, as well as an ongoing collaboration toward specific
cultural results.[30]

A theology that is understood through historical change will therefore need
to pay attention to the history of humanity and its culture as well as to the
interior subjectivity of believers. Besides outlining the terms and relations
that will provide a logical theory, and developing the systematic interrelation-

ships among those theories, it will need to understand the conditions of history and subjectivity that ground those interpretations of religious existence.

For a concrete example of the difference caused by looking at Christian experience through nature or history, let us look at the Christian sacraments. In a world dominated by nature, the meaning of the sacraments is primarily as a divine disclosure under physical, often spectacular, forms. The emphasis in classical sacramental theology, especially that of Baptism or the Eucharist, was on how God acted within water or bread and wine. Becoming a Christian happened at one moment, baptism, and there was either adherence or backsliding in relation to that one ritual event. If historical becoming is stressed, however, one is never a Christian all at once, but is one only slowly, painfully, with the ongoing conversion that sacramental life symbolizes. Christian Eucharist focused its meaning upon the way in which the community develops in relation to the tradition of believers who have shared the nourishing bread and the sacrificial cup. The historical self-gift of Jesus of Nazareth in his final supper with his disciples becomes the symbolic paradigm for Christian living. History includes natural objects, not the other way around. The history of Jesus of Nazareth determined the religious meaning of the sacraments; the natural values of the objects involved did not decide their religious value.

CONCLUSION

In the first three chapters of this book, we have developed the historical and experiential aspects of Christian life as a foundation for theological thought. The commanding character of conversion and discipleship and their history have dominated the way in which we have understood theology. But this is only the beginning of the journey. We have put together some definitions, conceptual distinctions, and basic elements that we now want to interrelate to show further aspects of theological foundations. Inside conversion and discipleship, there are cognitive and even normative dimensions of what it means to be Christian. In what follows, we will sort out the intellectual aspects of the experiential patterns we have outlined; then in chapters 7 through 9, we will clarify the way in which Christian theology claims its ability to establish standards or norms for both knowing and doing.

NOTES

1. Jean Piaget, *The Moral Judgment of the Child*, trans. Marjorie Gabain (New York: Free Press, 1965).

2. See, e.g., some of the critiques of Kohlberg's developmental theory in Christiane Brusselmans, ed., *Toward Moral and Religious Maturity: The First International Conference on Moral and Religious Development* (Morristown, N.J.: Silver Burdett Co., 1980).

3. Jim Fowler and Sam Keen, *Life Maps: Conversations on the Journey of Faith*, ed. Jerome Berryman (Waco, Tex.: Word Books, 1978), 34.

4. Lawrence Kohlberg with Clark Power, "Moral Development, Religious Thinking, and the Question of a Seventh Stage," in Lawrence Kohlberg, *Essays on Moral Development*, vol. 1, *The Philosophy of Moral Development* (San Francisco: Harper & Row, 1981), 345.

5. Lawrence Kohlberg, "From *Is* to *Ought*: How to Commit the Naturalistic Fallacy and Get Away with It in the Study of Moral Development," in his *Essays on Moral Development*, 147.

6. Kohlberg, *Essays on Moral Development*, 17–19 and 409–12.

7. Fowler and Keen, *Life Maps*, 36.

8. Ibid., 37.

9. Ibid., 24.

10. Ibid., 24–25.

11. Ibid., 39–41.

12. Ibid., 42–99.

13. See ibid., 82–101. For Paul Ricoeur's interpretation of the move from symbol, through criticism, to thought and the reappropriation of symbol, see his essay, "The Status of Vorstellung in Hegel's Philosophy of Religion," in *Meaning, Truth, and God*, ed. Leroy S. Rouner (Notre Dame, Ind.: Univ. of Notre Dame Press, 1982), 70–88. Ricoeur's articles in *Semeia* 4 (1975): 29–148 are also pertinent.

14. This interpretation revises Paul Ricoeur's "Toward a Hermeneutic of the Idea of Revelation," *Harvard Theological Review* 70 (1977): 1–37. For remarks about a generative poetics of religious language, see *Semeia* 6 (1976): 1–21.

15. Avery Dulles, "Revelation and Discovery," in *Theology and Discovery: Essays in Honor of Karl Rahner*, ed. William J. Kelly, S.J. (Milwaukee: Marquette Univ. Press, 1980), 1–29; and his subsequent *Models of Revelation* (Garden City, N.Y.: Doubleday & Co., 1983), esp. 3–154.

16. Bernard Lonergan, *Method in Theology* (London: Darton, Longman & Todd, 1972), 64–69, 73.

17. Although the language here embodies Dulles's use of Michael Polanyi (esp. *Personal Knowledge: Towards a Post-Critical Philosophy* [New York: Harper & Row, 1964], 120–31), we might also point to Lonergan's discussion of scientific procedures in *Insight: A Study in Human Understanding* (New York: Longmans, Green & Co., 1967), 3–102.

18. Ricoeur, "Idea of Revelation," 1ff.

19. Reginald Fuller, *The Foundations of New Testament Christology* (London: Collins Fontana, 1976), esp. 203–33. We have rearranged his data somewhat.

20. Compare Paul Ricoeur and David Tracy, *The Analogical Imagination: Christian Theology and the Culture of Pluralism* (New York: Crossroad, 1981), 259–87.

21. See *Semeia* 14 (1979) on "Apocalypse: the Morphology of a Genre," an issue whose guest editor was John J. Collins.

22. Lonergan, *Method*, 238–40.

23. Karl Rahner, "Theos in the New Testament," in his *Theological Investigations*, vol. 1, trans. Cornelius Ernst (Baltimore: Helicon Press, 1965), 79–148.

24. Bernard Lonergan, *The Way to Nicea: The Dialectical Development of Trinitarian Theology*, trans. Conn O'Donovan (Philadelphia: Westminster Press, 1976). See also the more circumstantial data in Aloys Grillmeier, *Christ in Christian Tradition*, vol. 1, *From the Apostolic Age to Chalcedon (451)*, 2d rev. ed., trans. John Bowden (Atlanta: John Knox Press, 1976).

25. *Summa Theologiae* I, Q. 1.

26. Walter E. Conn, "Conversion: A Developmental Perspective," *Cross Currents* 32 (1982):324.

27. Aristotle, *Physics*, trans. R. P. Hardie and R. K. Gaye, in *The Basic Works of Aristotle*, ed. Richard McKeon (New York: Random House, 1941), 236–41, (II.192b–95a). See Lonergan, *Insight*, 36; for our general interpretation, see Emil Fackenheim, *Metaphysics and Historicity* (Milwaukee: Marquette Univ. Press, 1961), esp. 17–34.

28. On the difference between classical and historical consciousness, see Bernard Lonergan, "The Transition from a Classicist World-View to Historical-Mindedness," in Lonergan, *A Second Collection*, ed. William F. J. Ryan and Bernard J. Tyrell (London: Darton, Longman & Todd, 1974), 1–9; and idem, "Theology in Its New Context," in *A Second Collection*, 55–67.

29. Augustine, *On True Religion* VII. 3, ed. Migne (Paris, 1841), 3:col. 128.

30. See Bernard J. F. Lonergan, "Theology and Praxis," in Lonergan, *A Third Collection*, ed. Frederick E. Crowe (New York: Paulist Press, 1985), 146–63, 169–249.

FURTHER READINGS

Marie-Dominique Chenu. *Toward Understanding St. Thomas*. Chicago: Henry Regnery Co., 1964.

Walter E. Conn. *Conscience: Development and Self-Transcendence*. Birmingham, Ala.: Religious Education Press, 1981.

Ronald Duska and Mariellen Whelan. *Moral Development: A Guide to Piaget and Kohlberg*. New York: Paulist Press, 1975.

Matthew Lamb. *Solidarity with Victims: Toward a Theology of Social Transformation*. New York: Crossroad, 1982.

Bernard J. F. Lonergan. *Insight: A Study in Human Understanding*. New York: Longmans, Green & Co., 1964.

Enda McDonagh. *The Making of Disciples: Tasks of Moral Theology*. Wilmington, Del.: Michael Glazier, 1982.

Paul Tillich. *Systematic Theology*, vol. 1. Chicago: Univ. of Chicago Press, 1951.

PART 2

COGNITIVE STRUCTURES
OF CONVERSION: THE NATURE
OF TRUTH CLAIMS

CHAPTER 4

THE SEARCH FOR NEW FOUNDATIONS— QUESTIONS AND CONTEXTS

"How in 'hell' are you going to recognize a legitimate holy man when you see one if you don't even know a cup of consecrated chicken soup when it's right in front of your nose? Can you tell me that?"

J. D. Salinger, *Zooey*

Christian holiness never lives in an abstract residence; it dwells within the ordinary categories of the everyday worlds in which we live. A bowl of soup and the chalice of salvation arrive in the same human hands. We must turn our attention down two paths: the way in which believers find that their society asks questions of them and the cognitive dimensions of morality and religion. Our world does not simply ask whether Christian experience has some meaningfulness to us; it asks whether it can be known to be true within the wider world of expanding populations, symbols, and science. Christians recognize that their faith is social, that the religious institutions that proclaim their beliefs in our contemporary world must be more widely credible, more ready to meet the often rigorous intellectual demands of the present.

The harshest climate for contemporary foundational theology can be overheard in one question: Why believe at all? This query asks us to outline a description and theory of human nature that answers whether there is, as some philosophers would put it, a "God-shaped blank" in human affairs.[1] Is there a question to which God is the answer? And what is the character of this divinity, if God does exist? Is there a God on the other side of our idols and authentic interpretations?

Not only the main object of faith is at stake; the mediations of divinity are also suspect. Can we credibly give ourselves to the Scriptures or ecclesiastical institutions without losing our freedom? Is there a way to read the language of the Bible which lies between the fundamentalism that holds onto the words for security and the liberal revisions that magically make content disappear with form? Is it legitimate to adhere to past witnesses to traditions? Is it possible to grant rituals, doctrines, or governing structures a measure of obedience without losing one's authentic humanity?

Foundational theology is forced to meet difficult intellectual questions directly. The challenge of the old Enlightenment, which Bertrand Russell (1872–1970) represents in our century,[2] asks Christians to express a way of believing in God and living their witness to Christ which promotes affective community, intelligent cooperation, and the reduction of suffering. Christians hide from the challenges only at the risk of remaining literally "uncultured," that is, without a social environment except their somewhat nostalgic ancient selves, caught in an isolation that can speak to no one. Since the New Testament witnesses to an energetic community whose boldness (*parrhesia*, 2 Corinthians 7:4) sent them well beyond the confines of their original worlds, contemporary Christians can hardly hope to do less.

For Christians, there is an important further context that requires attention. Even in the nineteenth century, it was still possible for people to conceive of the world in largely European terms. The culture that Europeans believed the world awaited was exported if not quite on wholesale terms, at least in extravagant quantities. When missionaries arrived, they brought with them European symbols, thought, languages, art, and government. Despite, and sometimes because of, the imported religion, Christian missions have thrived in South America and Africa and to a somewhat lesser degree in Asia. But after almost two thousand years of constant witness, all Christians together made up in 1966 about 30.9 percent of the world's population. Approximately 18.2 percent of this group were Catholic in 1971, the largest number in Latin America and the Philippines. Due to increasing population, primarily in non-European and non-North American countries, Catholics will drop to 16 percent by the year 2000. Christianity remains a minority religion in a world more and more dominated by Asian experience (Hinduism, Buddhism, Confucianism) or African tribal religions. Asians are approximately 54 percent of the world's population and by the year 2000, Asian countries will hold 60 percent of the world's population.[3]

The churches of the non-European world are a youthful community, with populations in their adolescence and early adulthood. Asserting independence from old colonial governments, they are jealous of their national and tribal autonomies. They are also, by and large, a suffering church, poor in the world's consumer goods, rich in resources and labor, and exploited by larger, more prosperous economies. In almost every case, there is a lack of institutionally arranged ministers. They are congregations of ordinary believers who take responsibility for their faith.

These churches find their way back into the European-based Christian communities not only through the newspapers and television accounts of their political, social, and economic difficulties but also through their refugee status. In almost every major industrialized country, there exist migrant or guest laborers who work in factories and agricultural fields. Whether present legally or illegally, these necessarily lower-class workers contribute to the national economies of developed countries without the security of knowing whether they will be able to share the profits of their own labor.

Christian churches must respond socially, politically and religiously to the changing shape of their own congregations. Just as in the nineteenth and early twentieth centuries in the United States, Catholic immigration changed the character of American Catholicism, so the contemporary migration of peoples from Asia and Latin America into North America, and from Africa, the Near East, the Balkans, and India into Europe and Japan, will so change. The complexion of Christian faith is recognizably more culturally varied than it was once understood to be.[4]

CONTEMPORARY FACTORS IN THE
SEARCH FOR FREEDOM

The pluralism of our world is not a neutral experience. The various cultures that impinge on an individual during any given day require attention, demanding room inside a psyche already struggling to maintain its unity. Generally speaking, this psyche can be described as one of secularity.[5] If *secularism* is the reduction of all meaning and values to what is empirically available, *secularity* may be more neutrally described as the independent moral values fostered by the Enlightenment of the seventeenth and eighteenth centuries. These imperatives include personal and national autonomy, scientific clarity, a pluralism of opinions, and historical change or development as the proper category for understanding individuals and nations. They are moral demands because we experience them as an "ought." It is "better" to be in charge of one's own history than subject to the tutelage of others. It is better to be clear and distinct, based in the methods of the natural sciences, than to be caught in opaque images or feelings. Secularity tends not to dismiss opinions; all must be equally entertained.

Secularity—or modernity, as it is sometimes called—has begun to show its limits as a cultural option. Though we will indicate its important values to theology, we should note the ways in which the moral demands of the Enlightenment have begun to pale as beacons of hope. Since all options must be fairly considered, we find ourselves often caught — located in the intolerable bind of being able to choose no particular person, place, thing, or idea for fear of alienating another justly entitled voice in the cultural milieu. Our histories become a serial sequence without an internal goal, radically contingent and fearfully paralyzed. All opinions become relative. The rejection of all authority not generated by the self so limits personal action that we feel constantly captured by our own bad consciences, which have not examined all the possibilities of existence. Recognizing that not all people have the rational distance to weigh incalculable alternatives, we nonetheless feel less than honest giving ourselves to poetry except as an escape from the hard work of living. The consequences of "daring to use our reason" drift toward a passivity that frightens us when we see the enormously complex tasks facing us when we try to govern our world. In what follows, we will indicate the internal poles of contrast that disclose the ambiguity of secularity.

Natural Science: Responsibility for the World

Copernicus (1473–1543), Galileo (1564–1642), and Francis Bacon (1561–1626) inverted the order of things.[6] It is true that the results of their thinking in physics and astronomy forced a revision of the way people looked at their world; but more important, they invited thinkers to move not from principles to their consequences (deduction) but from the data of experiments to limited, but empirically verified, conclusions (induction). Nineteenth-century studies in geology (with Charles Lyell, 1797–1875) and genetic biology (with Charles Darwin, 1809–89) applied experimental methods not just to things but to human beings.

What shifted for thinkers and believers were not so much the results as the way of proceeding to results.[7] What had been assumed now needed to be tested in laboratories. Where before the stress had been on the universal nature of things, now investigators were concerned with the particular. Where abstract principles were the procedural goal, now specific control of natural phenomena was primary.

Religious people responded suspiciously to the new science. They recognized, perhaps more instinctively than reflectively, that the empirical methods of natural science would directly confront their appeal to authoritative texts and doctrines and the primacy of the Unseen. In a sense, it was a struggle for control of the world. It was extremely improbable, believers thought, that one could grant people responsibility for the consequences of the world process *and* acknowledge divine care for the same world. The language and way of thinking about how God might be governing the universe would require revision.

More subtly, however, what was (and is) at stake in the conversation between believers and scientists is the how of divine-human interaction. Is there a way in which we can speak about human knowing and doing such that independence is granted men and women at the same time that we continue able to speak of God's action in the world? Is God's way of acting "alongside" human choice, "out there" in "nature," so to speak? Or is free human activity exactly where God operates? If this is so, then how do we not turn ourselves into demiurges, remaking the earth in our own quite limited image?[8] How do we keep from turning the ecology of nature into neutral, valueless putty in our less than careful hands? What appears, in other words, in the debates between scientific methods and religious institutions is a new version of the problematic relationship between divine and human freedom.

Subjectivity: The Possibility of Freedom

The discovery of interior human history is not a new phenomenon, since Augustine's *Confessions* displayed his inner story with considerable acuity. The conviction that personal perspective affects our vision of the world is also not particularly novel, yet the attempt to integrate explicitly the role of the human subject in knowledge can be said to stem from Immanuel Kant. The *Critique of Pure Reason* hoped to provide an antidote to the skepticism of David Hume about the certainty of our sense knowledge and the natural sciences based upon it. By clarifying the schemata of our understanding, Kant believed that he had provided a base for the results of natural scientific experiments. By knowing *how* we know, we can know *what* we know. He was attempting to justify in a theory of knowing the Newtonian sciences.[9]

The language about the subject's knowledge effected a philosophical revolution. Recognizing that human faculties constitute the way the world is for us re-created all realms of endeavor. Whether the topic was science, human emotion, industry, or social relationships, it became necessary to introduce the "filter" of human subjectivity. This could be reduced to a shallow perspectivism—holding that all human beings have a different relative viewpoint—or it could be treated more philosophically in the idea that the structures of knowing complement the structures of the known. But in all cases, it was a discovery that the interior life of human beings was in some way directive of the way the world is.

History: The Self-Making of the Individual[10]

If knowing the natural world required attention to conscious human operations, then knowing oneself demanded equal analysis. It quickly became clear that the changing patterns of one's own experience were also understood through the schemata of one's understanding. Much of the philosophical and theological discussion of the nineteenth century centered on the ways in which history could be interpreted. Just as Newtonian science looked for the regularities in physical elements and Kantian philosophy sought to ground those regularities in the patterns of human cognition, so thinkers such as G. W. F. Hegel (1770–1831) analyzed the schemes of recurrence in change.

The interest in "thinking change" was partially due to the newly won empirical bent of historical research. In the late eighteenth and early nineteenth centuries, there was an extraordinary growth of collections of artifacts from the past and a renewed interest in ancient cultures. The increase in data about the past and its differences from the present required attention to the possibility of continuity. Can we be said to belong to the same human race, if Persians, Medes, Romans, Greeks, Chinese, and Japanese had such different practices in religion, philosophy, science, and the shape of everyday life?

When this particularizing analysis was applied to the Bible, compared with other ancient Near Eastern cultures, it became necessary to understand how Christian religious understanding "fit into" historical change. It was clear that the long Judeo-Christian tradition had its own empirical contradictions and contrasts. Scriptural texts were not all written at the same time; they contained prescientific expressions; they did not always cohere with what researchers knew from sources outside the Bible. Christians needed to face the fact that they too had a history. Just as a vintage wine remembers its autumn of harvest, so too human experience, including religion, betrayed its particular origins.

The first aspect of crisis for Christian history, therefore, turned upon the factual character of its data. Were the texts authentic? What was their provenience? Could they be verified? But the stories contained in the texts were also scrutinized. Were the stories that the New Testament told accurate? What did it mean to trust these witnesses? What weight could be given to conflicting reports of the same events? All the resources of historical research began to be applied to the Hebrew and Christian Scriptures.

The second problem for believers was equally important. Not only were Christian data being compared to other historical information for validation, but questions were asked about the judgments and decisions that had made

Christianity what it was in the present. History was not only collecting the fragments of the past but also recognizing that those parts constructed a present whole. Human beings were involved in the making of themselves. If this was a generally recognized principle, then one had to ask how and in what ways decisions had affected the style in which the Christian Scriptures had been written and the shape in which religious traditions had been fashioned. If we were the makers of our own history, then were we also the creator of our own gods? And if we were not, then how could this be the case? How can revelation be experienced as gift from an authentic Other?

Religious thinkers applied the techniques of historical-critical method to determine "facts" and implemented the insights of comparative religion and literary criticism to understand the "shapes" or genres of Christian expression. So D. F. Strauss (1808–74) attempted to distinguish "history" and "myth" in the stories of Jesus. If Christian texts were the product of human contexts and human minds and hearts, then questions could again be raised about how the Bible was not simply a word about God but the Word of God speaking. Is the self-realization of human beings in conflict with the presence of God?

Praxis: The Authentic Action of Society

The term "praxis" has its origins in Aristotle where it tends to mean the activity of a free human being.[11] He distinguishes between *praxis* and *poieisis*, that is, doing something and making something. Making has a goal outside the activity, a product; doing has its own end, born of purposeful human choice. As linguistic usage has evolved, the English word "practice" has begun to mean something more like "making" than "doing," applying what we already know to some material outside ourselves, shaping it according to a preconceived idea. The use of the word "praxis" in English attempts to correct that, to point to the intrinsically intellectual and evaluative dimensions of human activity.

Action can, of course, be a skilled application of some notion previously worked out in our heads. But we recognize that if we waited to act upon clear ideas, we would not likely accomplish much of anything. Human action has a priority to our theories; indeed, thinking itself is a praxis.[12] Human activity contains within itself the cognitive and affective elements that guide our choices and shape our understandings. The key to an intelligent theory is to see how it emerges from the ordinary human actions that pose questions to us.

Nineteenth-century discussions began to focus upon praxis as an antidote to broad generalizing abstract philosophies. Karl Marx's eleven theses upon Ludwig Feuerbach (1804–72) end with this statement: "The philosophers have only *interpreted* the world in various ways; the point is, to *change* it."[13] In the course of his philosophical development, Marx moved from an early struggle with Hegel's theology to a critique of Hegel's political thought. In his attempt to act on the Enlightenment's courage to trust human activity, to wrest his own freedom from its limiting social conditions, Marx realized that the social subjects could not take responsibility for themselves through theory alone. Criticism and then transformation of the subject in its social context were the only way to freedom. Philosophy ends in revolutionary praxis, because within transformative human activity, there is an intellectual, critical moment.

Beyond the intrinsic concerns of Marx's thought, there remains the fact that his interpretation has affected philosophy, religious understanding, and politics. Holding correct philosophical positions or religious doctrines, without the activity to support them, was to oppress through an abstract, alienated vocabulary those whose experience operated at other levels. Reflection upon human activity also made clear that it was not possible simply to entertain the maximum number of available possibilities. One finally needed to choose, to take a position, to become partisan to a side. Not to do so was to continue to support the majority or the elite, in essence, to remain in a posture determined by others. Freedom required personal adherence and the option of "taking sides." It meant opting for yourself against those people and things who could separate you from your rightful public identity.

The World Religious Impulse and Secularity

Each of the themes we have mentioned above has profoundly affected Christian experience and theology. The conflicts that have emerged since the seventeenth and eighteenth centuries have required clearheadedness and affective loyalty on the part of believers. Both have not always been in evidence. The emphasis of the Enlightenment upon autonomy faced a religion whose foundations had been an authoritative book and a traditional history. The stress upon inductive experience rather than deductive principle threatened the basis for authoritative statements. The nature of evidence had changed.

The emphasis upon the subjective in knowledge met religious objectivity, the assertion that God was "already out there" without our cognitive powers. The introduction of historical research into religion demonstrated the relative change in Christian thought within the Bible and beyond it. The recognition that human beings were in some way the cause of their own histories put believers in the awkward position of being either against freedom or against God's free action upon the world. Late nineteenth-century emphasis upon praxis challenged a religious identity that had seen itself as contemplative, as vulnerably passive before divine love, waiting for God's work in the world.

Christian response to these polarities was not uniform. Just as there were those who collapsed Christian experience into the secular search for autonomy, subjectivity, historical knowledge, and revolutionary change, so too there were those who doggedly held for authority in social life, objectivity in religious doctrines and texts, an unchanging essence despite the historically secondary accretions, and divine transformation of the world.[14]

In our contemporary experience, options remain open. There are Christian institutions that form themselves according to classical principles of stratification, as in the nation or monarchical state; there are those which mirror nineteenth-century political liberalism with its hopeful tolerance of all available options. Some Christian organizations see themselves as a kind of welfare state. Lately, churches seem to be assuming the mantle of bureaucratic efficiency. In a sense, each shift has been an attempt to settle with rising modernity, to be able to maintain maximum freedom in a startlingly pluralist society.

Simultaneously, there has been a flight from reason and a growth in loyal adherents to the literal truth of the biblical text or of the ecclesiastical tradition.[15] The fear of technocratic reason has promoted a rise in astrology, the occult, and magic—manipulative attitudes that parody scientific control and prediction. For the loyalty to such prescientific motifs is not naive; it is in reaction to what already exists as a differentiated option within society. The rush toward mystical traditions and imaginative discourse can be equally destructive—a wish that science's "shortfall" in the transformation of the world be supplemented by ecstasy. It is as though technological mistakes and disasters gave us permission to leap over the restrictions of our ordinary vocabulary and syntax and to merge in nostalgic anonymity.

In the world of classical philosophy, metaphysics provided a common language for analysis, criticism, and constructive dialogue. With Kant's demolition of the cognitive framework on which this language could be built, little has taken its place. The common language of social criticism seems to have become psychology.[16]

Unfortunately, it is not a reflective psychology warranted by slowly emerging analyses of patterns and generalities but a "psychologism" that often reduces all extraempirical identities to innerworldly events. Divinity too easily becomes a projection onto the universe of Oedipal fixations. Religious men and women as well, finding themselves without a common social language, have resorted to psychology as their primary mode of analysis. And although such language can be used as an exploratory structure for human interiority, it can be forgotten that these metaphors disclose the world of the divine. Inner mechanisms lose themselves on the way to God.

The harsh polarities of autonomy vs. authority, subjectivity vs. objectivity, history vs. unchanging nature, and contemplation vs. action, have bred a new apocalypticism as they work themselves out concretely in our social and personal lives.[17] The ancient world knew the apocalyptic genre as a way of describing the bankruptcy in contemporary social mediations of the good and the true. Only God could intervene to save the truth. Repaying good and evil, God would return to draw suffering people into freedom. Contemporary speakers focus upon either the anarchic debilities of contemporary social terrorism or the totalitarian repression that dialectically spawns to counter it. Prophets from the right generally take the religious message as a paradoxical criticism of a society in which pornography, abortions, divorce, and murder seem rampant. God must be coming soon. Critics from the left pronounce terminal doom on a social system that must develop a police state to maintain its middle-class consumerist privileges. Neither is interested in determining the legitimate means that might mediate between the polarities of our modorn world.[18]

Nor is modernity itself without faults. This has become clearer in our century, with its wars to end wars and its peace which is a "cold war." Technological advance, the scion of scientific experiment, no longer seems to promote the goals for which it was intended. Analysts in the United States Department of Defense have documented that the mere addition of further sophisticated techniques to more complicated machines will only increase the mismatch between the goals of self-defense and the operation of the technology.[19]

Subjective cognition has given many people an important sense of their responsibility for the world. Human being was not simply fated to react to natural causes. It has also idealized the task of human responsibility so much that people expect either absolute control or complete passivity. Trying to take charge of one's own world by oneself is not a totally unambiguous enterprise.[20] Subjectivity needs to face the limits that emerge from the power of others and that finally end in death. We are not the complete causes of ourselves. Trying to take total responsibility for ourselves can lead to self-annihilation or destruction of the very world we were seeking to shape.

Still, to retreat from this subjectivity either by privatizing all values (including religion) or by a leap toward a new objectivism is altogether unsatisfactory.[21] Neither narcissism and self-absorption nor externalization of the self and nostalgic play seem sufficient. Bureaucracies attempt to satisfy all the individual needs of consumer societies. But the compartmentalization necessary to accomplish this satisfaction of desire only isolates people further. Finding oneself in the logo of designer clothes seems like the final objectification of the subject, turning personal identity into a purchased commodity.

Yet personal existence remains part of the directive character of the future. Without the individual novelty created by people in conversation, no plans would come to fruition. Personal decision for or against value changes the way in which social events occur. We may not be totally free agents, but in the limited choices of legitimate means for accomplishing values, we do create ourselves as well as our world. As we enter a postmodern world, a universe in which the unlimited hope for autonomy, subjectivity, history, and praxis is rather chastened, we will reassert the values of secularity, but within the proportions recognized as partial embodiments of a whole.

CLASSICISM AND MODERNITY: SOME GENERALIZED ATTRIBUTES

What we have been describing in sweeping terms and fleeting allusions is a shift in culture.[22] The movement from the medieval world, through modern science, into industrialization and the technological bureaucracies of this century occurs within the patterns, carriers, and structures of human interest and meaning. In the conflict of these cultures, we have a difference of horizon, which affects the way in which contemporary constructive theology based upon the Bible or a systematic theology rooted in traditional doctrines is accomplished. And if it is not already obvious, the changing cultures affect the way in which foundations are laid. Let us point to the general principles of each culture and then notice the way they affect theology.

Classicism depends upon an unchanging human nature, always the same in every place at every time. Its content is clear, its processes certain. Science is largely stable and deductive, drawing consequences from first principles and universal concepts. Culture is defined by a normative grid of determined formulas involving language, manners, social identity, and ethical standards. Living by the rules is important; responsibility tends to be individualized though not isolated.

Modernity uses inductive scientific procedures that are empirically warranted and dynamically open-ended in their goals. It tends to see human nature as an embodied subjectivity, relative to different spaces and times, shaped by the symbols, stories, and psychologies of many peoples. It develops new disciplines to study these changing phenomena: psychology, sociology, anthropology, and their cognates. Instead of applying a single set of rules everywhere, it attempts to adjust and adapt, recognizing that the best results for understanding another culture will be probable and incomplete. When normative statements emerge, when people determine ethical standards, they emerge from within the personal and social history of the communities involved. Authority gains its role not so much by accession to office as by competence. The checks upon competence involve the development of governmental social controls that stress collective responsibility for the values of a society and the necessary flexibility to transform those that are inadequate.

The Christian faith looks quite different in each of these cultures. In classicist cultures, Christianity will be stable, focused upon cultural similarities rather than differences, applying its ethical norms and doctrinal statements uniformly. When it travels to non-European lands, it will carry with it a particular European culture, assuming that it is the most advanced, best-developed form of Christian life. Sin will be individual failure; if public structural problems exist, they will be corrected by appeal to individual conversion. Affect, developmental history of individuals, and empirical warrants for truth or falsity will remain primarily peripheral concerns.

On the other hand, in contemporary cultures, Christianity will differentiate into various societal forms. It will stress the experiential, the affective, and the symbolically expressive. Institutional structures will begin to embody differing cultural languages, developing alternate governments in patriarchal and tribal societies, in consumerist democracies and in authoritarian socialist economies. The reflective features of ethics and doctrine in distinct Christian cultural embodiments may be more analogous than uniform.

The issue in contemporary Christian experience is not, therefore, the forced replacement of one cultural form of Christianity by another. Nor is it a matter of settling disputes on some overarching basis about which culture is superior. Rather it is a question of determining within the dialectic the legitimate mediations that will continue to communicate the gospel. How do we imagine the moderately successful positions between absolute autonomy and totalitarian authority? What does it mean to think through human nature as a historical reality? Can the experience and expressions of interior subjectivity become a basic metaphor and fundamental concept to disclose the reality not just of self but also of God? Can we recover the nonrational aspects of experience without capitulating to unreason? How do we recognize the important advances of technology and scientific experiment without capitulating completely to the crass manipulation of nature?

THE CHRISTIAN MINISTER:
BETWEEN TWO CULTURES

The people most often caught in the throes of translation from one religious culture to another are the pastors, preachers, priests, and ministers of congregations. The classicist order of ecclesial experience has largely collapsed; the ready bonds of comradeship between ministers have ruptured. Where there was once a clear teaching church and a group of faithful listeners, we are as likely to have a discussion group coming to consensus about the meaning of the gospel. Ethical decisions are no longer made by simple declaration of an ecclesiastical position. Doctrinal language cannot be merely repeated and thereby understood. If the problem is finding the legitimate means to promote the gospel in complex, aggressively pluralist cultures, then the way leaders of congregations identify themselves in this cultural incoherence is crucial. We will look at the various aspects of modernity and their effect upon the leaders of worship, preachers, and pastors.

In a classicist world, the minister, like the blacksmith or tinker, had a single role. He wore a particular dress, which he took on from the moment he assumed his authority. The minister was regularly male. A universal definition satisfied the sense of a worldwide order. In a contemporary culture, the priest or pastor defines his or her role within the situation, part of it determined by the way the community requires pastoral presence. The pastor has moved from defining the ministerial role as salvation of souls to counseling, facilitation of group consensus, and challenge to social responsibility.

Historical sensibility has also changed the way priests and pastors look at themselves. It is a shift from spatial definitions of role to a temporal one. In a classicist world, pastors are defined by their geographic parishes, territory defining work, with a primary responsibility the buildings of the congregation. Church becomes physical space rather than people. Pastors now tend to define their work in terms of the number of services performed and the amount of time taken for work oriented toward people.

This also entails a shift from things to persons. In the classicist mold, the most important work of the pastor or priest was sacramental or administrative. Younger clergy find it difficult to sit still for budget meetings or to relegate their identities to liturgical services. Their focus is upon the actions that gather the congregation, giving them a sense of social identity. What concerns them is not so much passing on a tradition to children but the active involvement of adults in their own religious education.

We have also begun to shift from absolutely necessary institutional rules to an emphasis upon transient transactions. In the classicist world, belonging to a church meant keeping the rules. If you were a Catholic, you followed Friday fasting laws, went to mass on Sunday and dutifully lived by the pronouncements of pope and bishops. If you were Protestant, you adhered with some doctrinal specificity to the confessional catechism that defined your tradition. Modernity stresses quite other aspects of Christian experience. Pastors know who belongs by the amount of visiting they do with parishioners. They are expected to have good personal skills, so that congregants feel that they are being met by a human being rather than through a role. Ministers hope to intervene at the critical moments in their parishioners' journey of faith. Both believers and pastors would feel cheated if the personal dimensions of ministry were denied them.

The contrast between autonomy and authority in the cultural shift catches pastors first. Wanting to promote Christian freedom, they are convinced that only surrender to God can provide authentic independence. Believing in the dynamics of history, they must wait upon the developmental psychology of the faithful to experience religious change. Whereas in the classicist world, the authoritative mediations of God's presence included the pastor and the sacraments he served, in the world of modernity there is an innate suspicion of all activity that is not self-generated. Form is to be distrusted; spontaneity must be freedom.

In such a cultural shift, it is to be expected that the minister, as one of the primary translators of religious meaning, should be confused about his or her identity. For every individual who has collapsed Christian values into modernity, there is another who has held fast to the classicist mentality, refusing admittance to the hydra of historical relativism. Yet part of the argument of this book is that from the experience of modernity, there emerge the concerns of classicism: tradition, authority, cognitive or intellectual truth, objective values, and law. The entry to theology through experience does not necessarily end in surrender to confusion.

FINAL REMARKS

The language of this chapter has been primarily common sense. But it is a common sense that has its origins in theory. Behind the problem of subjectivity lies the name of Kant and the *Critique of Pure Reason*. Beneath the shapely play of history is the study of Hegel. Underlying the language of praxis is the power of Marx. And Friedrich Nietzsche, Sigmund Freud, and Carl Jung have studied the role and expression of affective symbol in our experience. The reason that the chapter has remained largely descriptive is not that these thinkers' analyses are not genuinely intelligent and monumentally intriguing in themselves; it is that for our present purposes, the questions rather than the answers of modernity are the major concern. If foundational theology is to be at all adequate, it must first recognize the questions, then establish a procedure for answering them.

The topics for consideration are these: How do we know what we know? When does this happen so that we can say as a part of historical development that we know something or love someone? When and how can we be responsible for the world as we know it? What motivates our search for independence, responsibility, and knowledge? Can another legitimately stimulate our quest for personal and social value?

These questions lead toward disciplines that exceed the scope of this volume but that this work must use to sort through the issues. The answer to the first question about knowledge must develop a cognitional theory that understands the problems of scientific interpretation and knows where to locate religious knowing among other kinds of knowledge. The problem of history must be met by a science of religious narrative that meets the criteria for historical data, as well as an understanding of what it means to be created by change. Marx forces believers to develop a philosophy and theology of politics, economics, and public responsibility for the world. Finally, one must develop a discipline that can understand the objectivity of symbols and personal stories, permitting the possibility of discerning inauthentic from genuine motivation toward God. Foundational theology must set up the footings and the architectural struts by which it becomes possible to recognize holiness in the ordinary and the ordinary as the most extraordinary event of divine presence.

NOTES

1. See the discussion of "Theology and Falsification," in *New Essays in Philosophical Theology*, ed. Antony Flew and Alasdair MacIntyre (New York: Macmillan Co., 1964), 96–130; and Frederick Ferré, *Language, Logic, and God* (New York: Harper & Row, 1969), esp. 18–41.

2. "The whole conception of God . . . is a conception quite unworthy of free men" (Bertrand Russell, *Why I Am Not a Christian and Other Essays on Religion and Related Subjects*, ed. Paul Edwards [New York: Simon & Schuster, 1967], 23).

3. Walbert Buehlmann, *The Coming of the Third Church: An Analysis of the Present and Future Church*, trans. Ralph Woodhall and A. N. (Maryknoll, N.Y.: Orbis Books, 1977), 19–24, 129–66; see also idem, *God's Chosen Peoples*, trans. Robert R. Barr (Maryknoll, N.Y.: Orbis Books, 1982).

4. See Louis J. Luzbetak, *The Church and Cultures: An Applied Anthropology for the Religious Worker* (Techny, Ill.: Divine Word Pubs., 1970), 226ff., 285ff.

5. The discussion of secularity or modernity is indebted to Marshall Berman, *Everything That Is Solid Melts Into Air: The Experience of Modernity* (New York: Simon & Schuster, 1982); and Langdon Gilkey, *Naming the Whirlwind: The Renewal of God-Language* (Indianapolis: Bobbs-Merrill, 1969), esp. 31–71. For a critique, see Christopher Lasch, *The Culture of Narcissism: American Life in an Age of Diminishing Expectations* (New York: W. W. Norton & Co., 1978); and idem, *The Minimal Self: Psychic Survival in Troubled Times* (New York: W. W. Norton & Co., 1984).

6. See Herbert Butterfield, *The Origins of Modern Science, 1300–1800* (New York: Free Press, 1966).

7. B. J. F. Lonergan, "The Ongoing Genesis of Methods," in Lonergan, *A Third Collection,* ed. Frederick E. Crowe (New York: Paulist Press, 1985), 146–65.

8. See Berman, *Everything Solid,* 37–86, on the second part of Goethe's *Faust.* Mary Shelley's *Frankenstein* (New York: E. P. Dutton, 1970) also portrays the ambivalent feelings at the beginning of the romantic period concerning human historicity.

9. For Immanuel Kant's program for self-emancipation in knowledge and action, see "What is Enlightenment?" in *Kant On History,* ed. Lewis White Beck, trans. Lewis White Beck, Robert E. Anchor, and Emil L. Fackenheim (Indianapolis, Ind.: Bobbs-Merrill, 1963), 3–10. For comments on the problems this creates for history, see Hayden White, *Metahistory: The Historical Imagination in Nineteenth-Century Europe* (Baltimore: Johns Hopkins Univ. Press, 1973), and Paul Ricoeur, *Time and Narrative,* vol. 1, trans. Kathleen McLaughlin and David Pellauer (Chicago: Univ. of Chicago Press, 1984). For the ways in which these issues create moral problems for religious knowledge, see Van A. Harvey, *The Historian and the Believer: The Morality of Historical Knowledge and Christian Belief* (New York: Macmillan Co., 1966). For a discussion of the role of myth in religious self-understanding, see Elinor S. Shaffer, *"Kubla Khan" and the Fall of Jerusalem: The Mythological School of Criticism and Secular Literature, 1770–1880* (Cambridge: At the Univ. Press, 1975).

10. Gilkey, *Whirlwind,* 365–70; B. J. F. Lonergan, "Natural Right and Historical Mindedness," in *A Third Collection,* ed. Crowe (New York: Paulist Press, 1985), 169–75; and Emil Fackenheim, *Metaphysics and Historicity* (Milwaukee: Marquette Univ. Press, 1961), 1–34.

11. See Richard J. Bernstein, *Praxis and Action: Contemporary Philosophies of Human Activity* (Philadelphia: Univ. of Pa. Press, 1971), and Nicholas Lobkowicz, *Theory and Practice: History of a Concept from Aristotle to Marx* (Notre Dame, Ind.: Univ. of Notre Dame Press, 1967), esp. 3–139.

12. See Matthew Lamb, *Solidarity with Victims: Toward a Theology of Social Transformation* (New York: Crossroad, 1982), esp. 61–99; and Francis Schüssler Fiorenza, *Foundational Theology: Jesus and the Church* (New York: Crossroad, 1984), esp. 296–311.

13. Karl Marx, "Theses on Feuerbach," in *The Portable Karl Marx,* ed. and trans. Eugene Kamenka (New York: Penguin Books, 1983), 158; Bernstein, *Praxis and Action,* 11–83; and Lobkowicz, *Theory and Practice,* 149–257.

14. For Catholic theological responses, see Gerald McCool, *Catholic Theology in the Nineteenth Century: The Quest for a Unitary Method* (New York: Seabury Press, 1977), and Thomas F. O'Meara, *Romantic Idealism and Roman Catholicism: Schelling and the Theologians* (Notre Dame, Ind.: Univ. of Notre Dame Press, 1982). For two different Protestant responses, see Karl Barth, *Protestant Theology in the Nine-*

teenth Century: Its Background and History (Valley Forge, Pa.: Judson Press, 1973), and Paul Tillich, Perspectives on Nineteenth and Twentieth Century Protestant Theology, ed. Carl E. Braaten (New York: Harper & Row, 1967). For an unbiased history, see James C. Livingston, Modern Christian Thought: From the Enlightenment to Vatican II (New York: Macmillan Co., 1971), 80–300.

15. See below, chap. 6, pp. 126–28; see Edward Farley's critique of the "house of authority" in his Ecclesial Reflection: An Anatomy of Theological Method (Philadelphia: Fortress Press, 1982), 47–168; and Peter Berger's sociological description of the reaffirmation of tradition in his The Heretical Imperative: Contemporary Possibilities of Religious Affirmation (Garden City, N.Y.: Doubleday Anchor Books, 1980), 30–86.

16. See Lasch, Narcissism, 3–26.

17. Berger, Imperative, 20–23; Langdon Gilkey, Society and the Sacred (New York: Crossroad, 1981), 3–14, 90–103.

18. For a theoretic proposal, see Matthew Lamb, History, Method, and Theology: A Dialectical Comparison of Wilhelm Dilthey's Critique of Historical Reason and Bernard Lonergan's Meta-Methodology (Missoula, Mont.: Scholars Press, 1978), esp. 2–54, 357–455.

19. John R. Boyd, "Patterns of Conflict," Department of Defense briefing, May 1984; and Franklin C. Spinney, "Defense Facts of Life," Department of Defense briefing, 5 December 1980; idem, "The Plans/Reality Mismatch and Why We Need Realistic Budgeting," Department of Defense briefing, December 1982; and idem, "Defense Program Analysis and Evaluation: Is History Repeating Itself?" Department of Defense briefing, 22 March 1984.

20. See Ernest Becker, The Denial of Death (New York: Free Press, 1975), esp. 115–24.

21. Richard J. Bernstein, Beyond Objectivism and Relativism: Science, Hermeneutics, and Praxis (Philadelphia: Univ. of Pa. Press, 1983), 1–49.

22. Cf. George Steiner, In Bluebeard's Castle: Some Notes Towards the Redefinition of Culture (New Haven: Yale Univ. Press, 1971), esp. 97–141; and B. J. F. Lonergan, "Belief: Today's Issue," in Lonergan, A Second Collection, ed. William F. J. Ryan and Bernard J. Tyrell (London: Darton, Longman & Todd, 1974), esp. 90–99.

CHAPTER 5

THE COGNITIVE DIMENSIONS
OF MORAL CONVERSION

Truth is the secret of eloquence and of virtue, the basis of moral authority; it is the highest summit of art and of life.
Henri-Frédéric Amiel (1821–81), *Journal Intime*

The breakdown of the classical and medieval syntheses and the emergence of modern consciousness with its attendant emphases on autonomy, pluralism, history, scientific clarity, and praxis have resulted in a multitude of conflicting interpretations concerning the cognitive status of moral statements — concerning, that is, the question whether, and how, moral statements can be bearers of truth and falsity at all. As we saw in the last chapter, in the classical horizon or world view most theologians began with abstract universal principles that were considered to be true because based on either the static nature of humanity or the content of Scripture. Then they proceeded, primarily through deduction, to arrive at conclusions they supposed always to remain certain and the same.

In the everyday moral life the believer attempted to conform moral activity to preestablished norms and authority. The emphasis was on duty and obligation to reproduce the established moral order either of the universal natural law or of the divine will manifested through the Scriptures. In sum, the cognitive status of moral statements in this horizon was considered objective and sure. Individual autonomy and subjectivity, pluralism and history were at best downplayed, and often no room was left for them at all in the determination of morality.

With the dawn of the European Enlightenment, the star of the reigning classical horizon began to lose its glimmer. Kant's turn to subjectivity, Hegel's turn to history, and the turn of Friedrich Schleiermacher (1768–1834) to experience all signaled a change in the way truth was thought to be attained. The emergence of modern science also greatly influenced the modern world view and the procedures it considers adequate for discerning the true and the real. More and more emphasis was placed on the experience of the particular, and the method of moral inquiry shifted to the inductive, in which room is left for incompleteness, possible error, and revision. Historical consciousness sometimes led in the early phases to cultural relativism and to doubts about the reliability of any moral statements or norms.

THE EPISTEMOLOGY OF MORAL
APPREHENSIONS AND
THEIR COGNITIVE STATUS

Within the two fundamental horizons or world views there are conflicting interpretations concerning *how* we come to know value and *what* the status of these value judgments is. Thus, we must discuss the issues involved in moral epistemology and the cognitive status of moral judgments and statements.[1] In earlier chapters we have dealt with the questions of moral meaning and what gives rise to such meaning. Now we must attend to the questions of moral knowledge, objectivity, and truth.

There are three main theories or schools of thought that attempt to explain the grounding of moral knowledge and the cognitive status of the moral interpretations that emanate from moral apprehensions. First, there is the relativist school, which can be divided into the social-relativist wing and the personal-relativist wing. For the social relativist, moral evaluations are governed by the culturally available categories of a given society. What we know in moral apprehensions are the particular mores, folkways, or customs of a particular society or social group. On such a view, there can be no universal moral truth that could be apprehended by and applied to every culture. There can be no universal agreement because all moral statements contain an egocentric reference, that is, a reference to one's own group or society.

For the personal relativist, moral evaluations must find their ground in personal feelings or emotions. Accordingly, an action becomes right or wrong by reference to whether one approves or disapproves of the action and feels happy or sad when the action is performed. Clearly, the concerns for moral truth and objectivity are undercut in this view because, beyond self-satisfaction, there is no reason or ground for moral discussion, argument, or debate about values and actions.

Both wings of the relativist school are naively empiricist in the sense that they believe we can test the validity of moral statements empirically. For the social relativist, we can test the validity of the moral statement "Torture is wrong" by using the methods of sociology to see whether most or all of the members of our society disapprove of torture. Similarly for the personal relativist, we can test the validity of the same statement by using the tools of psychology to see if the individual really does disapprove personally of torture. The problem with both positions, however, is that neither of them answers the open question whether torture *really* is wrong *in itself* beyond the disapproving of the action.

The second main theory of moral knowledge is found in the noncognitivist school. It has found its expression in the tradition of positivism of A. J. Ayer, Rudolf Carnap (1891–1970), and others.[2] For the members of this school, which has a somewhat diverse constituency, our moral statements are in no way objective and verifiable statements about our moral life together. Moral "statements" are not even statements about the speaker's feelings. They are simply emotional utterances like "Hurrah for truth telling!" or "Boo for torture!" No rational justification can be offered for moral interpretations on this view, since the view's proponents argue that all moral evaluations are an expression of subjective emotion. The unfortunate consequence of accepting this position is that there would be no way moral debate and discussion could be carried on between members of our society. If the expression of moral evaluations is a subjective eruption, then we are simply unable to debate the validity of various moral assessments on complex issues that confront our society, for example, nuclear warfare and national unemployment.

In contrast to the relativist and noncognitivist schools, which view moral judgments as in principle incapable of objectivity, there is the absolutist school. There are several branches to this school, but we will look only at two of them to illustrate the central characteristic of this theory of moral knowledge before sketching our own position. Briefly stated, those in the absolutist school argue that moral statements are about objective common human reality, and thus, that in principle there can be universal agreement about the truth or falsity of any particular moral claim. The use of the term "absolutist" does not entail that moral apprehensions and interpretations must be deduced from some universal, static human nature. On the contrary, for several members of this school moral judgments may be situationally unique, and they may even be situationally relative. The central reason there should be universal agreement is that all humans are looked on as attempting, however imperfectly, to determine a judgment that comes from a *single source*.

Supernaturalistic Absolutism. We find this view frequently represented in the writings of some twentieth-century Protestant Reformed theologians and Catholic neo-scholastic authors.[3] Supernaturalistic absolutism holds that an action is objectively right or wrong by reference to God's explicit will. In fact, to say that an action is right means the same as "God decrees it" or "God approves of the action." Because there is only *one* God, there can be only *one* correct judgment about the morality of an action.

Reformed theologians especially argued that moral apprehensions depend intimately on religious experiences of the one God. However, such a view does entail the proviso that on the same moral issue, for example, abortion, God could command one action (to abort the fetus) in some circumstances and the alternative action (not to abort the fetus) in other circumstances. As long as our religious-moral apprehensions find their source explicitly in God's will for humanity, proponents of this theory reason, there is only one correct judgment that can be discerned.

Intuitionistic Absolutism. This branch of the absolutist school finds its modern origin in the writings of G. E. Moore (1873–1958).[4] Though Moore denied that the properties referred to by words like "good" can be defined in nonethical terms, he maintained that all should agree in principle on the moral rightness or wrongness of specific acts. We apprehend value intuitively, and the moral rightness or wrongness is transmitted through some form of intuition. All persons possess this faculty of intuitive apprehension of values, and the knowledge obtained cannot be achieved through standard empirical observation using our sensory faculties. Although the knowledge is gained from some sort of extrasensory process, its objectivity resides in the perception of an objective nonnatural quality, which in turn refers to something real about the world of being human. In sum, moral knowing is true knowing of a reality independent of social-personal preferences and emotion.

Of the three main theories of moral knowledge, the absolutist school is clearly where our own position lies. For us, moral apprehensions, and the concepts and propositions that are formulated from them, contain and convey knowledge of an aspect of human reality and of the way human relations should be structured. Human reality, or the world mediated by meaning, is not that of the naive realist or empiricist. Knowing human reality is not like taking a look at what is already out there to be looked at. Reaching an objective judgment is not just verifying that something is true or real or valuable by using the standards of empirical observation based on our sensory faculties. The sources for the real, true, or valuable always have reference to the invariant process of human self-transcendence in the operations of attentive experience, of intelligent understandings, of reasonable judgments, and of responsible deliberations. Furthermore, the criterion for all valid and objective moral knowing and moral judgments of value is the human being self-transcending through personal exercises of freedom in the conversion processes.

Our position on the issues of moral knowing (as well as of religious knowing) and the cognitive status of moral claims is a form of absolutism called critical realism that can be best described as *noetic praxis*. We argue that not only is moral knowing (noetic) a way of apprehending a dimension of human reality, namely, the value of persons and their needs, but the knowledge gained is true, objective, and valid insofar as it results from the various conversions (praxis). In other words, we come to know moral reality through our imagining, intending, deliberating, deciding, and thoughtful acting by reference to the four conversions.

The cognitive aspects of moral interpretations arise from within the dynamics of moral experience itself. Moral judgments are not something extrinsic or "added on" to moral experience. To appreciate the significance of this statement, we must return to the bipolar sources of moral experience and discover how we come to know value. As we shall see, all practical knowing, that is, knowledge about values, is born of our affections, deliberations, and doing. Stated another way, practical knowledge is acquired in the crucible of noetic praxis.

THE PREDISCURSIVE APPREHENSION
OF VALUE

We have argued in chapter 2 that the foundational moral experience is the experience of the value of persons and what befits their well-being. From within this experience we apprehend in a prediscursive way the primordial worth of persons and the values that fulfill their basic needs. By calling apprehensions prediscursive, we mean that our apprehensions are primarily via the affections and the imagination and not through a discursive or reasoned process. The value of persons, then, is not known by way of a thought process that can be represented by a syllogism and hence subjected to proof. Although we would certainly argue that the apprehension of values can be supported by a reasoned process with corresponding syllogisms, such apprehensions are not fundamentally established through acts of the intellect.

To argue that all value is primarily apprehended by the affections is not to lapse into either a noncognitivist or an intuitionist position on moral knowledge. For when we speak of the affections, we are not describing the emotions that come and go as the passions are called into play. On the other hand, knowing through affect is not some kind of extrasensory process as described by G. E. Moore. Affective knowing refers to what could be called the apprehension of value through feelings as intentional responses.

We need to distinguish feelings as nonintentional states and trends from feelings as intentional responses.[5] Nonintentional states can be illustrated by such states as fatigue, irritability, bad humor, and anxiety, and, as such, they all have causes. Feelings as nonintentional trends or urges can be illustrated by hunger, thirst, and sexual discomfort, and they all have goals. In both cases, the feeling itself does not presuppose and arise out of perceiving, imagining, or representing the cause or goal. We only discover the state or trend and then diagnose that what we need is rest or something to eat.

Feelings as intentional responses always occur at the level of symbolic imagination, and thus they answer to what is intended, apprehended, or represented in the symbol. A symbol is an image of a real or imaginary object that will evoke a feeling or is evoked by a feeling.[6] Now, the objects that are responded to and apprehended in intentional feelings are values, and the primordial value is persons. Persons are values whose images are symbols that evoke in us a feeling and that drive us to a response, and so we see that the bipolar structure of a drive-draw operates within the very origins of moral knowing.

It is necessary for feelings to reveal their objects (values) and, inversely, for objects to awaken feelings in us. In what we have called the foundational moral experience, we apprehend the primordial value of persons in feelings (affect) and respond imaginatively by attending to their needs so that they might flourish. In the corresponding moral conversion, we now adopt these values as the criterion of decision and choice.

There is another aspect to feelings as intentional responses. There is not only an absolute aspect that concerns the recognition of value, there is also the relative aspect that concerns a preference or hierarchy of values.[7] Feelings respond in accord with a scale of values that can be arranged in an ascending order of importance from vital, to social, to cultural, to personal, to religious. As we recall from chapter 2, this scale of values is the same as the hierarchy of human needs that drive us outside ourselves for meaning. Whereas the basic needs and desires constitute one intrinsic drive to moral meaning (value), the objects and relations that fulfill these needs are apprehended prediscursively in our feelings. We are also drawn by these objects of value, and once again, it is in our feelings that we are awakened in imagination to their presence.

Response to value through our intentional feelings is indeed a mode of self-transcendence. But, as with all modes of self-transcendence, our feelings are not guaranteed. We are neither born with fully constituted sets of feelings toward value nor inexorably led by our feelings to the worth of persons and those goods which fulfill human needs. In other words, our intentional feelings need to be developed, refined, and reinforced over a period of time. We need continually to scrutinize our feelings and their implicit scale of preferences. Much of the moral life is a process of education of our feelings by fostering and developing a climate of discernment and taste. Also, because some of our feelings come and go and others are open to personal and cultural aberrations that can distort both the value of persons and the hierarchy of goods, there is a necessity for the conversion of feelings. Moral conversion is certainly the beginning of the process of discernment and development of adequate feelings. Yet, as we have seen before, moral conversion is more a challenge than an achievement.

There is the further necessity to undergo an affective conversion in which our horizons are expanded by questions of the *love* of value. In affective conversion we are enabled to withdraw regularly and consistently from our own egocentricity and the cultural biases and prejudices that infect our intentional feelings. By loving persons and the values making up the hierarchy of goods, we learn to know a dimension of reality that until that moment was unknown by us. In this knowledge now born of love we know the true giftedness of the other and of all reality, and thereby we become aware of what the virtuous life is. Being loving means being just, truthful, chaste, prudent, and all the other qualities that lead us to value for the sake of persons and the fulfillment of their needs.

Disciples of Jesus enjoy a distinctive climate in which to educate and refine the intentional feelings. This distinctive climate is the ecclesial community and its noetic praxis. The disciples' religious experience and commitment to the person of Jesus engage their imagination at levels deep within themselves. Christian religious affections, which are born of the love of God in Jesus, become powerful resources for the education and reinforcement of the moral affections. They not only sustain and deepen but also confirm the moral feelings that have arisen in our moral conversion. The giftedness of the other and of all reality, which is made manifest in affective conversion, is now seen to be ultimately confirmed and guaranteed by a loving God who calls us to share in the community of the triune life (religious conversion). The moral project of self-transcendence to value is no longer radically questioned, for now the disciple has at last discovered an adequate answer to the question, Why be moral at all? As Kohlberg himself has claimed, an answer to this question can only be framed within a religious-moral context.[8]

The distinctive resources of the ecclesial community are also important for the education of moral affections. The Christian stories, myths, and symbols enliven the disciple's imagination and sensitize moral sensibilities. These resources aid us in focusing our gaze on the scale of values against the cultural biases and prejudices of our society.[9] The liturgical celebrations and prayer life of the Christian community become sources for our moral self-understanding and commitments as well as resources for understanding the meaning of the virtuous life.[10]

In addition, the prophetic witness of the ecclesial community to the in-breaking reign of God enlivens the disciple's imagination to develop eschatological virtues such as humility, gratitude, vigilance, serenity, joy, and especially hope.[11] These eschatological qualities of the disciple awaken and sustain the intentional feelings to value especially in times when the disciple is confronted with difficult situations in which others are going either to one extreme by losing all hope in the transformation of society or to the other extreme by absolutizing the available cultural values.

Certainly, one very important contribution the resources of the ecclesial community can make to the moral imagination of disciples is to sensitize their feelings of commitment to the plight of the poor and oppressed. To become a disciple of Jesus is to take on his story of preference for those who are the most disadvantaged in society. The narrative of Jesus' life is an invaluable resource for education of the moral affections into a life of commitment to the Christian orders of charity and justice.

It might be helpful to summarize how and what the disciple knows in the prediscursive apprehensions of value. The knowledge that is born in affect is true and real knowledge of human reality. How and what we know in affective-evaluative knowledge is not the same as how and what we know in Euclidean geometry or in the study of the complex structure of the DNA molecule. Only the unreconstructed rationalist or empiricist believes that all knowledge must be gained by either the intellect or sensory perception. What we know through affect is a world and a set of human relations that are mediated by value meanings.

The old Latin adage that states that "nothing is loved unless it is known" (nihil amatum nisi praecognitum) is true as far as it goes. Yet, the insight of Blaise Pascal (1623–62) is more to our point. When he stated in his famous book *Pensées*, "The heart has its reasons, which reason does not know,"[12] he was claiming that we know truth not only by reason but also by the heart. We could understand Pascal's phrase "the heart's reasons" in terms of what we have called "feelings as intentional responses." Thus, with regard to the knowledge of the value of persons and the goods that fulfill their needs, it might be more appropriate to reverse our Latin adage to read "nothing is known unless it is loved" (nihil cognitum nisi amatum). In this way, we come to understand that the knowledge of moral reality, which is a dimension inherent in our everyday experience of the world, is evaluative knowledge of persons, born of our affections.

Although evaluative knowledge is infinitely more complex and subtle than our knowledge of mathematical or scientific realities, it too issues forth in cognitive claims about human reality. To make the claim that some actions are right (e.g., keeping our promises to a dying friend) and others are wrong (e.g., torturing a child) is to state what is true about human reality. The origin of these moral truth claims is found in our intentional feelings toward value (promise keeping) or repulsion from disvalue (torture). As we recall from previous discussions of intellectual conversion, the criterion of judgment of these cognitive claims about value or disvalue is our self-transcendence within the four conversions. In fact, the knowledge and the truthfulness of moral claims are verified according to whether they proceed from the conversions themselves.

VALUE AND THE ROLE OF
DISCURSIVE ANALYSIS

What we know in prediscursive apprehensions are the truly valuable and disvaluable and the better and the worse. Once these apprehensions take place, it is the role of discursive reason to analyze what our intentional feelings have grasped. Through the methods of discursive reason we seek scientific clarity. What we intend to know by asking questions about why persons are good or evil and certain actions are right or wrong is once again the valuable or the better, now at the level of analysis. Our practical reason, like our intentional consciousness, is not value-neutral, and so the very questions we ask at the level of analysis are inherently value-laden. Stated simply, our practical discursive reason seeks to know and analyze value.

There are several critical tasks that discursive reason performs in achieving scientific clarity about cognitive moral claims.[13] One task is to find and compare ethically meaningful empirical data. Not all data in a moral situation are morally relevant to the appraisal of the person and his or her actions. For example, a person's skin color is not morally relevant in questions of virtue or vice, but that a person was psychically impaired does count in such questions. The circumstances in which actions take place are also important, but not every circumstance is relevant to moral judgments of rightness or wrongness. Answers to such questions as how, why, when, where, and with what consequences are all relevant in judging actions that affect human and even nonhuman welfare. In sum, we need to analyze and compare critically the data before jumping into the business of moral judgment.

Analysis is necessary to search for the unasked questions about the valuable or the disvaluable. Often we are quite content to be unimaginative in the questions we ask, and so one critical task of analysis is to force us out of our matter-of-fact ways of looking on reality. We are prone to accept uncritically the regnant authorities of our society, whether they are persons or cultural mores, and so ethical analysis serves as a way of testing these authorities. Nowhere is this task more important than in cases of uncritical moral conversion where we simply identify the value of persons and their needs with the regularly expressed views of cultural authorities. Critical distance from our own biases and prejudices can also be enhanced through moral analysis. Our own myths and cultural filters are often inaccurate representations of human reality, and so they need to be corrected and refined to meet the demands of the moral life.

Not only does moral analysis enable us to cope with the inevitable partiality of our knowledge of what constitutes the truly human, it also fights against the allure of too facile a consensus. We want others to approve of what we do, and they desire the same of us. This kind of mutual-admiration-society syndrome can be counterproductive to the growth in moral maturity. The building of moral consensus always follows a difficult and rocky path, and shortcuts to spare ourselves and others the hard analytic work are not helpful. In the Christian community the call to perfection, illustrated in the life of Jesus and in the lives of the saints who have most closely followed in his steps, stands against any such easy consensus building in moral matters.

Moral analysis is also helpful in jogging our lazy memories. We so easily forget the past, and often we doom ourselves to repeat the moral stupidities, errors, and atrocities of our own heritage. A sense of history and its critical methods of analysis are crucial so that we do not fall into the very moral pitfalls our ancestors did. In addition, moral analysis can aid us in remembering what J. B. Metz (b. 1928) calls the "dangerous memory of the freedom of Jesus Christ."[14] The Passion, death, and resurrection of Jesus have won for us a new freedom to be for others, especially the poor and oppressed in society. What it means situationally to be a person for others cannot be decided in the abstract. It must be decided always in the concrete, based on proper moral analysis.

Another critical task of discursive reason is to break the stranglehold of our own habits. How often have we heard the famous phrase "We have always done it this way" uttered in the complacency that therefore it.must be right? Christian holiness and perfection call us to be free from all false habituations and to assess anew the needs of the neighbor. The "old self" about which Saint Paul so often spoke needs to be put off so that the "new self," fashioned through the conversions and enlightened by critical analysis, might serve the neighbor.

Furthermore, critical practical reason attempts to solve the inevitable conflicts between principles. For example, moral analysis seeks to resolve the conflict between the principles of nonmaleficence (do no harm) and beneficence (do good for others). There is also the necessity to reformulate and correct moral principles in view of new experiences and further advancements in moral conversion. Finally, moral insights need to be communicated to those within and outside the ecclesial community. It is the role of discursive reason to develop the proper forms of systematic moral theory by which these insights may be handed on and understood.

FROM DESCRIPTION TO PRESCRIPTION
IN MORAL INTERPRETATIONS

Moral interpretations are primarily vehicles by which we intend moral meaning or value. Yet there is another side to these interpretations, and we have said very little about this side up to now. In this section, then, we must address the foundational experience of moral obligation and the "authorities" that ground statements of moral oughtness.

Moral interpretations move from description to prescription, not in the reverse order. By description we mean statements of fact ("is" statements), and by prescription we mean statements of obligation ("ought" statements). In the classical period of moral theory, for example, in the writings of Aristotle and Thomas Aquinas, we find an intimate relationship between these two types of statement. It was with David Hume in the eighteenth century, at the peak of the Enlightenment, that a wedge was driven between descriptive and prescriptive statements that has perdured into the present. In his famous text, Hume appears to protest that we cannot logically derive "ought" statements from "is" statements.[15] While we intend neither to debate the proper interpretation of Hume's remarks nor to adjudicate the polemics in contemporary moral philosophy over this issue, we must admit at least that there is a problem in formulating the proper relation between descriptive and prescriptive statements.

We argue that the ground and parent of responsible judgments of both value and obligation are objective judgments of fact about the world and human reality. Judgments of fact are achieved by moving through the invariant operations of attentive experience, of intelligent understandings, and of reasonable judgments. When they are concerned with investigating the moral life, these three operations constitute reason in its practical mode, and they arrive at descriptive statements of fact.

In judgments of fact we grasp in reflective understanding what we call the "virtually unconditioned," that is, a conditioned whose conditions are fulfilled.[16] In other words, when we are attentive in experience and intelligent in understanding the data before us, when we can find no further relevant data on which to make a judgment and no further relevant questions can be raised for reflective understanding, then the judgment that follows has all its conditions fulfilled and the judgment is probably true. Once further relevant data become available, or further relevant questions can be raised about the data, then the judgment of fact is open to revision. By adopting this critical realist understanding of practical reason, it is obvious that we have adopted, but also critically interpreted, many characteristics of the modern horizon or world view, for example, the critical turn to the subject as the criterion of truth, the need to be open to further revision in our judgments, etc.

Practical judgments of fact are the beginnings or springs of judgments of value and prescription. This requires that we have intelligent understandings and correct judgments about two sets of data that are relevant to making moral decisions: the data of consciousness and the data of science. The former include facts about the drive to human self-transcendence through the operations of experience, understanding, judgment, and deliberation. The latter include facts about the empirical world, human persons, and their basic needs. Moral obligation presupposes these two sets of facts, although it cannot be reduced to them. Thus, moral judgments of value and claims about moral obligation can be cognitively unwarranted to the extent that they deny or neglect the best factual (empirical and nonempirical) knowledge available in economics, psychology, sociology, philosophy, and theology.

Moral interpretations of value and obligation are as concerned with what *might be* as they are with *what is*. Therefore, value judgments and moral obligations presuppose knowledge (correct judgments) of human possibilities proximate and remote, and the probable consequences of projected courses of action for human and nonhuman welfare. This kind of knowledge is fashioned in both the imagination and the critical tasks of discursive moral reason. Without attention to the possibilities of what might be, the disciple of Jesus either becomes dull or simply absolutizes the current values of a culture as the ground of all value or obligation.

Moral interpretations that result in judgments of value rely not only on correct judgments of fact but also on our intentional feelings. Between our judgments of fact and judgments of value we apprehend values through our feelings. We reach correct judgments of value in a way similar to how we reach correct judgments of fact, namely, by reaching the virtually unconditioned in the practical life. If there are no further morally relevant data to be gathered and assessed by discursive reason nor any further relevant questions to be asked about the values at stake, then the judgment of value is probably correct. Like judgments of fact, the criterion of truth or falsity of judgments of value is in the authenticity or lack of authenticity of the subject. If the criterion of value judgments lies in the authenticity of the subject, the meaning of the judgment is objective.[17] As we have seen before, authenticity in the subject always relates to the conversions and the necessity for proper moral affections.

Moral interpretations that result in moral prescriptions rely on correct judgments of value. Therefore, any misapprehensions of value, or any misrepresentations of how persons come to judgments of value and their criterion of truth or falsity, will lead inevitably to either a false sense of obligation or a skewed formulation of moral obligation. We are now in a position to define the foundational experience of moral obligation: it is the experience of the need to conform our decisions and life to our judgments of value. We must live by the answers we have arrived at, and the necessity to conform our decisions and life to these judgments is what constitutes the experience of moral oughtness.

Moral obligation is not something that is arbitrarily imposed on the disciple of Jesus by some outside source, for example, ecclesial authorities or even God. The experience of moral oughtness arises from within the self, and its criterion of truth is the authenticity of the subject seeking to live out the moral life according to truthful judgments of value. On the other hand, the experience of moral prescription is not a *separate* experience from the experience of value. Experience of obligation is simply a further dimension from within the experience of value itself. In other words, there is a singular movement with distinct, but not separable, moments in the process of self-transcendence to moral interpretations. For example, when we come to judgments of the value of persons and their needs, we experience from within ourselves the duties to be open to and to act in behalf of these values when we can as well as not. Clearly, then, our perceptions of duty rely on and emanate from our perceptions and judgments of value.

MORAL NORMS AND THEIR AUTHORITY

It is not our intention in this volume to undertake a full discussion of the nature and function of moral norms. That is the task of a systematic study of moral theology. But because moral norms are formalized statements of our moral obligations, a brief discussion of them might be helpful in making concrete some of the issues we have already raised.

Moral norms can be divided appropriately into two groups: formal norms and material norms. Formal norms attempt to formulate into imperative statements those moral qualities essential for humans to live well in the moral life. In other words, these norms are concerned with requiring those qualities of the agent called virtues, for example, to be loving, to be just, to be chaste. Although they do not tell us what those qualities mean concretely, formal norms are necessary to remind us of what we too often forget about ourselves. Because formal norms apply to everyone and in all situations—that is, there are never situations in which we may not be just or chaste—they are considered universal and exceptionless.

On the other hand, material norms seek to formulate into imperative statements various judgments on concrete actions judged conducive or not conducive to the fulfillment of human needs. These norms are concerned with requiring (prescriptive norms) or forbidding (proscriptive norms) actions in view of our interpersonal and social life. They seek to specify in content what the formal norms require. Material norms, then, tell us concretely what it might mean to be loving, just, and chaste in our personal and social life with others. For example, the norm "one ought not to engage in premarital sexual relations" seeks to make concrete the virtue of chastity in the unmarried life, and it makes a proscriptive statement about the human need for sexual intimacy among the unmarried.

Unlike the formal norms, however, material norms are not universal and exceptionless. The simple reason is that we cannot always reach the "virtually unconditioned" in concrete matters of the moral life in such a way that the result would apply everywhere and in all cases. All the relevant data, circumstances, and questions need to be considered and appraised before a concrete norm can be adjudged exceptionless and universally applicable. In other words, we would have to conceive of *all* the morally relevant data and circumstances ahead of time and formulate them in the norm itself before we could issue a truly exceptionless material norm. This task would be truly daunting, since the enumeration of all these data and circumstances is beyond the moral imagination of even the best of us. Nonetheless, material norms are valuable and necessary to lift us to some minimal level of knowledge about what we ought and ought not do for the working of a humane and just society.

It should be clear that the two groups of moral norms do not express our emotions about the moral life, nor do they simply express our attitudes. Formal norms function to express truths about the qualities necessary for living the moral life well. Material norms function to express truths about the relationship between events, states of affairs, and action, on the one hand, and the satisfaction of human needs, on the other.[18] Both sets of norms presuppose other truths about the world and the makeup of persons in their personal and social lives. Because moral norms are really indicatives formulated in the imperative mode, they have the authority of truth, no more and no less. Although the relation between moral truths and our lives is usually more complex than the relation between other kinds of truth and our lives, for example, truths about the structure of the DNA molecule, moral truths do not, for this, lose the cognitive status of truth. They state what is necessary for the moral life and they tell about actions in relation to the fulfillment of human needs. Once again, moral interpretations, whether they are of value or duty, relate us to a world and a set of human relations that do not yet exist but are capable of coming into being.

CONCLUSION

The movement in moral interpretations is from description to prescription. Thus, the ultimate court of appeal in morality is the facts. We must recall, though, that "facts" cannot be interpreted in an empiricist way. We gain knowledge of the facts about human reality and human welfare, that is, the world mediated by meaning, from a number of sources, not all of which are empirical. We need to rely on the best insights of the empirical and human sciences, for example, biology and psychology, the normative science of philosophy, and the religious sciences. As disciples of Jesus, we can trust in critical religious experience and the reflections of the ecclesial community to offer valid insights into the nature of a humanity created, fallen, redeemed, and called to a future beyond this history.

What is important is that we not reduce the ultimate authority in morals to one or another of these sources alone. To do this would be to fall into some form of empiricism, naturalism, or theologism. Conflicting interpretations between the various sources of the "facts" will no doubt arise. When they occur, however, we must seek to resolve some of these conflicts by reference to a normative noetic praxis, that is, by reference to right doing informed by the four conversions.

NOTES

1. Much of this section is a brief summary of Robert M. Veatch's article "Does Ethics Have An Empirical Basis?" *Hastings Center Studies* 1 (1973): 50–65.

2. A book that represents this school of thought is A. J. Ayer, *Language, Truth, and Logic* (New York: Dover Pubs., 1952 [1946]).

3. For the Reformed theologians, see Karl Barth, *Church Dogmatics* II/2, trans. G. W. Bromiley et al. (Edinburgh: T. & T. Clark, 1957), 509–781; and Paul Lehmann, *Ethics in a Christian Context* (New York: Harper & Row, 1963). For a helpful discussion of the Catholic neo-scholastic theologians, see Vincent McNamara, "Religion and Morality, Part II—Traditions," *Irish Theological Quarterly* 44 (1977): 175–91.

4. G. E. Moore, *Principia Ethica* (Cambridge: At the Univ. Press, 1966 [1903]).

5. Bernard Lonergan, *Method in Theology* (New York: Herder & Herder, 1972), 30–31.

6. Ibid., 66–67; see also above, pp. 16–18 and 63–65.

7. Ibid., 31–32.

8. Lawrence Kohlberg with Clark Power, "Moral Development, Religious Thinking, and the Question of a Seventh Stage," in Lawrence Kohlberg, *Essays on Moral Development*, vol. 1, *The Philosophy of Moral Development* (San Francisco: Harper & Row, 1981), 311–72.

9. Richard A. McCormick, "Theology and Biomedical Ethics," *Eglise et Théologie* 13 (1982): 315.

10. Enda McDonagh, *The Making of Disciples: Tasks of Moral Theology* (Wilmington, Del.: Michael Glazier, 1982), 38–59. For a more detailed discussion of the relation between liturgy and Christian ethics, see the special issue entitled *Focus on Liturgy and Ethics* in *Journal of Religious Ethics* 7 (1070).

11. Bernard Häring, *Free and Faithful in Christ: Moral Theology for Clergy and Laity*, vol. 1 (New York: Seabury Press, 1978), 201–8.

12. Blaise Pascal, *Pensées*, trans. W. F. Trotter (Chicago: Great Books, Encyclopaedia Britannica, 1952), IV.277, 282. For a recent and insightful discussion of the role of the affections and imagination in Christian ethics, see Philip S. Keane, *Christian Ethics and Imagination: A Theological Inquiry* (New York: Paulist Press, 1984), esp. chap. 4.

13. The following section relies on some of the insights in Daniel C. Maguire, *The Moral Choice* (Garden City, N.Y.: Doubleday & Co., 1978), chap. 8.

14. Johann B. Metz, *Faith in History and Society: Toward a Practical Fundamental Theology*, trans. David Smith (New York: Seabury Press, 1980), 88–99.

15. David Hume, *A Treatise of Human Nature*, ed. L. A. Selby-Bigge (Oxford: At the Clarendon Press, 1888), 469–70.

16. Bernard J. F. Lonergan, *Insight: A Study of Human Understanding* (New York: Harper & Row, 1978), chap. 10; and idem, *Method in Theology*, 75.

17. Walter E. Conn, *Conscience: Development and Self-Transcendence* (Birmingham, Ala.: Religious Education Press, 1981), 139.

18. Gerard J. Hughes, S. J., *Authority in Morals: An Essay in Christian Ethics* (London: Heythrop Monographs, 1978), 83.

FURTHER READINGS

Anthony Battaglia. *Toward a Reformulation of Natural Law.* New York: Seabury Press, 1981.

Charles E. Curran and Richard A. McCormick, eds. *Readings in Moral Theology*, no. 1, *Moral Norms and Catholic Tradition*. New York: Paulist Press, 1979.

James M. Gustafson. *Ethics From a Theocentric Perspective*, vol. 1, *Theology and Ethics*. Chicago: Univ. of Chicago Press, 1981.

Janine Marie Idziak. *Divine Command Morality: Historical and Contemporary Readings*. New York: Edwin Mellen Press, 1979.

John Macquarrie. *Three Issues in Ethics*. London: SCM Press, 1970.

William A. Spurrier. *Natural Law and the Ethics of Love*. Philadelphia: Westminster Press, 1974.

CHAPTER 6

THE COGNITIVE DIMENSIONS
OF RELIGIOUS CONVERSION

You cannot create this obscure and marvellous field of energy—*le bonheur*—by advocacy or the whip, by force or by guile, but only by pleading. Poetry begins there, and prayer also; they lead you to a thought, and science comes out of that thought. But the pedigree is long.

Lawrence Durrell, *Constance, or Solitary Practices*

Although Christians find themselves in a new world that emphasizes subjective pluralism, relativized values, and historical differences, they assemble in prayer, possessed by the same stories and symbols as their religious ancestors. The hymns to Jesus as Lord, the prophecies about the lion lying down with the lamb, the good news told about the resurrection, and the practical demands made of apostolic believers enshrined in the texts of the Scriptures symbolize the faith expressed in their converting lives. To speak about the Father of the Lord Jesus in other than biblical language might seem second- or third-rate at best, a betrayal at worst. Our objective is to show that this is not so.

Religious experiences and their symbolic expressions contain more than they realize.[1] Just as the moral dimensions of conversion develop into cognitive, discursive analysis, so too Christian stories implicitly hold a grammar that unwinds into further sentences about God and salvation. The constantly pregnant symbols give birth to new religious insights for every age. This occurs at both the individual and social levels in Christian experience. Indeed, the "individual" intellectual meanings from religious poems and prayers have inherently public aspects. Why and how are cognitive Christian statements made? How does the language of doctrine, truth, dogma, and tradition guide our conversions?

THE DEMAND FOR COGNITIVE
CLARITY WITHIN FAITH

In the later social contexts of the New Testament, defined by the so-called catholic epistles (James 1 and 2; Peter 1–3; John; and Jude), there already appeared false teachers. In 2 Pet. 2:1– 3:3 (similar to Jude 4–18), authors warn against incorrect interpretations of the original message. They are "waterless springs and mists driven by a storm" (2 Peter 2:17), caught in licentious whim and speculative lust. No moderate condemnation of falsity! So a letter of John recommends maintaining allegiance to the official teachers (2 John 9–10); Titus suggests that the person chosen to lead the community be a faithful teacher (Titus 1:9–10). A letter to Timothy (1 Tim. 6:2–5) promotes the "sound words of our Lord Jesus Christ and the teaching which accords with godliness" (see also 2 Tim. 1:13; 3:2ff., 14–17). From the beginning, there were conflicts of interpretation.

How do we account for truthful understanding? This question meets our culture directly; it asks any society that permits plural perspectives on its laws, constitutions, and benefits to sort out what counts as a fair, adequate interpretation of its own identity.

The Cognitional Shape of a Truthful Faith

The patterns that determine the nature of moral knowledge and judgments also shape the appearance of truthful statements from faithful symbols. What we know in faith is not like "taking a look at God," an "already out there now" transcendent thing, liable to simple empirical validation. The critical appropriation of our faith is accomplished within the convergence of our affects, decisions, and cognitive abilities.

The foundational religious experience is the uncanny sense of the Other that constantly obtrudes in our daily questions, evaluations, and situations of limit and crises of threshold. Just as our feelings reveal intended moral values, so their symbolic re-presentations invite and persuade us toward a consenting trust in an ultimately benign universe. As the Other draws us toward its own mystery, we see our need to purify and change ourselves through the experience of conversion, falling in love with the transcendent beyond all finite reality. When we take on the story of Jesus of Nazareth within the community of believers, we opt for a horizon in which all God's gracious love is mediated through the radically igniting experience of the cross and resurrection.

Faith in the preaching, life, death, and transformation of Jesus takes on a new dimension when a believer affectively converts. Trusting in Christ becomes not only an assent to revelation as proposed by God in the church but a personal event in which all one's loyalty shifts from satisfying one's own desires to encouraging the will of God in the world. Faith assumes a dynamic exigency that challenges the Christian to be consumed by a love that knows no limit. Grasped by attachment to an ultimate concern, believers search for the most appropriate specific aesthetic symbol through which to express their new engrossing interest. Many of the most startling stories of Christian conversion (e.g., John Wesley, 1703–91; or Thomas Merton) are of individuals who had assented to Christianity in some way but only later affectively gave themselves to God.

Knowing the "truth" of or about one's faith, therefore, already involves at least two dimensions: the affective eros toward the transcendent which occurs in our feelings and their symbolic expressions, and secondly, the assent to the identification with the story of Jesus of Nazareth. The feelings operative in Christian love are transitive; that is, they drive us toward a valued object — the person of the Christ and the community for which he died.

From within the praxis of attachment to the body of Christ, believers discern the specific shape of the values chosen. Discursive analysis sorts out the data relevant to religious self-understanding; it discriminates which facts and judgments of value will contribute toward the kingdom to which the church aspires. It seeks to understand the individual or social conditions and criteria through which Christian life can be developed and inauthentic experience overcome.

Finally, by firmly establishing itself within intellectual patterns, it discovers that the criteria for the truth of religious discourse take place in the transformative praxis of religious, affective, and intellectual conversions. Believers appropriate a critically mediated Christian conversion. They clarify the conditions within which Christianity will be known as true in our contemporary society. Religious seekers will study the data of social living in our world and the nature of individual and communal change. They will recognize when no further relevant questions need be asked to validate not only their own but the community's discernment of authenticity.

A critical Christian faith therefore involves reflection upon the cognitive, affective, and moral conditions that permit the judgment that the symbols are true or false. Because none of the "conditions" (right or wrong, divinity or malice, attachment or detachment) are purely empirical, they must be interpreted by disciplines that can encompass the data of consciousness as well as the transcendent. Classical theologies used Plato and Aristotle; reformulated theories and systems about Christian doctrine and ethics will require appropriately revised metaphysics, individual and social psychology, anthropology, and other social disciplines.

The Social Truth of Christian Faith

If the achievement of a critical Christian conversion seems too austere, we should note that analysis of religious experience does not necessarily reflect the ecstasy of faith nor does it indicate the usual mode of emergence. Just as the moral life of the believer occurs within the affective values of the church, so Christian loyalties to God are fostered, refined, and guided by witness and worship, engendered by preaching, and supported by neighborly service. The experience of Christian faith always occurs within the community.

The first emergence of controversies about the truth of Christian beliefs occurred not in the context of the Enlightenment search for individual intellectual validation but in the social establishment of Constantinian Christendom. The first questions appeared when the Judaic language and customs required translation into Hellenistic social forms. The doctrines of Nicaea and Chalcedon were not impositions upon the community but grew from the intrinsic demands of faith. They established not only what seemed true to believers but what was the case for the world as well.

To describe what we mean by doctrine, it may be useful to begin with a specific example of such a teaching in ecclesial life—the statement at the Council of Nicaea that Jesus is consubstantial with the Father.[2] The Greek word *homoousios* over which much ecclesiastical and civil warfare was launched is not to be found in the Christian Scriptures. Yet the council fathers felt it necessary to use it. Why?

The conflict arose because it was possible to disagree about the meaning of the claims concerning who Jesus was and is. The prayers and hymns (e.g., Phil. 2:1–11; Rev. 5:9–10), and the images of Jesus as Lamb (Revelation 5:6), shepherd (John 10:11), light (John 8:12) and the application of many other titles (law, dayspring, name, Son of man, Son of God, and Lord) did not immediately reveal to the earliest hearers the answers to questions their faithful attachment provoked. The symbols informed their lives, criticized their social ethics, and provided a basis for catechesis, but they did not answer the question Arius (ca. 250–336) asked: Was the Christ on the side of creatures or of the Creator?

Early teachers like Origen did not hesitate to say that as Lord, Jesus was of divine origin. But what exactly was his "location" in relationship to the Father? After all, Jesus did say, "The Father is greater than I" (John 14:28). Arius was quite clear. Christ was a mixed being, halfway between human and divine realities. That, of course, is why he could save us: he had a bit of both worlds. Though many found this a convincing, even rational, argument, it quickly became clear to some thinkers (e.g., Athanasius, ca. 296–373) that to speak of Jesus as partially human and partially divine would compromise the gospel of salvation altogether.

The various images and sayings of the Scriptures did not immediately command solutions to the problem but provoked further conflicts of interpretation. It seemed necessary to employ a nonbiblical word to describe what the community meant: *homoousios*, "of the same being" as the Father. If Jesus was not truly God, then he could not have saved us; if he was not completely human, then it is not we (or not all of our humanity) who are saved. This was not to add to the meaning of the life of Christ but to examine in another culture what the language of the Gospels had said.

The teaching or doctrine of Nicaea was expressed in creedal form, to be avowed by believers, to be experienced as binding upon all the faithful. Symbols are multivalent, opaque, and born of a particular culture's common sense; they operate the way metaphors do in poetry, awakening us to some new resemblance in our world, shocking us into discovery.[3] Doctrines do not substitute for symbols but answer the need to notice one crucial point within a community—a point that, if misunderstood, might compromise the story itself.[4] Implicit within the symbols themselves is a descriptive moment that is explicated by the "new" doctrine.

The doctrines that answer our questions about faith have many functions.[5] Besides the *cognitive* dimension we have just mentioned which clarifies a controverted interpretation, doctrines also *counsel* us to pay attention to certain aspects of belief. They provide new insights that *constitute communities*, informing our living, our actions, and our common knowledge. They also *establish a tradition*, an often sharply worded way of handing on our faith in the form of stated beliefs. And as we shall see more fully later, they intrinsically claim to be a norm for those who believe with us.

Doctrines establish the common teachings of a church in such a way that to contradict some of them would be to refuse participation in the community. To disagree with certain doctrines, therefore, is not only to have a scholarly argument but to ask for a reshaping of the community. The noncognitive functions of doctrine (the affective suasions, the traditional communications, and community-constituting factors) often make disagreement violent. The religious and social fabric of people's lives is scorched, ripped, and sometimes only modestly patched.

Doctrines are a transition in the life of a community. They mark a shift from one literary form of expression to another: from the affective scriptural address to the whole person, to an appeal to the mind to focus on a single truth. Besides the difference in genre, a corresponding subjective change is required. Doctrine asks that individuals develop their own way of understanding belief, of shifting from one form of consciousness to another. The new pattern assumes that it is worthwhile to sort out the questions we have about belief, that we value the mind itself as religious. Finally, doctrines assume that we say something true about what is real and that what is religious is altogether real. Doctrines do not make clear what was unclear in the Scriptures (Paul, Mark, and Luke believed Jesus to be Lord); rather, public teaching puts into another form what was said in a metaphoric manner in the Gospels. Doctrines add to the church's understanding of the Bible; they do not replace it.

REFUSALS TO ADMIT DOCTRINE
TO THE REALM OF FAITH

We have presented public doctrines and cognitive teachings about faith as a natural and necessary growth from the stories of Christian conversion. Many find the contentious rivalry of doctrinal schools something to be rejected, not condoned, in the life of the church. Why? What are some of the reasons that believers prefer to leave doctrines aside when discussing their faith? We can clarify what we mean by the personal and social cognitive dimensions of conversion by understanding three forms of doctrinal rejection: biblical fundamentalism, religious agnosticism, and the contemporary fear of ideology.

We have already distinguished the world of immediacy and the world mediated by meaning.[6] We have indicated how the dimensions of meaning grow from learning basic skills at a common-sense level to a search for coherence and consistency to establish systematic procedures and divisions of labor. Systems ask for definitions, models, and well-ordered explanatory terms; but at the same time, systems distance those who use them from the ordinary understandings of common sense. Some groups of people can use both common-sense and systematic languages; some can only use common-sense speech.

Beyond system is method. Methodologists look not so much at the contents of systems as at the way in which they work, the way in which they interrelate with nonsystematic languages. They place the operations of common sense, system, and theory into a dynamic context. Method reflects upon the structural conditions that permit the multiple ingenuities. People explore their own interiority, the feelings of subjectivity, and the patterns of their own knowing processes.

Differentiations of human consciousness point out the pluriform ways in which the doctrines of a religion can emerge and be accepted. Although public teachings originally appear because there is some converging set of questions within common sense, they go beyond the symbols and stories and add definitional clarifications and propositional statements meant to sharpen the believers' understanding of what they already know. Though the questions may seem pertinent in one context, they may not find a ready hearing in another, and equivalences, analogies, and translations are required. Translation is never exact; translators may not be sufficiently aware of the common sense within which the problem surfaced. Scholarship may determine that the original context no longer exists; ordinary people may feel that doctrines formulated in other situations are existentially irrelevant. What was argued and developed at one level of differentiation may be given to a society and culture where that question is not yet or no longer significant. Methodologists with highly nuanced doctrinal vocabularies may believe that the language of religious common sense should be corrected or even discarded. And thus Christians whose beliefs are lived in the pews of their neighborhood church and in the marketplaces where morality is of crucial importance wonder if thinking about their religion does not automatically distance them from their faith. Doctrines seem more trouble than they are worth. Unused, unpreached, they disappear by neglect.

Fundamentalism: Distinguishing Reflection from Common Sense

Fundamentalism as a movement began in evangelical Protestant circles at the turn of the twentieth century.[7] In 1895, the founding Bible conference issued a statement maintaining five points: the verbal inerrancy of the Scriptures, the divinity of Jesus Christ, the virgin birth, a substitutionary doctrine of the atonement, and the physical resurrection and bodily return of Christ. Early in the new century (1909), eminent American preachers wrote a series of tracts called *The Fundamentals*, which were widely published. Much of what was taught became the basis of evangelical preaching—especially American evangelical preaching—during the next fifty years. In the popular mind, fundamentalism has most often been identified by its first tenet: the belief that the words themselves of the Scriptures are the inspired Word of God, and that they are entirely free from any conceivable error.

If we look at the fundamentalist movement through the prism of the differentiation of consciousness, we can refract several different colors. Fundamentalism is first a response to nineteenth-century biblical scholarship that attempted (for good or ill) to situate the Scriptures within their original communities of common sense. This scholarship, in its turn, reacted to methodological positions that had located religion in an ongoing context in which philosophy and science seemed to have surpassed it. The scholarship of the nineteenth century originated as part of the ongoing quest to determine the unique character of Christianity within the world of religious experience and expression. Fundamentalism noted, however, an important problem in such scholarship: it did not necessarily take account of the existential significance of the texts for believers.

More important, scholarship refused to reinsert itself within the ultimate claims of the Bible—that it was not just a human word about God but the Word of God speaking. Rather than answer biblical critics on the basis of more differentiated scholarship, the movement chose to reassert an identity between the literal text and its contemporary meaning. It was socially and politically crucial, believers felt, to emphasize that these words were God's Word.

Second, fundamentalism may have rejected the kind of teaching that biblical scholars provided, but it did not refuse to teach. Though it seems to deny the possibility of doctrines, the five tenets of the movement are a doctrine about the Bible, not a repetition of the scriptural words. The argument between fundamentalists and exegetes on the meaning of the Bible is a disagreement about which doctrinal method should be applied in reading the texts. As a result, a discussion must occur that studies the adequacy of the various doctrines to the nature of the Bible itself.

Finally, the evidence that will decide the discussion will differentiate common sense from reflective doctrines. To determine the status of doctrines on the basis of common sense will not be adequate; it would be like deciding the nature of the moon's orbit and phases by what we see most evenings before we go to bed. Just as human experience in other realms requires differentiation, so the cognitive dimension of Christian conversion emerges at several levels.

Agnosticism: The Relativism of Feelings and Language

By agnostics we do not mean here those who bracket whether their reason knows or does not know that there is a God; we mean those believers who think that statements about their faith are mostly a matter of perspective.[8] On the agnostic view, everyone is entitled to his or her own opinion about what the symbols, stories, hymns, and prayers mean. Since religion is really a private view on the world, no one can say for sure what is true or false about such religious experience.

Like fundamentalist adherence to the literal meaning of the text, agnosticism in Christianity refuses to express religion beyond its own common sense. Seeing that there are conflicting interpretations of the symbols of faith, it prefers to remain "unknowing" whether one or another aspect might be true. Just as fundamentalism is a fixist fusion with the biblical text, so contemporary religious agnosticism is a perspectival relativism that privatizes biblical faith. The former assumes that there is a single imperial way in which to capture the present situation through strategic proofs from the text; the other recedes to individual enclaves and nurses its battle wounds inflicted by the conflicts of scholarship, confessional disagreements, and theological arguments.

The agnosticism of which we speak has both affective and linguistic dimensions. Linguistically, it refuses further clarification of its own common sense; words, especially austere, reflective concepts, cannot express the surpassing meaning of the aesthetic symbols of faith. Affectively, it finds its own feelings, its religious intensity, more important than whether religious experience has a dimension of truth or an impact upon the wider world of science, technology, and politics. Such agnosticism is a spiritual anemia, a fear that if "my" symbols become part of the larger social world, they may evaporate like the ghosts of personal security they are.

The Fear of Cognitive Norms

To grant doctrine a legitimate place in faith establishes an intellectual norm, both a guide and a prompt to belief. A doctrine says not only what Christians have believed but what they ought to believe. Doctrines become authentic teaching as opposed to aberrations and errors. After the Nicene definition, it no longer made sense to adhere to Arius's theological positions or to their equivalents.

Doctrines have authority, and contemporary life bridles at authoritative statements. The assumption inherent in doctrine is that it is not that the teaching does not fit the times but the believer does not yet experience the whole of faith. Instead of changing the doctrine, one should transform oneself.

All the current fears about losing one's freedom, about not being able to choose, about not fulfilling one's own true destiny become operative.[9] It is easier to think of doctrines as automatically suspect, as alien repressions of sovereign freedom, as thin meaninglessness in the face of emotional attachment.

One can reject as an illegitimate incursion upon subjectivity what one cannot avoid by reason of history.

Many would argue that there is an implicitly cognitive aspect within revelation itself.[10] God's gift of self-presencing love announces something about the nature of the world; it maintains that "I" am not the norm of the way the universe is. Rather, God is the authentic speaker who tells the truth. When we reflect upon that revelation, we put forward our thoughts as partially normative. We assume that an aspect of what we conceptualize is the authoritative dimension. People ought to see the world in this way, for this is the way God understands the world. Normative teaching becomes what the church has called dogma.

DOGMA: THE EMERGENCE OF
NORMATIVE TEACHINGS

Though we have used the Nicene statement as an example of doctrine, it is also a dogma — a truth available in revelation, solemnly defined by a council in union with the whole church, and proposed as binding upon all by reason of its inclusion within the regular and general teaching of the church.[11] All theological thinkers implicitly put forward their studies of faith as a representation of the original revelation, but not every theological position, however commonly taught, becomes dogma. Dogma is an ecclesial event in which the members of the church, including those who argue for or against the dogma, commit themselves to this aspect of revelation.[12]

As an exercise of faith, dogma sees the Scriptures as the absolute norm of the original revelatory experience but provides a verbal, conceptual orientation in a particular culture, especially when that biblical experience is threatened. Establishing a linguistic map through difficulties, dogma focuses through one small point of light a coherence in the theological positions taken within the church. Since we are shaped by the languages we speak, agreed dogmatic statements create a solidarity of vocabulary around which the community can rally. Insofar as they are exploratory, a discovery within a conceptual realm of some particular meaning of revelation, they can become a source of faith itself by reflecting back upon the other beliefs of the church. In this sense, official doctrines of a church are more a beginning of a new discussion than the end of an old one.[13]

Some would like to forget the existence of dogmas because they have been used to club opposite ways of thinking into submission. Service unites; doctrines divide; or so the saying has it. Ecumenically, the differing doctrines of the Christian churches and the weight that each gives them have made contemporary dialogues difficult, if not heated. But believers cannot avoid making statements about their beliefs. What the interecclesial discussion has wanted is no longer a clearing away of mistaken positions, historical inaccuracies, and projected stereotypes, but a developed "further" position that can encompass both partners in dialogue. This "further" linguistic statement will not be so much a return to the biblical language as a serious search for a common conceptual, that is, doctrinal, vocabulary that can include and transform both (or all) traditions. The seeming hiatus in the ecumenical discussion except at the local level, where destruction of prejudice is still crucial, is probably caused by this necessary shift in attention.[14]

The intellectual, cognitive, and affective aspects of doctrine and dogma may be clarified through the church's experience with heresy.[15] Heresy does not mean mere opinion, a candidly held disagreement or dissatisfaction with the formulation of one or another of the church's official positions. Rather the community's belief that heresy is possible assumes that dogmas deal truthful statements about reality. Some consciously and strongly held positions can cut us off (*airesis*) from our relationship with the originating event. For some fundamentalists, historical-critical method, because it does not pay explicit attention to the divine origin of the biblical text, is heretical.

To be a heretic means not just to hold a silly or false opinion but deliberately and obstinately to deny or doubt, while retaining the name of Christian, some truth within faith. To hold on to an opinion about Christian realities when the rest of the community believes otherwise can be a sign of culpable ignorance.

The problem is that disagreement can also be a sign of prophecy. The common understanding may be common confusion. To stand against the whole body of believers on a certain issue might witness to a lost or forgotten truth or a knowledge that is yet to be born in the heart of believers. We shall speak about dissent from common teaching in chapter 9.

The reality of heresy in the church recognizes both the cognitive and moral dimensions of faith. Just as there are evaluative, affective, and moral conditions that become the criteria for knowing the truth of Christianity at an individual level, so too the public teachings of the community may demand important transformative conditions that require articulation at the social level.

The distinction between authentic faith and heresy is based not on the fact that some people have different opinions about doctrine but on the fact that some are willing to enter into dialogue and others are not. If companions in dialogue remain docile to that larger position on the subject matter which may emerge, then it is plausible that both the "orthodox" and "heterodox" positions may be transformed into a "further" language that neither yet knows. Though doctrinal statements cannot be given up once they are enunciated, they can develop if the community believes that its previous insights into the gospel have been preserved and even advanced. Christian dialogue, both inside individual churches and between churches, is at this threshold.

DOCTRINES AND HISTORY: THE
APPARENT CONSENSUS

The problem of conflicting claims concerning beliefs makes it clear that not all the dimensions of faith are cognitive.[16] For example, in the context of trying to develop a balanced position between fideism (the "I believe because it is absurd" position) and rationalism (the "I will believe if and only if I have clear and distinct reasons" position), the First Vatican Council (1869–70) offered the following definition of faith:

> Faith, which is the beginning of human salvation, is a supernatural virtue, whereby, inspired and assisted by the grace of God, we believe that the realities God has revealed are true; not because of the intrinsic truth of the realities, viewed by the natural light of reason, but because of the authority of God himself who reveals them, and who can neither be deceived nor deceive.[17]

Faith comes from God, who operates as both the interior assistance of the Holy Spirit and the external help of the outer words of the Scriptures, miracles, prophecies, prayer, and the worshiping life of the church. Human beings do not will themselves into conversion, nor can they argue themselves into it. We believe because we encounter an ultimately truthful speaker who discloses a personal love for the world. We do not believe because we have figured out the necessary structures of what we are told. Rather we trust someone who tells us the truth.[18]

The first motives of faith, therefore, are not rational; they are rather the trustworthiness of the speaker. Reasonableness functions on the other side of faith to provide "some understanding" of the mysterious presence of God that will always exceed our ability to interpret it. "Even when delivered by revelation and received by faith, [the divine mysteries] remain covered with the veil of faith itself, and shrouded in a certain degree of darkness, so long as we are pilgrims in this mortal life, not yet with God."[19]

The last hundred years of theology have tried to determine some of the characteristics of the intersubjective trust that operates as the first moment of faith. The nonrational historical motives for faith (affective maturity, moral values, the apprehension of beauty, the stability of order, the boundaries provoked by crises) are certainly as important as "having the correct opinions" before (or for that matter after) the first moments of faith in God. Catechetical disciplines, theories of communication, evangelization proposals, homiletics programs, and liturgical renewals have been the direct result. No one will be propelled into faith only by having the right reasons; faith is a gift between God and the community of believers. Part of the truth of a historically conscious faith remains this intersubjective witness and the concrete conditions that permit and encourage its emergence.

THE IRREFORMABILITY OF DOCTRINE

The introduction of witness, intersubjective trust, the moral stance of the individual, into the motives and conditions for allowing faith to be disclosed makes some people nervous. Are not the doctrines of faith to be held irrefutably—once true, always true, not just under historical conditions? Dogmas are irreformable doctrines—yet they travel through history.[20] How can the two notions be reconciled?

The church makes the claim that the revelation in Christ is definitive, final in the sense that here God has been disclosed totally. It is not that we cannot learn more or will not, but that our knowledge will always be in reference to the particular data present in Jesus as universal Lord. In this event, Christians have a constructive common history through which we are what and who we are. We cannot be otherwise. Holding to specific formulations about the revelation maintains that this decisiveness would be compromised if the history of Christian understanding were truncated or aborted. Yet the teachings of Christ must appear in every culture and in every time. How can the two understandings hold together? How can there be both change and identity in the same doctrine?

The community of believers has taken two different positions on this topic. On the one hand, the Catholic church has a firm teaching that says that doctrines, at least those declared by the pope or councils under strict conditions, are irreformable of themselves, not as a result of the consent of the church.[21] Once stated, always true, irrespective of audience. Pope Paul VI maintained that there are some concepts that are "not tied to a certain definite form of human culture," scientific progress, or a theological school.[22] Yet the *Decree on Ecumenism* from the Second Vatican Council (1962–65) maintained that the tradition given by the apostles was received in different forms from the beginning and had a varied development dependent upon natural gifts and environment. It saw these differences as often complementary.[23] The same council in the *Constitution on the Church in the Modern World* spoke of the revealed truths as one thing, and the manner in which they are formulated without violence to their meaning and significance, as another.[24]

Catholics resolve this difficulty through the notion of the development of doctrine,[25] which argues that there is in the primary revelation given by God to believers more than the faithful can possibly understand in first fervor. Not only does our affective attachment deepen over the years but our conceptual understanding of the truth illuminates self, world, and God. The nature of the message requires development; the developments are called doctrines or dogmas; and they are binding insofar as they crystallize the truthful meaning of the original revelation.

Three basic theories have been proposed about development of doctrine: (1) a logical or classicist understanding, (2) a transformist or "liberal" interpretation, and (3) a reflexive position.

1. In the *logical theory*, there is an assumption that our knowledge about God is tied to a particular vocabulary, that to change those words is to falsify content and to undermine the authority of revelation itself. Classicism believes that there is a single cultural form universally true and valid, that the invariance given to faith by believers is to be found in its formulations. Theories of doctrinal development that focused upon the form of dogma tended to discuss whether reasonable conclusions drawn from revelation should be accorded the same weight as the Bible. They believed that it was possible to derive through some syllogistic form later doctrinal positions. What was implicit and opaque in earlier formulas became explicit and clear through the agency of the authentic teaching offices of the Christian community. Its usefulness was that it took formulations of doctrine seriously; its fundamental drawbacks remained all those related to classicist culture, including the location of revelation in propositional forms. It was assumed that when God did not speak logical sentences, there were intelligent and infallible interpreters in the present who could.

2. In reaction to such a narrow, if sometimes elaborate, view of historical change, nineteenth-century liberal theologians rejected the normative character of concepts. Intellectual knowledge is always growing and changing. The situated nature of our questions limits the ways in which we can believe in the answers. *Transformism* emphasized the affective piety of believers and the symbolic expressions that shaped their faith. Personal, even mystical, adherence to Christ was much more important than externals. Theological doctrines, especially ecclesiastical dogmas, were simply human work about divine revelation rather than a representation of God's word for a given culture. Without the continual adaptation of vocabulary to every place and time, there could be no divine presence. Truth never appears in formulas; rather,

it discloses itself in trusting attachment to Jesus. Between one century's formulation and another, there need be continuity not at the level of expression, only at the level of interior faith.

If in the logical theory of development, truth must appear in the lapidary prose of formulaic repetition, in this interpretation, truth transforms itself from age to age without ever quite appearing in the specific vocabulary of the church's beliefs. By stressing the affective dimensions of Christian experience, transformist theories of doctrinal development provided a relatively new component to the understanding of faith and its formulations. By not having the critical tools to describe the relationships between affective attachment and reflective forms, it ran the risk of denying any identity to the Christian kerygma. This interpretation invited the fundamentalist response in evangelical circles and the repressive magisterial response to Catholic modernism that marked the turn of the century.

A moderate position accounts for both the conceptual formulations of belief and their origins in affective, intersubjective faith. It is the interpretation that has been operative in our interpretation of the cognitive dimensions of faith. Contemporary theologians take seriously the prereflective character of faith, its origins in the gift of God's self-revealing presence, and the operative interior, more often affective, attachment that occurs in the believer. The initial reflexive appearance of this faith is to be found in symbols. Christian conversion manifests itself as operative in the enthusiasm and the peace and joy which incline toward worship. It tells its own tale in gospels, letters, and visions. It begins to reflect upon itself in creeds and doctrines.

3. The *reflexive theory*, therefore, understands both symbols and doctrines as forms or genres of Christian revelation, founded in the transcendent love of God for our humanity and epitomized in the person of the Christ. This prior care of God for the universe judges all formulations and requires that Christians study the interconnections between conceptual and symbolic forms of revelation. The only access we have to the primordial divine presence is through the symbols and our conceptual reflection upon them. Our adherence to the traditional symbols and our ongoing noetic articulation of their meaning is our way of maintaining Christian identity within the change that constitutes our lives. If we do not revise the conceptualizations, we run the risk of no longer seeing the truth that is available through the symbols. We grant the tradition of symbols and dogmatic formulas a prior claim on our faith because we trust the truthful witness of previous speakers of Christian experience.

The prereflexive-conceptual theory offers stability to the Christian tradition within dynamic movement by focusing mutual reciprocity between concepts and cultural change. Faithful formulas can criticize the culture; cultural problems can require new articulations of belief. Conceptual doctrines can authentically generate a disclosive experience for believers; the romanticist belief that images alone must provoke faith is a blind spot of culture. The position recognizes that the authority of an authentic tradition is a complex interaction of the entire interpretive community, the authoritative teachers, the receptive sense of God's faithful people, the vocabulary and grammars of the past, and the transforming possibilities for a future. Christians may not exit from faith either by blind authoritarianism (whether of Bible or tradition) or by subjective relativism (which collapses faith into self-worshiping agnosticism).

TRADITION: CRITERIA FOR
CHANGE AND IDENTITY

In the search for an articulation of the truths of faith, however, what count as criteria to distinguish the tradition from the traditions?[26] How do we tell the difference between human opinions and God's revealing presence (Mark 7:8)? The work of understanding the original revelation in Christ asks us to maintain identity within change, unity within plurality, and coherence among legitimately differing options of expression.

Christianity cannot solve this problem in isolation. Since the problem of determining an authentic faith occurs within a society, some of the conditions for maintaining the community in truth will depend upon the implementation of those social conditions that correspond to the affective, moral, and intellectual conversions.[27] What Catholics have called *development of doctrine* is an instance of a cultural experience (pluralism within one societal identity and the relationship of developmental processes and stable goals). Christianity must help frame these questions socially and thereby assist in the transformation of the social systems to which it belongs, or it will remain a monologue.

Tradition consists of both active and objective dimensions.[28] It is not first the thoughts or ideas transmitted but rather the process of transmitting for others through the activities of the community. In moral witness, narrative preaching, hymnic worship, apocalyptic visions, believers offered to others the vehicles by which the living Christ was disclosed.

How do we distinguish the human elements from the divine presence? There are two unintelligent extremes: (1) to say that the "real" Christ is present in the active underlying process but is not available in the institutional, material elements of the church; (2) to say that Christ is present only in the institutions, sacraments, and doctrines of the church and is inaccessible elsewhere.[29] Both positions are unacceptable, the first because it does not take the incarnation seriously, the second because it does not recognize the inexhaustible operations of the transcendent Spirit.

Vincent of Lérins (ca. 450) offered a classical formulation to determine what was authentic Christian tradition — that which was believed everywhere, by everyone, for the longest time (what possessed universality, consent, and antiquity). Unfortunately, it was difficult to prove that a tradition satisfied the criteria. Not all the earliest authors (the fathers of the church) agreed. Arianism could appeal to an older pedigree in its explicit formulas. The sense of the faithful was often divided. If one made Vincent's formulation a negative criterion, it might be more useful: what was never believed by anyone in any place at any time must be a bizarre un-Christian novelty.

Criteria for authenticity grew — the canon of the Scriptures, the example of early teachers, the worship of the community, the pastoral leaders, incipient creeds worked out in preaching, and the witness of holy lives. When these all agreed, there was little difficulty. When they did not, the community began to ask which speaker of truth demanded priority. Did we have standards that permitted linking the authorities together?

John Henry Newman (1801–90) was one of the first English-speaking theologians to answer this question.[30] Partially as a result of the experience of defending his own conversion to Catholicism, partially from his deep understanding of the church fathers, Newman proposed seven norms for the truthful development of Christian teaching.

There must be (1) preservation of type, in which the development of a specific tradition must fit within the tradition as a whole, a part of the entire church's life. There must also be (2) continuity of principles. Taking the image of organic growth, Newman pointed out that a naturally developing organism always has hidden conditions that guide it toward maturity. The new doctrine must have a genuine (3) power of assimilation, capable of incorporating all the previous elements of the church's teaching into a new synthesis. If it does not account for what was true in the past, then it is more often than not truncating the tradition. Newman maintained that authentic development would have a (4) logical sequence, not in the classicist form of a syllogism but rather as an informal inference, which would often appear to have coherence only much later.

A new doctrine should not simply complete past programs, but should also include (5) anticipations of the future. Implicit within its new images and interpretations, there should be foreshadowings of future positions. In past doctrinal positions, there should be, as well, the same "anxiety of anticipation" toward the present development. Though the new doctrine should be a (6) conservation of the past, it must be written in a creative, dynamic fashion. Finally, doctrinal development should show (7) chronic vigor. A healthy social body cures itself over the long haul — even when the processes of decay and enfeeblement seem preponderant. In Christian society, there is a genuinely self-correcting spirit to which the new doctrine should contribute.

Newman's highly descriptive and somewhat abstract proposals do not satisfy us, because of the complexity of the tradition and because of the contemporary need for interlocking analyses at the level of textual criticism and social efficacy. What distinguishes sheer force from authentic redescriptive power in social discourse? Why have some Christian positions succeeded and others not? Recent work in literary criticism,[31] social psychology,[32] and social philosophy[33] will contribute to our understanding of this process.

CONCLUSION

Pointing to the emergent cognitive dimensions of Christian conversion, we have shown how faith leads to understanding not only on an individual basis but also in the church and society. Teachings appear not through an irrational need to preserve formulas nor in an act of divisive cruelty or extreme philosophical acculturation, but as a descriptive and prescriptive witness to the truth of the evangelical narratives.

Doctrines discern the church's mind, particularly when it is confused by opinions or torn by doubt. Though conceptual formulas intend to express socially the truth of the gospel, they are enshrined in relative statements that require revision to meet contemporary experience and to re-present the ancient meanings of Christian experience. Older formulations cannot answer questions unasked in their own age; but new teaching can be equally shortsighted, and reflection may be required upon doctrines that seem to it of little import.

Just as we sometimes meet ourselves going through our desk drawers, finding a paper here or there we remember as significant, so the Church confronts its own history in various doctrines. Assuming responsibility for its own cognitive past by rethinking it or revalorizing its focus means being available for a creative future. Without knowing how we are bound by our own historical understandings, we will too often tragically try like amateur magicians to accomplish dangerous feats and find ourselves drowning.

NOTES

1. See Paul Ricoeur, *Symbolism of Evil*, trans. Emerson Buchanan (Boston: Beacon Press, 1969), 3–24, 347–57; and idem, *Interpretation Theory: Discourse and the Surplus of Meaning* (Fort Worth: Texas Christian Univ. Press, 1976), 45–88. See also Karl Rahner, "What Is a Dogmatic Statement?" in his *Theological Investigations*, vol. 5, trans. Karl-H. Krueger (Baltimore: Helicon Press, 1966), esp. 57–93; and Francis Schüssler Fiorenza, *Foundational Theology: Jesus and the Church* (New York: Crossroad, 1984), 38–46.

2. See Bernard Lonergan, *The Way to Nicea: The Dialectical Development of Trinitarian Theology*, trans. Conn O'Donovan (Philadelphia: Westminster Press, 1976), and idem, *Method in Theology* (London: Darton, Longman & Todd, 1972), 305–8.

3. See Paul Ricoeur, *The Rule of Metaphor: Multidisciplinary Studies of the Creation of Meaning in Language*, trans. Robert Czerny with Kathleen McLaughlin and John Costello (Toronto: Univ. of Toronto Press, 1977), esp. 216–56.

4. See Rahner, "Dogmatic Statement," 51.

5. Lonergan, *Method*, 298–99.

6. Ibid., 302–18. On patterns of experience, see idem, *Insight: A Study of Human Understanding* (New York: Longmans, Green & Co., 1967), 181–89.

7. For this entire section, see James Barr, *Fundamentalism* (Philadelphia: Westminster Press, 1977, 1978), and René Marle, "Hermeneutics and Scripture," in *Problems and Perspectives of Fundamental Theology*, ed. René Latourelle and Gerald O'Collins, trans. Matthew J. O'Connell (Ramsey, N.J.: Paulist Press, 1982), 69–86.

8. For a sociocultural description of this *Zeitgeist*, see Christopher Lasch, *The Culture of Narcissism: American Life in an Age of Diminishing Expectations* (New York: Warner Books, 1979). For a philosophical description of relativism, see Hans-Georg Gadamer, *Truth and Method*, trans. Garrett Barden and John Cumming (New York: Seabury Press, 1975), 51–73, 192–234, 305–41. For the way in which these problems have an effect on theology, see David Tracy, *The Analogical Imagination: Christian Theology and the Culture of Pluralism* (New York: Crossroad, 1981), 3–192.

9. Avery Dulles, *The Survival of Dogma: Faith, Authority, and Dogma in a Changing World* (Garden City, N.Y.: Doubleday & Co., 1973), 32–33, 80–81.

10. Rahner, "Dogmatic Statement," 53, 61; idem, "What Is Heresy?" in his *Theological Investigations*, vol. 5, trans. Karl-H. Krueger (Baltimore: Helicon Press, 1966), 468–512; and Dulles, *Survival of Dogma*, 42–43. Cf. George Stroup, "Revelation," in *Christian Theology*, 2d ed., ed. Peter C. Hodgson and Robert H. King (Philadelphia: Fortress Press, 1985), 116–26, 137–38; and in the quite different evangelical context, the emerging discussions in John Jefferson Davis, ed., *The Necessity of Systematic Theology*, 2d ed. (Grand Rapids: Baker Book House, 1980), esp. 61–74, 169–85.

11. Gerald O'Collins, *Has Dogma a Future?* (London: Darton, Longman & Todd, 1975), 1–8.

12. Avery Dulles, "The Church: Sacrament and Ground of Faith," in *Problems*, ed. Latourelle and O'Collins, esp. 263–73; and Fiorenza, *Foundational Theology*, 213–45.

13. Karl Rahner, "The Development of Dogma," in his *Theological Investigations*, vol. 1, trans. Cornelius Ernst (Baltimore: Helicon Press, 1961), 39–77.

14. Dulles, *Survival of Dogma*, 155–75.

15. Karl Rahner, "Heresy," 468–512.

16. Juan Alfaro, "Theology and the Magisterium," in *Problems*, ed. Latourelle and O'Collins, 340–42; Gerald O'Collins, *Fundamental Theology* (New York: Paulist Press, 1981), 130–56; Avery Dulles, "The Theologian and the Magisterium," *Proceedings of the Catholic Theological Society of America* 31 (1976): 235–46.

17. "Dogmatic Constitution on the Catholic Faith," in *The Teaching of the Catholic Church*, ed. Karl Rahner, trans. Geoffrey Stevens (Staten Island, N.Y.: Alba House, 1967), 32–33; translation slightly emended.

18. Bernard Lonergan, "Natural Knowledge of God," in Lonergan, *A Second Collection*, ed. William F. J. Ryan and Bernard J. Tyrell (London: Darton, Longman & Todd, 1974), 117–33; and idem, *Method*, 115–19, 320–24.

19. "Dogmatic Constitution," 36.

20. Dulles, *Survival of Dogma*, 192–212.

21. "First Dogmatic Constitution on the Church of Christ," in *Teaching of the Catholic Church*, ed. Rahner, 229.

22. Pope Paul VI, "On the Mystery of Faith," *Acta apostolicae sedis* 57 (1965): 758.

23. "Decree on Ecumenism," pars. 14–16, in *Vatican Council II, The Conciliar and Post-conciliar Documents*, ed. Austin Flannery (Northport, N.Y.: Costello Pub. Co., 1975), 464–67.

24. "Pastoral Constitution on the Church in the Modern World," pars. 4, 58–62, in *Vatican Council II*, ed. Flannery, 905, 902–00.

25. For this entire section, see John Hendrik Walgrave, *Unfolding Revelation: The Nature of Doctrinal Development* (Philadelphia: Westminster Press, 1972), esp. 119–347.

26. Gerald O'Collins, "Criteria for Interpreting the Traditions," in *Problems*, ed. Latourelle and O'Collins; idem, *Fundamental Theology*, 208–24.

27. Fiorenza, *Foundational Theology*, 166–70.

28. Yves Congar, *Tradition and Traditions: An Historical and a Theological Essay* (London: Burns & Oates, 1963), esp. 156–493.

29. Ignace de la Potterie, "History and Truth," in *Problems*, ed. Latourelle and O'Collins, 87–104.

30. John Henry Newman, *Essay on the Development of Doctrine* (New York: Appleton Co., 1860), esp. 20–48.

31. Terry Eagleton, *Literary Theory* (Minneapolis: Univ. of Minn. Press, 1983); Frank Lentricchia, *Criticism and Social Change* (Chicago: Univ. of Chicago Press, 1983); and Fredric Jameson, *The Political Unconscious: Narrative as a Socially Symbolic Act* (Ithaca, N.Y.: Cornell Univ. Press, 1981).

32. See Alvin Gouldner, *The Coming Crisis of Western Sociology* (New York: Basic Books, 1970); Lloyd H. Strickland, Frances E. Aboud, and Kenneth J. Gergen, *Social Psychology in Transition* (New York: Plenum Pub. Co., 1976), esp. 107–51.

33. For examples, see Jürgen Habermas, *The Theory of Communicative Action*, trans. Thomas McCarthy (Boston: Beacon Press, 1984), and its critique in Helmut Peukert, *Science, Action, and Fundamental Theology: Toward a Theology of Communicative Action*, trans. James Bohman (Cambridge: M.I.T. Press, 1984), and J. B. Metz, *Faith in History and Society: Toward a Practical Fundamental Theology*, trans. David Smith (New York: Seabury Press, 1980).

FURTHER READINGS

Paul J. Achtemeier. *The Inspiration of Scripture: Problems and Proposals*. Philadelphia: Westminster Press, 1980.

Wayne C. Booth. *Modern Dogma and the Rhetoric of Assent*. Notre Dame, Ind.: Univ. of Notre Dame Press, 1974.

Charles C. Hefling, Jr. *Why Doctrines?* Boston: Cowley Pubs., 1984.

George A. Lindbeck. *Nature of Doctrine: Religion and Theology in a Postliberal Age*. Philadelphia: Westminster Press, 1984.

Sheldon Sacks, ed. *On Metaphor*. Chicago: Univ. of Chicago Press, 1979.

PART 3

NORMATIVE STRUCTURES OF CONVERSION: THE NATURE OF ARGUMENT

CHAPTER 7

PATTERNS OF THEOLOGICAL INVESTIGATION

The community in which we live will hardly bear to be told that every man should be open to ecstasy or a divine illumination.

Saul Bellow, *Herzog*

If your own development or decline in conversion, faith, and moral progress has been named, if you have struggled to articulate the intellectual dimensions of value and truth, if you have noted how these religious experiences and concepts have their uneasy home in the contemporary world, then you have already been engaged in theological "work." Our book argues that all conversion will gradually issue in conceptual clarification (whether moral or doctrinal) and that implicit within individual and ecclesial praxis, there is a normative dimension. Conversion and theology tell us the way things are as well as the way things ought to be.

Theology may be defined as reflection upon conversion in a culture.[1] In previous chapters, we have outlined the way critical reflection emerges from the Christian experience of conversion and discipleship; we have described important, crucial features in our culture. Now it becomes important to show how these investigations formulate coherent patterns of understanding. What counts as a theological argument? What evidences are pertinent to theological discussions in doctrine or ethics? In the following chapters, we will show the ways contemporary theologians reason. To do so, it will be necessary to remind ourselves of two factors: the distinction between faith and beliefs, and the conflicts of culture in which we live.

FAITH AND BELIEFS REVISITED

Faith is what we know by virtue of our newfound attachment to God in Christ.[2] First a reason of the heart, rather than of the head, faith apprehends

145

transcendent value in our world. Believers are seized existentially by a fulfillment of their thirst in going beyond themselves in truth and love. Knowing
that this desire is infinite, faithful people discover that their quest is being
completed by a power not their own.[3]

The new horizon opened by Christian conversion reveals both new information and new abilities. We discover both who we are and who God can
be for us, as well as the way to set out on the continuing journey of personal
self-identification and our encounter with divine generosity. For Christians,
this transformation is accomplished by identifying with the tragic and glori-
ous story of Jesus of Nazareth — both the content and form of Christian
change. Faith reshapes us, removing us from the patterns of concrete social
decline created by our sins and our own honest, if stupid, mistakes. It becomes possible to entrust our efforts to others in the world and to overcome
the resentments and angers that poison human collaboration.

Beliefs are rooted in faith. Communion with God invites common expression when believers gather. Worship, symbols, and stories register the multifaceted experience of turning toward God; from these, concepts and
propositions grow and develop. Preaching and teaching become traditional,
passed down through generations. Beliefs are compiled, added, and reshaped
in accord with the originating faith of the community. They are often the initial creedal reflection within faith. Conversion can appear in both the serene,
mystical attachment of faith and the complex conceptualizations of doctrines.
Attempts to clarify beliefs make use of theory, establishing terms and relations
that will sharpen understanding. Systems coordinate beliefs into coherent
patterns, and methods try to understand the dynamic origin of belief from
faith and to articulate the grounds in interiority by which that passage
occurs.

Converting faith is always embodied in a particular culture; its beliefs have
the characteristic tone and color of the society's mores, attitudes, and intellectual frameworks. Contemporary theology thinks through the connections between faith and its cultural incarnations in its past formulations and
articulates those of the future. Theological understanding self-consciously
mirrors these two poles of Christian experience.

CONFLICTS OF THEOLOGICAL CULTURES

Given the major shift in our cultural self-understanding, however, it is not
surprising that theologians, like ministers, priests, and pastors, as we discussed earlier, find themselves caught between two contrasting notions of
what arguments count in a thoughtful faith. Dedicated as scholars to the in-

tellectual value of inquiry and convinced that Christ came to save minds as well as hearts, theologians must often place themselves between the polarities of our competing social systems. To locate themselves in one or another school can seem counterproductive. Where classicism stresses stable and universal concepts, logical inference, and uniform cultural embodiment, modernity will appear flimsy, irrational, and relative. When modernity focuses upon empirical induction, adaptation, cultural adjustment, and nonrational symbolic expression, classicism will emerge as rigid, unfeeling, and authoritarian. Eclectic inconsistency is often the result.

We have opted in this text to think Christian experience systematically through the language and processes of modernity. It is our conviction that within secular culture there is an emergent normative dimension that the Gospels can transform. In the description of phenomena, there is an intrinsic noetic thrust toward prescription: what does the collection of data mean? Secularity is concerned not only to determine the many ways in which things work but to discover the best way. It wants to know on what basis the best is derived. Implicit within the tolerant, sometimes lazy, pluralism of Enlightenment reason, there exists a sense that what we say should fit the realities we experience. Can all positions on a topic be equally plausible? If there are conflicting claims about what is true, who or what decides the criteria for discrimination?

A theology mediating between modern culture and faith will not avoid these questions but answers them within an empirical, inductive framework. It searches out the appropriate expressions and legitimate intellectual means for embodying itself within the culture. Where these expressions do not exist, such a theology will have the creative imagination to invent the new. Where newer concepts envelop the old, making them obsolete, theology will avow its willingness to change. Theology becomes the interpreter for the two cultural forms as they encounter each other in piety, intellectual investigation, and social involvement.

Christians can, of course, capitulate to one or the other side of the conversation. They can see in classicist formulations of the past the only way to be a believer; they can celebrate the new culture as the embodiment of Christian love without remainder. But these naive options are simply no longer useful. An equally unhelpful conversational stance is to declare that the two cultures are paradoxically related and that Christians should see themselves standing beyond classicism, yet refusing modernity. In this light, believers can be, and supposedly are, countercultural, opposing through their oxymoronic stubbornness the incarnation of their faith. Just as the identification of faith with a particular culture melds Christianity into an unexceptionable alloy, so the refusal to allow faith to be the catalyst in a new cultural equation, except by negation, prohibits a new religious culture from being forged. In such stances one may take responsibility for oneself by awakening God's presence in the inner zone of one's subjectivity, but these stances leave the world illumined by faith to the progress of evil. Contemporary Christians and theologians must commit themselves to transforming the intellectual and moral dimensions of their common world.

THEOLOGICAL REFLECTION

A Brief History

Theology has not always been understood as reflection.[4] According to early believers, "theology" appeared in all the expressions of Christian faith, whether symbols, gospels, icons, architecture, or academic learning. Only with Peter Abelard (1079–1142) do we have a clear differentiation between the doxological, illustrative, narrative dimensions of faith and the reflective, conceptual, and dialectical moments. Abelard, quite to the dislike of Bernard of Clairvaux (1090–1153) and others, proposed questioning the traditional authorities of faith found in the Scriptures, the fathers, and councils. Since they did not always agree with one another, decisions for or against important issues had to be made on the basis of reasonable principles. To Bernard this not only gave reason power over faith, but it ignored the spiritual unification that was at the heart of the meditative assimilation within the tradition. Bernard's motto was an Augustinian "I believe that I might experience" God. To think without immediate attention to prayer was insanity.

Those who believed that differentiated reflection could function within faith turned to Anselm of Canterbury, who enshrined what has become the fundamental definition for theologians: theology is "faith seeking understanding." Anselm's authority in formulation and practice weighed heavily in favor of his interpretation. In the course of his analysis of redemption, he used questions as tools in a dialogue to untie the various metaphorical images (ransom, payment for debts, satisfaction) of salvation. He was convinced that a God who created both faith and reason would not place them in contradiction; rather, a thoughtful analysis of faith would indicate that the most necessary of reasons functioned within divine mystery. Ultimately this could lead the thoughtful inquirer to union with God.

Anselm is considered the progenitor of scholastic theology, that is, of the theological reflection associated with the cathedral schools and growing medieval universities in Paris (originating about 1207) and Oxford (originating about 1214). With Thomas Aquinas, we have a developed differentiation between praying to God and thinking about God. For Aquinas, however, study was as much a religious activity as was explicit prayer.

In the first question of the *Summa Theologiae*, Aquinas maintained that Christian theology (*sacra doctrina*) was first the knowledge God has of himself and that which he shares with the blessed. God has chosen to impart his knowledge to human beings and it takes three forms: faith, science, and vision. The first is the primary apprehension of divine presence through the gift of the Spirit which illuminates our hearts and changes our lives so that we can hear the Scriptures and the authentic doctrines of the tradition. Science is the systematic reflection upon one's faith, necessary because human beings have minds and because questions arise. Vision is what we shall receive when we know God even as we are now known. Reflective knowledge within the praxis of faith is what we are given until we die.

Abelard, Anselm, Bernard, and Aquinas — and thinkers into the eighteenth century — reflected upon God's revelation from the standpoint of a culture that thought of itself as the only legitimate form. Amalgamated of Hebrew wisdom, Greek philosophy, Roman laws, and barbarian energy, this culture imposed itself upon settlers within Europe and upon natives it discovered outside Europe. But with the divisions among Christians due to the Reformation, the burgeoning explorations into oceans and continents unknown to Europeans, and the revival of interest through archaeology and language in pre-Christian Roman and Greek cultures, a leavening agent had entered. Perhaps other cultures were not in every way subordinate to European Christendom.

Though detailed aspects of developing modernity can be seen in our earlier exposition, we need to note the effects secularity has had on theological reflection. Our understanding of contemporary life is that it contains a plurality of cultures striving toward normative interpretations of themselves. A theology that mediates between faith and this set of cultures will need to be empirical and dynamic in its description of religious data. But it will ask how the various elements it gathers are interrelated. It will focus on incarnate subjects embodying themselves in feelings, histories, and symbols. But it will ask what constitutes a human being: Are those who are now at the edges of human existence — the senile, the dangerously handicapped, the aborted — human? Modern culture hopes to adopt policies that will produce the greatest number of goods for the largest populations. But that assumes that we know what the best products are and that all societies can produce them. What is the best product? And what happens when the resources to build that product and the capacity to enjoy and pay for the product are not in the same hands? Moreover, many world cultures have varying differentiations of philosophy, religion, economics, and ethics. If Christianity is inculturated in each of these, will all the theologies produced be equally valid?

Implicitly then, the pluralism of cultures dynamically moves toward norms. We want to take responsibility for the motion of these processes and the disciplines that reflect upon them. In our post-Enlightenment knowledge of the world, it is no longer plausible to leave the direction of such complex systems to drift. If we do, we risk allowing mere force to take charge, authoritarian imposition of a single perspective rather than the dialogical development of an authentic human polity. The culture, therefore, within which faithful reflection occurs is modernity struggling for its own authentic sense of responsible freedom.

Reflection — Invariant Operations

The reflection[5] of which we speak is that described earlier in this text as intellectual conversion. It involves knowing not only *that* we know things truly but *how* we know them. Critical self-appropriation is a process in which individuals become clear about the way in which perceptual, conceptual, and judgmental operations can be considered true or false. This process is invariant; that is, it occurs whenever we wish to know, in whatever situations in which we find ourselves, even when we hope to understand how we know. To be critically tuned to oneself means to be able to produce the conditions and warrants under which knowledge will authentically take place.

In the development of one's faith, reflection functions beyond the stage of rejecting parental images of God and the revolutionary replacement of these by one's own; it takes place when the symbols of childhood have been reassigned a home in one's religious universe after they have passed through the fires of critical experience. Self-appropriation knows how to distinguish between poetic speech, theory, and ordinary common sense, but it also knows how to interrelate them. It does not reject one for the other or refuse to grant one realm its due. It knows that Christian conversion will appear in all three kinds of language. The intellectually converted person will, moreover, give an important place to thought in religion and will function as a theologian.

Method — Patterns of Reflective Relations

Method, says Lonergan, is a "normative pattern of recurrent and related operations yielding cumulative and progressive results."[6] Methodical operation is not conceived here as an art to be learned from another skilled master or mistress of the tasks at hand, though most of us learn first how to do something by imitating a teacher. Nor is method the kind of science that in a classicist world studies only the universals, excising accidental occurrences from imposed laws and principles. Contemporary method is conceived as a discipline that articulates the interlaced operations that accomplish the goals set forth. This process, which moves from data or information to results or achieved purposes, requires clarification.

The invariant pattern underlying human inquiry is the reflective series we have described here and elsewhere. There are operations of seeing, hearing, tasting, imagining; understanding, conceiving, reflecting; marshaling and weighing evidence, judging; and deliberating and evaluating. These activities are transitive; that is, they intend objects: by our processes of knowing, we become aware of realities. These operations occur because there is an operator, a subject who acts. When we sense or feel something, we are conscious of ourselves as operating. Indeed, we can turn the invariant process upon itself and become conscious of our own intentional operations.

Theologians are human beings with intentional processes. When they operate theologically, they are engaged in the invariant process of sensing religious data; formulating and understanding concepts about God, humanity, the church; judging the evidence of truth or falsity for ideas and propositions; and evaluating the worthwhileness of the items judged. There are always empirical, intellectual, rational, and responsible levels of theological activity. Rooted in our natively spontaneous need to question the world and ourselves, theology can be thematically articulated on the basis of these interlocking operations. To articulate it in this way is to be methodical in our sense of the term. To recognize that this method is not only useful but imperative if theological activity is to be organized and understood is to see the normative nature of method.

Although the results of contemporary method (whether in theology or in science) are cumulative and progressive, theological activity is not like a laundry—"Bring in any confused information and we will clean it up for you." Because method resides in the individuals who think theologically, method is primarily a way of describing the self-correcting activities by which theologians can order, display, and transform their own lives and work.[7] The normative character of theological method is therefore primarily formal, that is, a heuristic structure that can underlie any series of investigative data, from icons to insufflation. Theology may be understood as progressive and cumulative in the sense that its work can lead from obscurity to greater clarity or from less information to further elaborate syntheses. It can provide a sustained succession of discoveries, as in the rejection of human slavery based upon the worth of created and redeemed realities, though such developments are regularly slow, even intermittent. Because such a method is dependent upon the interiority of theologians, it is conceivable, even likely, that such thinkers will also participate in the various blind spots of their culture, the biases of their individual histories, and genuine confusions about the nature of understanding itself. Revision in theology will focus not upon the methodological operations that accomplish the task but upon the results. The structures of human consciousness will continue to operate. They are the basic anthropological component of human knowing and therefore of theological investigations.

Theology Reflects Upon Conversion in a Culture

Reflection upon Christianity can be divided, therefore, in three ways: by dividing and subdividing the fields of data, by organizing the results of inquiry, or by sorting the stages of a process that moves from data to results.[8]

Theology articulates its own method: what set of operations must one perform to obtain the goal sought? The constantly subdividing fields of contemporary theology—scriptural studies, patristics, doctrinal history, liturgy, ethics, feminist studies, black theology, ecclesiology, ministry, and so on— require their own complex interdisciplinary techniques. Each has its own integrity and belief in its own centrality to the theological enterprise.

To study the field of Scripture, for example, one ought to know multiple languages, engage in or evaluate the findings of archaeology, develop the sensitivities of a critic of literature, study the geography, weather, and culture of the ancient Near East and so on. To be a theological historian means not only knowing the data of the period one studies but knowing the various ways thinkers have told its narrative interconnections. So there are romantic histories that focus on biographies, dramatic incidents, and tragic consequences; anecdotal histories that detail illuminating tales and odd incidents; positivist histories that capture serial data without clear interconnection and undertake research into particulars by means of graphs, charts, and percentages; and philosophical histories that describe sweeping patterns without attention to detail. To be a theological historian would require understanding why such differences occur and interrelating the differences coherently. Not all differences in the way history is written are simply a matter of missing data. Interpretations vary; good historians will understand why.

To study method means to be able to articulate the basic operations theologians must perform on the material studied to answer the questions asked. It does not mean that method substitutes for the fieldwork that defines regions of data or replaces special techniques of retrieval and interpretation. That must be left to the experts in each area of investigation. Method will contribute toward the reasonable integration of the various specialized tools that permit theologians to come to their conclusions.

Theology as reflection on faith has evolved from being undifferentiated worship, preaching, gospels, and letters of the apostolic period, through a coherent doctrinally ordered systematics and an elaborate theory with technical terms and relations, to a method based upon the operative intentionalities of theologians collaborating within ecclesial traditions. An authentic method in theology, when reflecting upon itself, assumes the truths of previous patterns of understanding of theology and assists them in their evolution toward a more comprehensive position. Method then should include symbols, doctrines, systems, and theories, explain their previous success, and establish the basis upon which they have their present relevance.

BERNARD LONERGAN'S THEOLOGICAL METHOD

Functional Specialties

Much of what we have said about the nature of theological investigation is based upon the ideas of the Canadian theologian Bernard Lonergan. Lonergan's position has so shaped the contemporary horizon that it is impossible to understand present theological discussion without it. It has set a standard by which other positions are measured. In the remainder of this chapter and in the chapters that follow, we shall describe Lonergan's notions, qualify them with regard to ethics and doctrine, and argue for a position on the nature of theology based upon them.

For Lonergan, the theological process is the interconnection of methods within the various fields of theology. It remains an understanding of *the cumulative interrelated and interdisciplinary operations that function when theologians encounter religious data.* What does this mean? Though Lonergan believes that his doctrine on methods applies to more than simply one religious tradition, we will apply it here to Christianity alone. If we have developed the terms, relations, and cultural theories clearly enough in the first two parts of this volume, our remarks here should synthesize and systematize those reflections into a whole.

Religious data are those experiences we have when being grasped by the claims of ultimacy, in the moments of conversion enshrined in the documents of the Christian tradition. The mutual interdependence of symbolic expressions (in worship, texts, and ethical actions) and originating transformation is here assumed.

Theologians, with their reflective mode of inquiry—of asking questions, forming conceptual hypotheses, fastening judgments of truth and falsity on the basis of the appropriate evidence, and making decisions — are the operators of method. Their religious authenticity and reflection upon their own interiority, their self-involvement in ecclesial praxis, are at the heart of method.

The *interdisciplinary operations* that theologians perform upon religious data are those proper to the levels of individual and social inquiry. Thus, collecting data, codifying them, learning the proper vocabularies and grammars to decipher information, and so forth, have their own disciplinary demands. Bicycle mechanics cannot fix broken sprockets with inappropriate, outdated, or poorly honed tools. The research scholar requires the correct instruments to work on religious material.

To interpret what was intended in religious expressions, theologians must discern the contexts of texts and the subject matter intended. Studying the literary forms, the characteristic styles, and the effects upon audiences, among many other things, can lead to an understanding of the structures, meanings, and even failed enterprises of authors. Interpretation requires the literary-critical, philosophical tools that will permit a Christian thinker to sort out the world presented by the texts and actions shaping religious life.

To judge the truth or falsity of one's interpretations requires a historical knowledge of the tradition generated by the text. Was there something "going forward" in the data? And the ordinary tools of the historian are required to clarify the response.

To know whether the subject matter is worthwhile and when it can or should be transmitted into the future means looking into one's own sense of values and committing oneself for or against them. This requires the kind of skill on the theologian's part that pays attention to the theologian's own subjectivity and its religious embodiments. These disciplines sort out the nature of subjectivity and objectivity (how do we know?), study the interrelated nature of that knowing (why is doing that knowing?), and characterize what we learn when we say we know something (what is intended by knowing?). Moreover, there are the disciplines that objectify and criticize the thinkers' notions of value and the moral good, and apprehension of the transcendent. All of these will affect the way theologians encounter the religious data.

The characteristic disciplinary processes that function in relationship to all data, the most sophisticated tools that the natural and human sciences have to offer can and should be used to understand the experience of conversion and Christian transformation. A theology that attempts to mediate between contemporary culture and Christian experience will need to be as highly differentiated, as highly reflective, and as methodologically profound as its neighbors. Every level of interpretation has its own tools, its own techniques of "controlling" the data. None are abrogated; rather, they are connected by the dynamic ongoing process of inquiry that is taking place in theologians.

Lonergan describes the collaboration of these processes as interrelated stages in the single process of moving from data to results. So the interpreter takes over where the textual critic finishes; the historian assembles interpreted texts and creates a narrative from them. Each area of theology is a functional specialty through which a theologian or team of theologians handles an aspect of the entire project of theology, in order to achieve an understanding of the revelation given to us by God in Christ.

As Lonergan indicates, one discipline is in fact incomplete without the others; it only performs part of the task. Functional interdependence of the specialties divides the labor; it helps us to see the relationships between the fields of interest theologians develop and the results they achieve; and it assists in interrelating the continuous proliferation of new fields in theology, showing that there are often new data to be understood in ways analogous to previous interpretive strategies.

The Interrelationship of Functions in Method

With Lonergan, we will distinguish eight interrelated functional specialties: (1) research, (2) interpretation, and (3) history lead toward the decision-making process of (4) dialectics and (5) foundations, which in their turn ground the transmission of insights gained in (6) doctrines, (7) systematics, and (8) communications. The specialties are organized therefore in terms of the cognitive processes from data to results. This can be seen a bit more clearly, then, as an interpretive circle and communicative loop that in a spiral fashion continues to turn upon its own axis.

The first four specialties are determined by an ascending development from perceiving, interpreting, judging, and deciding, while the final four are characterized in reverse order:

Cognitional Pattern	Intentional Object	Specialty of Inquiry	Specialty of Transmission
experience	data	research	communications
understanding	concepts	interpretation	systematics
judgment	fact/value	history	doctrines
decision	choice/stance	dialectics	foundations

conversion

The inquiry process might be characterized as listening to the Word of God, while the second phase of theology, that of transmission, could be seen as bearing witness to the Word as loved, understood, and appropriated.

What moves theologians from inquiry through transmission is the continuing experience of conversion and its objectifications. Having gathered the appropriate information about Christ, having interpreted it correctly in its claims, and having developed a history of what was dynamically emerging in the Gospels, worship, preaching, and traditional creeds, theologians are placed before the claims and counterclaims that swirl around this Christ in terms of truth, value, and religious mystery. The only way to encounter those claims is to achieve the level of authenticity they demand. Personal transformation within one's community of faith and discourse either occurs or it is does not. Such a religious conversion, as we have argued, is the invariant base for the beginning of Christian devotion; when it is critically mediated to oneself and to others, it is the beginning of theology.

The process is an interpretive circle since what were initially data for analysis and appropriation can through dialectics and foundations be communicated both to oneself and others as further data for assimilation. It is a spiral because there is an ever-growing, ever-increasing progress or decline, depending not only upon whether there are further data and conceptual understanding but also on whether there is greater authenticity at the level of decision for or against the gospel. In an evergrowing authentic interpretive spiral, the process continues to emerge, as the philosopher Paul Ricoeur[9] would maintain, from first to second naiveté, through the critical questions that ask for deeper insight, sharper conceptualizations, more precise judgments, and better-warranted decisions.

The individual specialties have their own integral operative strategies. Research makes available any data it sees as relevant to theological discussion. Theologians begin where they are, but "some day, perhaps, [research] will give us a complete information-retrieval system."[10] Interpretation grasps the various meanings available in the data within their proper context. History tells us where and when what was done by whom, and who suffered reverses, successes, and influences from the events. It can specialize in particular areas of culture, such as institutions, or teachings on ideas. History aims for some approximately total view of what was "going on" during a particular phase of human experience. Just as history cannot get by without research or interpretation, so research and interpretation also have an intrinsic thrust toward the more comprehensive vision history provides.

Dialectics articulates the conflicts that appear in interpreting history, not only the disagreements of specific interpretation but the more fundamental oppositions from which appear the basic conflicts and confusions about what is real, what is valuable, and what is holy. Dialectics, in other words, does not just extrinsically sort the other person's prejudices and values; it excoriates, articulates, and enhances one's own. Ideally, theologians are intellectually, morally, and religiously converted individuals. They have not only learned certain critical research, interpretive, and historical skills, they have also refined their sensibilities to such an extent that they can articulate the significant differences in horizon that cause religious conflict.

When these differences are distinguished, argued for or against, embraced when known as true, good, and holy, and reversed when seen as false, evil, and demonic, then a critical religious, intellectual, and moral stance has been taken. Foundational theology has begun. Theologians make a fully conscious decision about their horizons for living and understanding the gospel.

This is not the case only with academically trained professors of theology. Part of our argument is that the Christian experience of conversion implicitly contains these dimensions. All of us operate from horizons about what counts as true, good, and holy. The foundational theologian articulates what is athematically or tacitly given in the performance of believers.[11] Most of us drift into some contemporary horizons; foundational thinkers exercise the skill of giving our choices a resounding voice.

Foundational theology faces the pluralism of expression and can understand which positions are legitimate and which are to be rejected. It can begin to develop general categorical definitions and analyses about what it means to be truthful, good, and holy in relation to the culture in which it is embodied; it will derive and clarify the confessional categories that will indicate how one's particular history of conversion illuminates the larger world of cultures and civilizations. These categories will be used in transmitting the Word one has heard. Based upon dialectics and foundations, the final three specialties critically mediate the experience of Christianity to the world.

Doctrines articulate the teachings that emerge from converted communities. From theological reflection and many other forms of teaching (e.g., prophetic witness), churches commit themselves to statements that are normative for believers. Doctrines attempt to understand and reformulate these teachings on the basis of the first phase of investigation.

Systematics is concerned with understanding, with promoting the coherence, consistency, and structural interconnection of the truths of faith. Doctrines are judgments made in faith; systematics tries to understand the realities affirmed in doctrines, yet it is perfectly clear that its interpretations will be incomplete and imperfect. While understanding the genuine continuities between past formulations and present ones, it nonetheless attempts to achieve continuity by reinterpretation from the basis of conversion to Christ in the present situation.

Communications turns the meanings achieved by the earlier specialties into the language of the marketplace and the pulpit. Here the contemporary church becomes through its various embodiments the transforming presence of Christ to the world. Theologians return to the world of common sense, now with the studied vision of the whole. The articulated religious stance, doctrinal language, and patterns of systematic speech are transposed into the stylistic keys of cultures already playing the melodies of other gods. And within those cultural syntheses, the theological process flourishes anew.

CONCLUSION

Theology as we have described it may seem an arduous discipline for a single individual. It is. In fact, the process from the data of conversion to communicating one's witness by the road of criticism requires multiple collaborations. What is described here is an ideal of interlocking interdisciplinary operations, some of which will be combined in a single individual, many of which will need to be underwritten by large communities of scholars. Each functional specialty will have its favorite partners in conversation. So dialectics and foundations may require dialogue with psychology, sociology, cognitional theory, epistemology, and metaphysics to help sort out the nature of truth, value, and holiness. Doctrines will need anthropology, economics, genetics, medicine, law, and business to articulate the appropriate Christian teachings in a given cultural matrix. Communications will require knowledge of contemporary media and patterns of rhetoric.

In an important sense, the theological method about interdisciplinary collaboration we have sketched here can be understood as a program for the renovation of contemporary cultures. Where the old classicist culture was conceived as primarily European in origin and imposition, the new culture will be polyfocal, multicultural, and federated in its legitimate polarities. The adoption of such a method will permit a multifaceted church to preach to an ever-diverse society without losing its identity in the gospel of Christ.

NOTES

1. Bernard Lonergan, *Method in Theology* (London: Darton, Longman & Todd, 1972), xi.
2. Ibid., 115–19.

3. David Tracy, *The Analogical Imagination: Christian Theology and the Culture of Pluralism* (New York: Crossroad, 1981), 201–18.

4. For a longer though still introductory survey, see Stephen Happel and David Tracy, *A Catholic Vision* (Philadelphia: Fortress Press, 1984) 61–76.

5. Lonergan, *Method*, 6–25.

6. Ibid., 4.

7. Ibid., 270.

8. Ibid., 125–45.

9. Paul Ricoeur, *Interpretation Theory: Discourse and the Surplus of Meaning* (Fort Worth: Texas Christian Univ. Press, 1976), esp. 71–95.

10. Lonergan, *Method*, 127.

11. Michael Polanyi, *Personal Knowledge: Towards a Post-critical Philosophy* (Chicago: Univ. of Chicago Press, 1958), esp. 69–245, 252–61; and idem, *The Tacit Dimensions* (Garden City, N.Y.: Doubleday & Co., 1966), esp. 3–25.

FURTHER READINGS

Henri Bouillard. "Human Experience as the Starting Point of Fundamental Theology." *Concilium* 6 (1965): 79–91.

Gerhard Ebeling. *The Study of Theology.* Philadelphia: Fortress Press, 1978.

Edward Farley. *Theologia.* Philadelphia: Fortress Press, 1984.

Ray L. Hart. *Unfinished Man and the Imagination.* New York: Seabury Press, 1968.

Theodore W. Jennings. *Introduction to Theology.* Philadelphia: Fortress Press, 1976.

John Macquarrie, *Principles of Christian Theology.* New York: Charles Scribner's Sons, 1966.

Randy L. Maddox. *Toward an Ecumenical Fundamental Theology.* AAR Diss. Series 47. Chico, Calif.: Scholars Press, 1984.

CHAPTER 8

THE NORMATIVE DIMENSIONS
OF MORAL CONVERSION

I refuse to accept the idea that the "isness" of man's present nature makes him morally incapable of reaching up for the "oughtness" that forever confronts him.

Martin Luther King, Jr. (1929–68),
speech accepting the Nobel Peace Prize, 1964

We have discussed in some depth how and why all theology is a reflective process. Now another set of questions must be sorted, and these issues are concerned with what the normative or "ought" status of our judgments is. In other words, once we have judged a certain value to be worthy of our attention (e.g., persons and their needs) or a certain religious statement to be true (e.g., that Jesus is one with the Father), what ought we to do about it? Is it good enough just to know value and truth, or must we do something as a result of this knowledge? What does it mean in contemporary culture to be a responsible actor and believer? If we must do the truth and not just know it, then how do we argue for the justification of our acts of the mind, heart, and will?

Our argument is that authentic moral interpretations (like religious ones) typically move from the symbolic experience of value, through affective-cognitive judgments of value, to normative (ought) claims and arguments, and justifications of moral action. This movement is cumulative and invariant, and it should be considered the norm in all authentic moral-decision making. Now the fact that this movement is normative does not derive from somebody's "ideal theory" about morality and moral experience; the normativity (oughtness) derives from the inherent unfolding structure of human self-transcendence itself. Stated simply, our minds, hearts, and wills quite naturally seek what ought to be done amid the complexities of daily life. What we need to do is become more consciously aware of this inherent movement in our everyday lives.

There are several reasons that the originating experience of value gives rise to normative interpretations. First, there is the process of self-transcendence itself. The human eros is such that we not only desire to know, love, and act, but we desire normatively to know, love, and act. It is not good enough to know just anything, to love just anything, or to do just anything; we inherently desire, and are drawn by grace, to know the truth, to love the truth, and to do the truth. In the practical life of moral action, this means that we desire normatively to know, love, and do value.

Second, although we inherently desire the normatively good in our thoughts, words, and actions, there is the persistent chatter of conflicting interpretations concerning what the normatively good is. This is nowhere more evident than in the highly pluralistic society in which we live. In addition, there are many sources that need to be consulted to arrive at normative decisions. Many of the complex issues confronting us today require the aid of the empirical and human sciences, the legal sciences, philosophy, and religion including the gifted discovery of revelation. We only have to think of such issues as fertilizing ova in petri dishes (in vitro fertilization) with the intent of freezing them for possible future implantation in surrogate wombs, or the world energy crisis, to get a sense of the complexity of the topics in our modern society. Conflicts of interpretation among the sciences arise not only about the relevant data for normative decisions but also about the conclusions. Unless these conflicts are resolved, the decision maker either will be paralyzed or will opt uncritically for one interpretation at the expense of the others. The result in either case is moral disaster for society.

Third, the drive to normative-decision making is the result of the desires for consistency, adequacy, and systematic understandings in our actions. We desire that our actions be consistent with one another and with our judgments of value. Furthermore, we desire that our actions adequately express and embody the originating value that gave rise to the actions. We also desire to understand how the moral life fits together into some kind of whole by which we can interpret and judge further actions. Such systematic understandings require a concept of the normatively good, and it is this concept we seek in the development of systematic theories on the moral life.

Finally, we seek normative moral discourse to create community. We could consider the ecclesial community a community of moral discourse, among other things. James Gustafson has defined a community of moral discourse as a "gathering of people with the explicit intention to survey and critically discuss their personal and social responsibilities in the light of moral convictions about which there is some consensus and to which there is some loyalty."[1] The ecclesial community needs normative moral discourse not only to inform moral action but also to help fashion the moral identities of those who claim a loyalty to Jesus. The mutual sharing of normative loyalties, commitments, and responsibilities which can result from open and critical moral discourse becomes one way of creating community.

NORMATIVE MODELS OF THE MORAL LIFE

The desires for consistency, adequacy, and systematic understanding in the moral life can issue forth into what are called normative disclosure models. Unlike picture models, which are nothing but scaled-down versions of something else (think, e.g., of a model airplane), disclosure models seek to disclose or re-present the realities they interpret. As such, disclosure models do not seek to provide pictures of the moral life; they attempt to gather together all the data of moral experience, organize it around a central symbol or image, and then arrange it along some scale or continuum. The purpose of this process is to interpret normatively how the moral life is to be viewed from an ideal or abstract point of view. The models, then, should be taken seriously but not literally.[2]

There are three principal normative models of the moral life, and they received their classical formulation in *The Responsible Self*, by H. Richard Niebuhr (1894–1962).[3] What Niebuhr did was take the two reigning normative theories in philosophical ethics, teleology and deontology, as well as one that he himself developed, relationality-responsibility, and interpret them through three images or synecdoches. His three images were: man the maker (teleology), man the citizen (deontology), and man the responder (relationality-responsibility). Each image singles out two elements from our everyday experience of the world and then interprets the agential aspect of the moral life through them. Thus, in the teleological model, the experiences of temporality and spatiality are dominant; in the deontological model, the experiences of bodiliness and living with others predominate; and in the relationality-responsibility model, the experiences of one's intentional consciousness and the need to interpret reality dominate.[4]

Teleology: A Value-dominant Model

The word "teleology" comes from the Greek word (*telos*) for end or goal. As a normative model for moral agency, teleology is really an umbrella for several positions that thematize moral experience around the concepts of end or goal. For example, there are virtue teleologies (Aristotle and Thomas Aquinas), which focus on the acquisition of virtues that lead us to specific ends or values; nature teleologies (some Catholic neo-scholastics of the nineteenth and twentieth centuries),[5] which focus on an abstract metaphysical nature that leads us to moral ends; and utilitarian teleologies (Jeremy Bentham, 1748–1832; and John S. Mill, 1806–73), which focus on consequences (ends) of acts that are intended and desired by the agent. Although there are significant differences between these three positions, what characterizes them all is the emphasis on the attainment of values as goals or ends in moral action. We can look on this normative model as a value-dominant model of moral agency and action.

The teleologist thematizes moral experience in terms of purposiveness. Moral agents, who act for the sake of purposes or ends, are viewed as giving shape both to themselves and to the world through the pursuit of values. Drawing on the everyday experiences of temporality and spatiality, the teleologist interprets the moral life as the capacity of human agents to stretch toward a future. Those who have employed the image of maker or artisan in moral self-understanding and in shaping their conduct have not, however, been unanimous in their choice of the ideals or goals to be realized. Some have claimed that the goals for which we act are pleasure; others have claimed that they are whatever serves the most needs of those in society; and others have claimed that the highest good for which we act is life with God.

Regardless of how the goal is defined, all teleologists are able to answer the question, What ought I to do here and now? only by raising and answering a prior question, What is my goal, ideal, or telos? In other words, those who are proponents of this view can only decide normative duties once the primary goal or value around which the moral life is construed is determined. For example, utilitarians can decide concrete duties only after they have determined that the goal of the moral life is to produce consequences (e.g., pleasure) that promote the greatest satisfaction of human needs for the greatest number in society. Thus, one's concrete duty in any given situation is to actualize this goal to the maximum extent possible. For nature teleologists, the goal of the moral life is to fulfill the universal tendencies they abstract from human nature, for example, the tendency that inclines us to sexual relations. Then they determine that our duties are to achieve those values toward which our innate tendencies lead us, for example, the conception of children.

Deontology: An Obligation-dominant Model

The word "deontology" comes from the Greek word (*deon*) for duty or obligation. Those who interpret the moral life around the central theme of duty do not deny the relevance of goals, the search for values, or the need to calculate consequences of actions. What they deny is that these factors should take primary place in the thematization of moral experience. Drawing on the everyday experiences of bodiliness and of life with others in society, the proponents of this normative model interpret moral experience as the fulfilling of moral duties to self, to others, and to God. We can look on this normative model as an obligation-dominant model of moral agency and action.

The deontologist thematizes moral experience in light of the special experience of personal existence. Life with others is viewed as requiring certain kinds of actions and personal relations, kinds of actions that define a just society. The primary emphasis here is not so much on the goals of a just society as on the right means to a just society. Moral self-understanding and conduct, then, are conceived by reference to agency interpreted as legislative and obedient. Individuals come to moral self-awareness, if not to self-existence, in the midst of mores, of commandments and rules, and of directions and permissions that govern our actions toward others.[6] Kant, with his emphasis on the will's function as legislating self-imposed duties, is a good example of deontology in philosophical ethics.[7] Many manuals of Catholic moral theology in this century, with their emphasis on fulfilling the commandments and ecclesiastical laws, are good examples of this normative model in theological ethics.[8] Whether the model is employed in philosophical or theological ethics, the primary characteristic of the moral life, through which all experience is interpreted, is seen as duty.

However one conceives the origin of duty, the deontologist cannot answer the question, What ought I to do here and now? unless he or she raises and answers a prior question, What is the duty, law, or rule of my life? Thus, the determination of one's concrete duties is made by reference to whatever law, rule, or commandment (e.g., Tell the truth, or Do not kill) is applicable to the situation, or by reference to whatever the authority (secular, ecclesiastical, or divine) says or demands of the agent. Whether the duty is determined from sources within the self (autonomously) or from sources external to the self (heteronomously), the result is the same: concrete normative questions are responded to by reference to more primary duties of one's moral life.

Relationality-Responsibility:
A Virtue-dominant Model

As Niebuhr originally conceived this normative model, the pattern of thought is interactional and relational. The moral life is viewed primarily in terms of our multiple relationships with God, neighbor, world, and self. This model does not deny the insights of the teleological and deontological models, but it refuses to interpret moral experience primarily in terms of either the search for the good (value) or the determination of the right (duty). Drawing on the everyday experiences of intentional consciousness and of the need to interpret all reality, the relationality-responsibility model seeks to highlight the discovery of meaning as central to moral experience. The primary emphasis, then, is on the subject and his or her regular self-realization through personal acts of freedom. Because regular self-realizations require not only the four conversions but also the virtues in the moral life, we could look on this model as virtue-dominant.

The proponents of the model thematize moral experience through the central image of responsibility (of persons as responsible). Although Niebuhr himself seemed to have limited this image to "responsiveness" in his four elements of responsibility (response, interpretation, accountability, and social solidarity),[9] we would prefer to interpret this image by reference to the self-transcending subjectivity of human persons: we become truly responsible to the extent that we embody the four conversions. In short, to be a responsible originator of value and of duty is to be a converted subject, an authentic disciple of Jesus. To interpret all moral experience through the central symbol of responsibility is to interpret the moral life in terms of conversion. In this case, greater emphasis must be given to character formation, virtue, and the development of moral discernment than in the two previous models.

As in the other models, questions about concrete normative decisions arise. The question, What ought I to do in this situation? can be answered only by raising and answering a prior question, What does it mean to be a converted person (morally, affectively, intellectually, and religiously)? The primary reference point, then, for all questions of concrete decision making is the self-transcendence of the subject in the conversions. What one who is authentically converted must do in any situation is conform one's decision to the objective judgments of value about persons and their needs according to a hierarchy of goods. The crucial notion here is that of the "fitting." Thus, whereas the teleologist is concerned with the good (value) in questions for normative-decision making, and the deontologist is concerned with the right (duty), the person as responsible agent is concerned with the fitting (both the good and right).

The search for the fitting in concrete decision making necessarily incorporates many of the insights and features of the two previous models. Value and duty continue to play an important place in the moral life. Indeed, both are essential characteristics of moral experience. But these notions are reinterpreted in the relationality-responsibility model in that they are construed relationally and are looked on as emanating from the authentic subjectivity of persons. Value is not something out there to be achieved; it is the harmonious relation between rational human needs and the objects capable of properly fulfilling those needs. On the other hand, duty is not experienced apart from our essential relatedness to others, the world, and God. Nor is duty an experience arising apart from our initial experience of value and its cognitive interpretations. We are the authentic and responsible originators of both value and duty to the extent that we undergo the conversions. Thus it is virtue, understood as the transformation of the self and society in converted life, that is the primary category through which Christian moral experience should be interpreted.

Because the relational and historical character of human reality prohibits us from viewing the moral life according to pre-fixed or static plans for decision making, we have argued that a new model is needed. The socially aware and converted individual is the one who can regularly and consistently respond to the call of the symbolic presence of the neighbor. It is the responsible person who can best discern the fitting amid the complexities of everyday moral living, and the daily practice of virtue is the surest avenue of attaining this discovery.

RESOURCES FOR MAKING NORMATIVE
MORAL DECISIONS

Anyone faced with a complicated moral situation must consult as many of the relevant sciences as possible. For example, when we are confronted with a socioeconomic issue like the fair distribution of benefits and burdens through tax structures, we are required to understand properly the sociological, economic, and legal data that are morally relevant. Unless we want to make decisions from ivory towers, we should know something about the methods and interpretive schemas of the relevant sciences. Similarly, when we are faced with medical-moral issues like organ donation, we need to know something about the medical procedures involved and the medical risks and benefits that might accrue to donor and donee. Although none of these empirical and human sciences are truly value-free in either their methods or interpretive models, the data produced from them do not in and of themselves generate value-meanings. Persons, not data, are the generators (and discoverers!) of value. So besides consulting the sciences and their methods, we must rely on evaluational processes whereby we arrive at truly normative decisions based on value-meanings.

When making normative decisions in concrete situations, disciples of Jesus have several evaluational resources available to them. We call these resources "evaluational" because they provide evaluative knowledge on which to base a decision.

There are ten evaluational processes and resources that are available to us for the normative-decision making: creative imagination, reason and analysis, principles, affectivity, individual experience, group experience, authority, comedy, tragedy, and religious experience.[10] Whereas such process provides evaluative knowledge, they must all be taken together and allowed to interact before a truly normative decision can be made. Since we have already dealt in some depth with the resources of principles, affectivity, and reason and analysis, we need not redescribe them.

Creative Imagination. Creative imagination is the supreme faculty of moral humanity. Through it persons perceive the possible that is latent in the actual but that would be unseen by any less exalted consciousness. Because the process of moral-decision making is not just a matter of passing judgment on the goodness and badness of persons or on the rightness and wrongness of actions, moral thinking at its best must perceive values that do not yet exist and must bring them into being through productive acts. Many times, it is creative imagination that makes between various values connections that have not been seen before. For example, before the twentieth century the marital sexual act was perceived by Catholic theologians as an act of nature directed toward the perpetuation of the race. Just before and at the Second Vatican Council, it was recognized that the marital act is an act of love between spouses which is at once responsible and fruitful.[11] It was an insight of imagination that perceived the interconnection between the values of love, responsibility, and fruitfulness.

Creative imagination, which apprehends and relates values at the symbolic levels of consciousness, needs to be enhanced and cultivated. Thus there are the constant needs for an excitement about life and value, quiet and thoughtful reflection, and a certain malleability or flexibility and openness in one's life. Disciples need to rely on the proven resources of the ecclesial community to enliven their imagination. As we have indicated before, Christian stories, myths, and symbols are resources not only for sparking the disciples' imaginative powers to be awakened to the excitement of life, but for informing and sustaining moral commitments to the poor and oppressed of the world. A life of prayer, personal and communal, provides the time and energy for thoughtful reflection and the occasions for being open to the Spirit's movements in our lives.

Because our imaginations can go astray and degenerate into uncreative imaginations — for example, in the contemporary buildup of nuclear weapons — disciples rely on an eschatological vision of the new heaven and the new earth for the trust and hope that moral efforts are not ultimately in vain.

Christians continue to hope that new and more creative solutions can be found to the complex problems that plague us, although disciples are always realistic about the systemic evil infecting our social structures and thwarting the development of a just society.

Individual Experience. Every individual is a unique font of ethical wisdom in his or her personal experience. Each of us is unique, because there are some things about us we do not share with others, for example, upbringing, education, temperament, and life experiences. When we enter situations that require moral decisions, we enter and interpret them from within our past histories. Our past moral histories do have a bearing on the way we decide, and thus the radical existentialists (e.g., Jean-Paul Sartre, 1905–80) and situation ethicists (e.g., Joseph Fletcher, b. 1905) who claim that our moral experiences are episodic and unrelated are at least incorrect on that count. However, what we do appreciate more today is the unique character of all moral-decision making and the necessity to look to individual experience as a valid source of moral insight. The waning of the classical horizon with its emphasis on a universal, static, and common human nature, and the rise of historical consciousness with its emphases on subjectivity and history, have no doubt paved the way for this insight.

Group Experience. We are not just individuals with our own experiences and interpretations. Although personal experience is necessary, it is certainly not adequate. We are embodied beings who come into human consciousness by and through living with others. All human consciousness is at the same time sociocultural consciousness. We think, talk, and act within a world mediated by social meanings. There is simply no way we can totally transcend the social matrix into some private asocial sphere in which to apprehend values and attain wisdom. All knowing is rooted in social reality and history, systematically learned from the community's resources of wisdom.

We are not complete originals; we do in fact share many things in common with others, for example, our basic needs. Unless each of us desires to reinvent the moral wheel, we must rely on the common understandings of our communities, both past and present. The principles, norms, and rules guiding and restricting our moral behavior in society are distillations of moral insight from the experiences of our ancestors, and thus they become mediations of past wisdom to the present. Christians trust in the ecclesial witness as one source of their own understandings and judgments of morals and faith. In fact, disciples possess their own religious faith through the mediation of the ecclesial community. Past witnesses to moral commitments and beliefs come to us through the daily life of the Christian community manifested in its liturgy, prayer life, and Scripture reading, and in the lives of faithful disciples.

Still, not all past moral wisdom is true or even applicable today. We all have the personal responsibility to take a critical distance from the deposits of moral insight contained in our civil and ecclesial societies in order to assess the truth and applicability of past moral understandings. In doing this, we neither retreat into some private realm of "pure subjectivity" nor become irreverent toward our ancestors or ecclesial traditions. What we seek in such explorations is a truth freed from error and from the cultural biases and prejudices that may have infected past formulations. For example, Elisabeth Schüssler Fiorenza has recently shown that many of the house rules (*Haustafeln*) that guided the behavior of the early Christian community (Col. 3:18 — 4:1 and Eph. 5:22 — 6:9) were formulated from a male-centered perspective. As formulated, these "house rules of the saved community" are alienating to women's contemporary experience of themselves and the world. They need to be purged of an androcentric bias in order that the lived ethos of the early Christian community can be discerned, evaluated, and then reinterpreted by universally transformative themes.[12]

In a slightly different way, one could consider, as the Second Vatican Council did, that the condemnation by Leo XIII (1810–1903)[13] of religious liberty and his formulation of the necessary unity of church and state are no longer applicable to the contemporary political experience of modern democratic societies. Leo's formulas, which were fashioned in a context of laicist polemics and biases, did not take into account the better elements of some democratic societies that sought to protect both the right to religious freedom of individuals and the freedom of the churches, for example, in the constitutional tradition of the United States.[14] *The Declaration on Religious Freedom* at Vatican II revised the papal position on religious freedom and declared that religious liberty is an inherent right of all persons that must be guaranteed in constitutional law.[15] By implication, of course, the council likewise considered the call for a unity of church and state to be no longer applicable.

Authority. It is probable that most of our moral opinions are not the result of a reasoning process but are due either to the influence of someone we admire or love, or to the influence of a traditional wisdom we have never questioned. In both cases, the decision maker defers to what might be called authorities. Authority in moral matters is not an alien intrusion on the autonomy of rational humanity. It is part of a system of reliance and trust that not only increases our contact with truth but also builds and sustains our relationships among persons. One insight of the morally and religiously converted person is that the quest for absolute autonomy in the moral life is an illusion. Commitment to, reliance on, and trust in others are all marks of the converted life.

Authorities in the moral life are not a luxury but an absolute necessity. We are communal beings who are socialized into a cultural heritage of language, customs, and moral codes. From a practical point of view, we need the authorities of our heritage in order to come into consciousness of a world mediated by social meanings. Furthermore, because our reason and experience are necessarily always limited, we must rely on and trust in others to expand our horizons and correct our deficiencies. To deny the necessity of authority in moral matters, then, is to deny both our limitedness and the social matrix of our reason and experience.

Disciples of Jesus also trust in the ecclesial authorities of Scripture, tradition, and the doctrinal and moral teachings of their church. Through the narrative accounts found in the Scriptures and the judgments of truth represented in the ecclesial tradition, disciples participate in a privileged knowledge about the nature and destiny of humanity created, fallen, redeemed, and called to a future beyond this history. This kind of knowledge is invaluable in moral-decision making because it provides an interpretive framework through which disciples can assess moral problems and situations. For example, disciples can use the insights from ecclesial authorities in interpreting and assessing the moral outrages of world poverty or of the worldwide buildup of nuclear weapons. The biblical notions of God's justice (righteousness) and of human pride (hubris) provide morally relevant insights into why these outrages have come to be and why they must be eliminated.

There are also human authorities in whom the disciple trusts for moral wisdom. First, there are our own families and the local Christian communities, who daily become a source of wisdom and inspiration in the moral life. Then, there are those who hold official offices within the church (deacons, presbyters, and bishops) whose functions are to preach and to teach the truth of the gospel message.

For the Roman Catholic community, there is also the moral and doctrinal teaching body (magisterium) of the church, which is constituted by both the episcopal and papal offices. Roman Catholics trust in these magisterial teachings, both ordinary and extraordinary, because they believe that the magisterium authentically interprets the gospel's call to moral and religious conversion.[16] Disciples also look to those who have special training and expertise in the religious sciences (theologians) for help in understanding the truth that has been preached and taught. Finally, disciples trust in the intrinsic authority of those persons whose lives have been exemplary in holiness and discipleship, for example, the saints.

There is always some danger that the disciples' legitimate trust in moral authorities may become misdirected. The danger is that we may give over all responsibility for discerning moral truth to authority and thereby refuse to use the other resources available, for example, critical reason and analysis. This would be simple idolatry. All the evaluative processes need to be employed in making normative decisions, so there is the necessity to look for instances in which some of these sources of wisdom are grossly or absolutely lacking. Moral decisions become truly normative to the extent that a healthy balance is struck among all the evaluative resources.

Comedy and Tragedy. Rationalism, as the attempt to reduce all moral experience and moral knowing to ideas and rational processes, is a danger in the moral life. The chains of this form of absolutism can be broken by a healthy sense of comedy (humor) and tragedy. Humor, as a form of moral wisdom, includes a response to the incongruities within human life, a sense of surprise, creative imagination, and affectivity. The moral life is not a casual living from day to day in a world that is humdrum and uneventful, although we do not doubt that some perceive it that way. Because it always takes place in the arena of living with others in a natural world filled with unexpected ecstasies and catastrophes, moral living needs to be imbued with a sense of dramatic incongruity and surprise.

The tragic elements in the human condition are grounded in our experiences of finitude and in the capacity for deep love. In our everyday experience of the world we are aware of our limitations in time and space, an awareness centered on the realization of our future deaths. Our ordinary experience also contains instances of love and the sense that our capacity to love is without limit. The love that prompts us to possess the beloved with absolute security is not possible. We love in a world that remains perilous. Pain and loss are simply facts of human existence. Nevertheless, suffering in the midst of tragedy can become a moral teacher when it draws our consciousness more deeply into the foundational moral experience of the intrinsic value of persons. Tragedy has a way of reminding us of what we seem to forget all too easily — the preciousness of life. Finally, tragedy can quickly remedy the arrogance and superficiality of intellectual smugness. Just when everything seems to be figured out and put into neat little categories, the world unexpectedly erupts into a tragedy that upsets our figures and categories. The comic and the tragic are dimensions deep within our consciousness of the world, and as such they are evaluative resources for moral-decision making.

Religious Experience. Religious experience, as the experience of giftedness of the whole, both informs and sustains moral experience. It informs moral experience not so much by offering content, for example, by giving an answer to the question, Why be moral at all? as by providing an abiding conviction that there is an ultimate moral power who wills the well-being of all creation, orders its preservation and sustenance, and creates conditions for new possibilities for moral action.[17]

The informing character of religious experience also becomes the sustaining power for moral living. The conviction that all, save sin, is grace or pure gift sustains the disciples' pursuit of value amid the cultural proclaimers of moral doom and decay, on the one hand, and the indifference of moral apathy, on the other. For the disciples of Jesus, religious experience is so much a part of their moral experience that the two spheres of experience are distinguishable only with the greatest of difficulty. Although we have argued throughout that these two realms of experience are conceptually distinct, in the everyday life of the disciple they should form one integrated whole that provide insights for daily living.[18]

ELEMENTS FOR MORAL ARGUMENT
AND MORAL JUSTIFICATION

After discussing the need for normative discourse and the various resources available for normative-decision making, we must now attend to the elements of moral argument and justification. Normative decisions need to be argued and justified, not merely asserted or proclaimed. Moral interpretations that result in judgments of value are truth claims about moral reality. To argue for the truthfulness of these judgments and to seek to justify them are neither extraneous nor alien to the originating event of value apprehension. Indeed, they are intrinsic dimensions within moral consciousness itself as it searches for the normatively good.

In earlier moral theologies, moral argument and justification proceeded deductively from well-established principles based on the nature of humanity. Nature was conceived in an abstract and metaphysical way that gave little or no attention to the realities of human history, grace, sinfulness, and eschatological destiny. The principles derived from nature were applied to the concrete situations of moral-decision making in a way similar to how one would arrange a major and minor premise of a syllogism. The conclusions reached were considered sure and certain to the extent that the deductive logic was correct. Any reference in the moral arguments to scriptural texts or to some types of ecclesial authorities (e.g., lives of the saints) was incidental. Many times, however, justification for a moral position was provided by reference to what had been earlier proclaimed by a church authority, for example, a pope or council. Thus, the beginning point of moral argument was with a *statement of principle* known to reason, and the end point was a conclusion reached by deduction and justified by logic and a narrowly conceived list of ecclesial authorities.

In contemporary moral argument, one does not begin with a statement of principle. Like the great scholastics Saint Thomas Aquinas and Saint Bonaventure (ca. 1221–74), one begins with a *question*: this is what opens the discussion for normative-decision making, and the question asked concerns the values and disvalues at stake in a moral situation. For example, when a competent patient is confronted with the moral dilemma of whether to undergo some medical treatment for a disease diagnosed as terminal, the first question to be answered concerns the values (benefits) and disvalues (burdens) of such treatment, as the disease progresses on to eventual death. Does the treatment offer some reasonable hope of pain relief (value), or does it only exacerbate the condition and cause further burden on the patient (disvalue)? Will the treatment allow the patient to remain conscious and functional (value), or will it cause persistent lethargy and drowsiness so that the patient cannot live to the fullest during his or her final days? Each question, then, illumines the values and disvalues implicit in the moral dilemma.

To answer the questions raised, we must turn to the resources of moral wisdom. As we have already seen, there are ten evaluative processes that can be used in coming to a normative decision. Finally, we employ these resources in the cumulative and interdisciplinary operations of moral argument. As we have explained earlier, normative reflection consists of gathering the data; interpreting it; consulting the historical judgments on the data and the values provided by our ancestors and ecclesial traditions; moving to a comprehensive viewpoint from which we can understand the relations and oppositions among the various data, interpretations, and judgments; assessing whether the conflicting interpretations and judgments emanate from a converted subject; then, in light of converted consciousness, making a judgment of value that is intelligible, that fits with other judgments made in similar situations, and that can be communicated to others. As cumbrous as this method of moral argument and justification might seem, we argue that it thematizes what is already operative, if unconsciously, in the moral thinking of all of us.

The evaluative resources of creative imagination, individual experience, religious experience, affectivity, and reason and analysis aid us in both gathering the data and interpreting it. The resources of group experience, authority, principles, and reason and analysis are instrumental in giving us insights into the past interpretations and judgments of our communities. To perceive both the relations and the oppositions among the results thus far, we must make reference to the four conversions. Because most persons who engage in moral argument are not converted at every level, it would be reasonable to assume that the evaluative resources used by them might still contain elements of bias and prejudice. For example, it would seem unreasonable to assume that every individual involved in a moral argument for or against the mandatory death penalty is morally, affectively, intellectually, and religiously converted.

The lack or deficiency of one or more of these conversions will skew not only the evaluative resources but also the normative conclusion. The individual who has never undergone the foundational moral experience (the experience of the value of persons and what befits their well-being), or the person who has never realized that knowing is not like taking a look, can hardly be expected to gather, interpret, and evaluate the considerations bearing on the complex issue of the mandatory death sentence. Similarly, one who has gone through the foundational moral experience yet uncritically has appropriated the cultural ethos on most issues, cannot always be trusted to make a correct normative decision. It is only when the conversions have occurred that an authentic and true judgment of value and disvalue can be attained.

Once we are converted, all the evaluative processes can operate to aid us in finding out if the judgment systematically "fits" with other similar judgments on related moral issues. As we have seen, the desires for consistency, adequacy, and systematic understandings need to be fulfilled, and that is what is sought in the search for coherence among judgments. For example, one would want to see how the judgment to mandate or not mandate the death sentence "fits" with other judgments on the killing of persons not considered innocent, for example, in a "just war" situation.

CONCLUSION

Our position has been that moral argumentation and justification should proceed from asking questions about the relevant values and disvalues implicit in a moral situation, to applying the evaluative resources for normative-decision making. These resources must be employed through the cumulative and interdisciplinary operations of normative reflection. The crucial moment in the entire process of moral argument and justification is found in the four conversions. Without them, the normative process itself runs the risk of making normative what is only unnoticed error, bias, or prejudice, on the one hand, or what is only a partial truth, on the other hand.

Even with the conversions, though, one should not get the impression that some once-and-for-all perfect truth in concrete moral matters is attainable. No one is ever converted enough, nor can any individual or society plumb the absolute depths of moral experience. As new questions directed toward moral meaning arise, and as further data become available, there is the need for revision of past normative judgments. With very few exceptions, the best we are able to discern in concrete moral decisions is the probable truth, and it takes a certain flexibility and openness to the Spirit of all truth to live with this fact.

NOTES

1. James M. Gustafson, *The Church as Moral Decision-Maker* (Philadelphia: Pilgrim Press, 1970), 84.

2. For a more extensive discussion of disclosure models, see David Tracy, *Blessed Rage for Order: The New Pluralism in Theology* (New York: Seabury Press, 1975), 22–42.

3. H. Richard Niebuhr, *The Responsible Self: An Essay in Christian Moral Philosophy* (New York: Harper & Row, 1963).

4. See Howard L. Harrod, *The Human Center: Moral Agency in the Social World* (Philadelphia: Fortress Press, 1981), 67–71.

5. For an excellent discussion of the Catholic neo-scholastic tradition, see Josef Fuchs, *Natural Law: A Theological Investigation*, trans. Helmut Reckter and John Dowling (New York: Sheed & Ward, 1965).

6. Niebuhr, *The Responsible Self*, 52.

7. See Immanuel Kant, *Groundwork of the Metaphysic of Morals*, esp. sec. 2; and idem, *Critique of Practical Reason*.

8. The early Jesuit and Redemptorist manuals of moral theology are most representative of this approach, which structured the moral life around the commandments. But not all the manualists organized their works around the theme of duty. Some sought to structure their manuals around the virtues, and more recently, a few authors, e.g., Gérard Gilleman and Bernard Häring, have organized their works on moral theology around the virtue of Christian charity. See Gérard Gilleman, *The Primacy of Charity in Moral Theology*, trans. William F. Ryan and André Vachon (Westminster, Md.: Newman Press, 1959); and Bernard Häring, *The Law of Christ: Moral Theology for Priests and Laity*, vol. 1, *General Moral Theology*, trans. Edwin G. Kaiser (Cork: Mercier Press, 1963).

9. For an excellent critique of Niebuhr's position on this issue, see Walter E. Conn, *Conversion: Development and Self-Transcendence* (Birmingham, Ala.: Religious Education Press, 1981), 18–26.

10. In this section we will be summarizing Daniel C. Maguire, *The Moral Choice* (Garden City, N.Y.: Doubleday & Co., 1978), chaps. 6, 8, 10, 11. Although we rely on

Maguire's book for a discussion of the first nine evaluative resources, many times the explanation of these resources is our own.

11. See "Pastoral Constitution on the Church in the Modern World (*Gaudium et Spes*)," nos. 47–52, in *The Documents of Vatican II*, ed. Walter M. Abbott (New York: America Press, 1966).

12. Elisabeth Schüssler Fiorenza, "Discipleship and Patriarchy: Early Christian Ethos and Christian Ethics in a Feminist Theological Perspective," in *Annual of the Society of Christian Ethics*, ed. Larry L. Rasmussen (Waterloo, Ont.: Council on the Study of Religion, 1982), 131–72.

13. Leo XIII, *Immortale Dei (The Christian Constitution of States)*, in *The Church Speaks to the Modern World: The Social Teachings of Leo XIII*, ed. Etienne Gilson (Garden City, N.Y.: Doubleday & Co., 1961), esp. arts. 29–35.

14. For an in-depth discussion of Leo XIII's positions on religious freedom and the relation between church and state, see John C. Murray, S.J., "The Problem of Religious Freedom," *Theological Studies* 25 (1964):503–75.

15. "Declaration on Religious Freedom (*Dignitatis Humanae*)," no. 15, in *The Documents of Vatican II*, ed. Abbott.

16. This distinctively Roman Catholic claim will be developed in chap. 9. It was necessary at least to state the claim here because the magisterium constitutes one of the important evaluative resources for the Catholic's moral life.

17. James M. Gustafson, *The 1975 Père Marquette Theology Lecture: The Contributions of Theology to Medical Ethics* (Milwaukee: Marquette Univ., 1975), 27.

18. For a more extensive discussion of the relation between moral and faith experience, see James J. Walter, "The Dependence of Christian Morality on Faith: A Critical Assessment," *Eglise et Théologie* 12 (1981):237–77.

FURTHER READINGS

Charles E. Curran. *Moral Theology: A Continuing Journey.* Notre Dame, Ind.: Univ. of Notre Dame Press, 1982.

Philip S. Keane. *Christian Ethics and Imagination: A Theological Inquiry.* New York: Paulist Press, 1984.

Herbert McCabe. *What Is Ethics All About: A Re-evaluation of Law, Love, and Language.* Washington, D.C.: Corpus Books, 1969.

Gene H. Outka and Paul Ramsey, eds. *Norm and Context in Christian Ethics.* New York: Charles Scribner's Sons, 1968.

Philip J. Rossi. *Together Toward Hope: A Journey to Moral Theology.* Notre Dame, Ind.: Univ. of Notre Dame Press, 1983.

Jeffrey Stout. *The Flight from Authority: Religion, Morality, and the Quest for Autonomy.* Notre Dame, Ind.: Univ. of Notre Dame Press, 1981.

J. Philip Wogaman. *A Christian Method of Moral Judgment.* Philadelphia: Westminster Press, 1976.

CHAPTER 9

THE NORMATIVE DIMENSIONS
OF RELIGIOUS CONVERSION

Now Mass is a serious affair, ever since the priests began to open our eyes and ears. One of them would always repeat to us: "To get to heaven, first we must struggle to create a paradise on earth. . . ." And we would ask them why the priests before them forced us to conform.

Manlio Argueta, *One Day of Life*

Just as ethical arguments are complex, so too contemporary doctrinal investigations have fielded many claims. We have organized the religious terms and relations into a general structure describing the nature of theology and of moral argument. Our discussions have turned on the nature of Christian data and the ways of appropriating them. The general shape of theology demonstrated the problems inherent in a discipline with sources containing emergent norms. Is it what is known or the way that it is known that is primary? What is the relative status of the sources of information in a specific case? Is the matter decided by pointing to the relative weight of the speakers of the normative languages? Is the standard for theology to be found in the active appropriation of the texts by believers? What weight do we give the quality of religious appropriation?

Method has been our way of coherently organizing some of these questions. By ordering theological study in terms of the intellectual and social processes from conversion to communication of the gospel to others, we have also shown how we will begin to solve the problem in individual theological investigations. If the goal is to preach and worship God by our adherence to Christ, the way proceeds through the ordinary human activities of knowing and loving truth and value as these are brought to full articulation.

We must now show how this general order for theology functions in relationship to the narrower ordering of specific problems and issues. Without

179

launching into vast arrays of new data, we need to indicate examples of theo-logical argument and the way in which contemporary theologians develop their reasoning. The first part of this chapter studies the various normative elements in theological arguments; the second section investigates several ideal types for theological reflection, providing models to help readers locate both themselves and other authors. In the next chapter, we will locate our-selves along the spectrum of theological discourse.

THE ELEMENTS FOR CONSTRUCTING
CHRISTIAN ARGUMENT

The normative character of Christian argument derives its imperatives both from the transformative power of the death and resurrection of Jesus as they convert the believer *and* from the ongoing process in human knowing, from data to results. Conversion seeks an understanding of itself; it hopes to find its place in a public world where it can continue to manifest God's pres-ence in Christ. The search for a communal self-definition leads to common teaching, creeds, the definition of doctrines, and the proclamation of dogmas. These are not separated from theology, but with their accession to the status of socially agreed propositions, they assume authoritative life. At no time in Christian history have these two dimensions of theological argument (faith and either public or private reasoning) been missing. Maintaining the intrin-sic interconnection between the two has not always been simple; expansion of the understanding of the poles of Christian theology has led in the present to a fertile period in religious thought and not a little dismay among some believers.

What is obvious is that theology, like any human discipline, has many sources for the data of its investigations. Reflection, affect, and Christian transformation in mind and heart are the basis, but many factors in moral knowledge (e.g., creative imagination, group experience, and a sense of the dramatic value of history) are important as well. To order the many sources, we must qualify the role each plays in establishing authoritative discourse.

The Classical Form of Christian Arguments

Just as moral theology, in the age of Reform and Enlightenment rational-ism, developed a style of reasoning that was deductive, propositional, and largely inattentive to affect, history, and personal circumstance, so too the the-ology of doctrines lost its rich insertion into the larger life of the commu-nity. What had been taken for granted because of a unitary ideal for culture during the medieval period was controverted by reformers, at first religious, then secular. Theologians found it crucial to organize the varying sources of religious argument, simply for the sake of coherence. From this, they derived a style of argument.

Melchior Cano (1509–60), a Spanish Dominican, is the classic exponent of the form.[1] In an influential posthumous text (1563), *De Locis Theologicis* (Concerning theological sources), Cano rationalized the competing sources of theological reflection in the following way:

L O C I	Proper	constitutive of revelation	Scriptures	[1]
			tradition	[2]
		interpretive of revelation	universal church	[3]
			councils	[4]
			Roman See	[5]
			fathers/church	[6]
			scholastics	[7]
	Foreign		natural reason	[8]
			philosophy	[9]
			credible witness	[10]

The proper and most important sources of theology were the Scriptures and tradition (note: not customs), but these originating documents and experiences were interpreted through five (occasionally differing) vocabularies: what was taught everywhere, general councils (such as Nicaea and Chalcedon), the practice and teaching of the Bishopric at Rome, the fathers of the church (such as Augustine), and the medieval scholastics (preeminently Thomas Aquinas). Reason, philosophy, and personal witness found their way into theology only as "external" validations.

Cano's scheme does, of course, recognize the genuinely dialogical character of theology. Since the authorities did not always agree, he provided a weighted chart for the map of a new era. Moreover, serious attention is given to the data of the past in the contemporary problems of the community. All the resources were consulted when they were relevant. The educated believer knew how to make use of valuable positions when they were effective. The codification of sources also shifted the theological discussion from polemics about the content of doctrines to what counted in a conversation. It permitted theologians to know the place from which their partners or adversaries were arguing, establishing Cano's framework as a highly interlocutory style. And finally, through the organization he matched the emerging arts (esp. rhetorical commonplace books) of the humanist context, constituting theology as an oratorical style alongside the public debating manners of law, medicine, and business.

From these sources, arguments could be shaped. There was (1) a thesis, a propositionally reformulated doctrine (e.g., that Christ instituted seven sacraments). There followed (2) a definition of terms ("Christ," "to institute," "seven," "sacraments") and (3) a declaration of the status of the proposition (see below) along with an identification of those who had denied it (e.g., Luther, Calvin). There was then (4) a search of the sources: by looking through the ten resources available, the theologian produced (5) a "proof" that his thesis was true. There might follow (6) a few corollaries, occasionally one that developed piety.

The status of the proposition, which was specified in step 3, was also identified by locating the proposition along a spectrum of possible theological sources. Each teaching had an exactly determined niche in the theological hierarchy. Some propositions (e.g., that of Jesus' divinity) were formally revealed truths, doctrines solemnly defined in councils of the early church; others were proximate to faith, most probable opinions derived from faith or ordinary ecclesiastical teachings that had never been publicly defined. Positions based only within the pious customs of witnessing believers were at the bottom of the scale, though disagreeing with them might still be offensive to Christian devotion.

Cano and his successors did not see the difficulties we find in this outline. Their lack of comprehensive knowledge concerning the historical, sometimes dubiously factual, character of their sources did not allow them to weigh evidence in the way critical scholarship might. In situations of conflict, which of the lesser sources was more important for making a judgment and then a decision was not always clear. If the Scriptures and the major traditions of the church made no comments, if a question arose that the fathers of the church and the scholastics could not possibly have treated (e.g., biogenetic engineering), then what should we use as warrants for a position?

The classicist solution to this problem was too often found not in the sometimes agonizing sifting through content but in the appeal to the status of authorities. The authoritative position of the speaker became the formal evidence for supporting or rejecting a position, rather than the intrinsic merits or demerits of the proposal. A sense emerged that reasonable syllogisms would solve problems for human beings, without any appeal to existential commitment. When rational argument failed, authority supplied the lack.

Contemporary theologians find this procedure insufficient for many reasons: (1) It too often limits the range of sources, so that the problems treated cannot be resolved. (2) It locates credible witness, that is, the converting experience of believers, at the end of the spectrum rather than at the heart of theological method. (3) It cannot clarify at all helpfully the relative weight of authorities after the Bible and tradition. (4) As a whole, the shape of the argument classifies history and historical development as at best a secondary warrant, and at worst mere moral example. What of religious practices, like the sacrament of penance and reconciliation, or theological teachings, such as Mary's motherhood of Divinity, that required historical reshaping to come to clarity? Can history be an intrinsic rather than an extrinsic factor in faith?

Contemporary Issues in Theological Argumentation

The problems in our culture have immediate ramifications in theological argument.[2] The narcissism that prefers its own judgment, however uninformed, neglects history and authoritative speakers in theology. Those existentially engaged in individual conversion or social transformation reject reflective or doctrinal norms that seem to lie outside their affective concerns. A poorly educated popular piety is likely to group together all official doctrines under a single heading entitled Authority and either accept or reject them in wholesale fashion, without nuance. Selective dissent appears distasteful, disloyal, or heretical.[3] Can we distinguish between authoritative teaching roles in the Christian community? Are teachers and research scholars held to the same vocabulary as preachers? Should preachers try to imitate the language of the academy so that absolute precision is maintained, even if it is unintelligible to congregations?

In the religious worlds of poetic, scientific, and ordinary speech, controversies have emerged concerning the weight various authorities have. We have made our position clear: the fundamental authority of Christian experience is to be found in the person of Jesus Christ and his obedient love toward the Father. His conversion, which the tradition has called incarnation, life, death, resurrection, and exaltation to God's right hand, makes him the primary norm for all human life.[4] Our participation in that event, through our own transformations from hearing the word and turning in worship to God, is the normative base upon which theological reflection occurs.

On the foundation of the interior and exterior event of conversion and discipleship, theological argument is born. It moves through the various reflective operations of human consciousness from data to results, probing for an understanding of the primordial disclosure of God in Christ. The historical growth of conversion in individuals and communities is elaborated into ever-complex theologies that mediate between the local or global culture and the faith of believers. On the basis of this adherence, we can outline a reasonable solution to contemporary theological problems with normative Christian discourse and shape the relative interacting value to be given to the differing sources of religious expression.

INSTITUTIONALIZED AUTHORITIES:
THE SCRIPTURES AND THE
ECCLESIAL TEACHING OFFICE

Protestants and Catholics find themselves largely in the same position in relationship to their traditional authorities.[5] Whether one appeals to the inspired text interpreting itself, to the official teaching of popes, or to the ordinary teaching authority of bishops, pastors, and priests, people distrust the institutionalized voices of interpretation. How is a community to understand the competing vocabularies, grammars, and propositions that argue priority for this voice or that?

Authority has meant two rather different things in the Christian tradition.[6] On the one hand, it has indicated that a book, a statement, a custom was "authentic," that is, that by all criteria, this expression, by virtue of its intrinsic competence, better described what was the case about Christ, God, and world. In this sense, the Scriptures were authoritative because they told us the truth about ourselves and God and continue to do so by provoking this set of insights. The official teachers within the community have gained authenticity not by accession to an office but by the intrinsic intelligibility they offered when interpreting the original experience of Christ. They have done this by the credible witness of their lives and the reasonable sense of their words. On the other hand, authority has also meant what is "official" in the power that pertains to office or status in the church. On this view, the New Testament was true not because of *what* it said but in virtue of *where* it was said. All apostolic positions (even, e.g., the Pauline permission for human slavery or Paul's attitude toward women) were correct simply because they were to be found expressed within the canonical words. The pastor and pope were correct because the office conferred the power, through both ordination and social legitimation, to interpret the tradition truthfully. Typologically, the first position on authority identifies itself with authentic content and the second with legitimate form.

Contemporary literary criticism and theories of interpretation find it more difficult to distinguish what is, in effect, divided above.[7] Is the meaning of a novel, a poem, a political charter, a speech, a parable, or a doctrine to be found in its form or in its content? Critics prefer to speak of the tenor of an expression — that is, its intention — and the vehicle or its method of conveying meaning, rather than of form and content. The way in which an audience "receives" the formed content also affects and effects what it means.[8] What tradition of interpretation has it generated? What community of discourse has heard the message and how were they formed by it? Contemporary issues of interpretation make the task of theologians who believe in authoritative texts more difficult as well as simpler. With the help of literary criticism, it has become possible to clarify some of the claims to authority and their meaning in a given set of religious statements.

In the work that follows, we will use examples of authoritative interpretation from Catholic life, since our own tradition makes the strongest claims for such normative speech. But it is our contention that the problems faced and the nuances found here apply to all traditions of Christian faith. Normative language, such as doctrine and dogma, necessarily emerges from the insistently particular experience of Christ. How does the contemporary world face those claims with any sense of hearing the Word anew?

The Catholic Concern for the Magisterium

Many of the primary conflicts concerning the role of authoritative speech focus upon the nature of the papal and episcopal magisterium. To clarify contemporary difficulties, it is necessary to outline the classical form of such teaching. The schema on the following page will be of assistance.[9]

The official teaching concerning various matters is carefully "graduated." At extraordinary times, councils meet to define the community's self-identity (Nicaea; Ephesus, 431; Chalcedon); the pope (under certain quite restrictive conditions, as we shall see) can define normatively in a dogma (the assumption of Mary, 1950). During the ordinary living of the gospel, the pope uses letters to the whole church (e.g., *Humanae Vitae*, 1968) or individual churches (*Mit brennender Sorge*, 1937) as a way of conveying important positions on various topics (on Nazism, on labor, peace, evangelization, and so on). Bishops also offer teaching that they believe to be universally binding when they discuss the nature of revelation or widespread custom. When they act alone or in collegial unity in episcopal conferences, they can propose nonuniversal teaching (the United States Conference, "The Challenge of Peace," 1983).

In its classic form, the infallible teaching of the papal office is strictly limited. "Absolutely infallible truth belongs only to God,"[10] stated one of the fathers of Vatican Council I, which defined the position. The pope must (1) act as a free human being without the evidence of force, threats, fear, or illness; and (2) meet all the conditions of infallible teaching. The latter requirements are extremely stringent. The pope cannot speak as a private person but

```
                          ┌ pope defines a dogma (infallibly)
                          │
O                         │
F    extraordinary   ⎰    │
F                    ⎱    │                        ┌ define dogma
I                         │  bishops define teaching │ proclaim the gospel
C                         └  in council          ⎰  │ or
I                                                ⎱  │
A                                                   └ pastoral council
L

                          ┌ papal encyclicals
T                         │   or letters
E                         │
A    ordinary        ⎰    │
C                    ⎱    │                        ┌ alone
H                         │              nonuniversal │
I                         │          ⎰             ⎰  │ in episcopal
N                         │          ⎱             ⎱  │   conferences
G                         └  bishops ⎰                └
                                     ⎱
                                     │              ┌ revelation-
                                     │  universal   │   interpretation
                                     └          ⎰   │
                                                ⎱   └ disciplinary matters
```

must speak as the teacher and pastor of the entire church. While making an appeal to his role within the apostolic authority as successor to Peter, he can only speak on doctrinal issues in the sphere of faith and morals. Mere precepts or common customs are not sufficiently integral to revelation. He must propose the doctrine as something to be held by the entire church.

The conditions just described are normative for the exercise of such an exercise of teaching, but it is assumed that other criteria are met as well: (1) dogmas must agree with Scripture and the universal tradition of the church; (2) they must articulate the present faith of the church; (3) the universal episcopate must agree; and (4) there must be sufficient intellectual and/or prayerful investigation.

The possibility of such a normative teaching authority as decisive for contemporary faith was based on the absolutely definitive character of Christ's salvation.[11] Just as believers have faith that Christ is the absolute mediator of salvation precisely within his particular history, so through an eschatological hope they are convinced that his body, the church, will never succumb to the errors that are often part of its daily identity. Christ's existence in our contingent world makes demands upon all areas of life, a fact we only gradually perceive. Even in the strongest Catholic support for a formal authoritative teaching office within tradition, there have always been serious reservations about its exercise and conditions concerning its content. Authenticity of content and formal office needed to coincide to be a proper exercise of doctrinal teaching.

Even these basic limits are further narrowed. To see the role of normative teaching within a Catholic understanding of revelation, we must recognize both ends of the spectrum: the transcendence of God's mysterious presence about which we speak and the limited historical transmission of the message. With this latter, we enter the realm of development of doctrine about which we have already spoken. The absolutely definitive teaching of God to the community of believers meets the equally absolute necessity for its historical development. One must be able to distinguish between official dogmas and other kinds of teaching, sorting out the appropriately normative character of each. Yet this cannot be accomplished by an interpretation that assumes there is an "interior" kernel surrounded by an exterior "husk."[12] Finally, there appears the limit of the human conscience, the border between private adherence and social acquiescence, the threshold of authenticity between willing conversion and moral refusal.[13]

Individual Dissent from Official Ecclesial Teaching[14]

The dissonance between adventitious customs and authentic Christian traditions has raised the contemporary question of dissent from official teaching. We know that some official teachings have changed.[15] Though the following list is incomplete and includes issues of varying importance or obligation, it illustrates that the norms of the community have shifted.

War and military service were once absolutely condemned; they found a modest Christian home only through the theory of a just war. The taking of interest in financial matters was forbidden. In the bulls or official decrees of Pope Saint Pius V (1504–72), *Cum Onus*, 1569; *In Eam*, 1581; and *Detestabilis Avaritiae*, 1596, the pope believed that he was performing an apostolic task, articulating the divine natural law and the positive law of church and society. Torture and trial by ordeal were once permitted. Religious liberty was condemned by the ordinary teaching authority of the pope as indeterminism, a heresy. And there are other examples.

The experience of change, even over centuries, makes the individual conscience careful, less willing to invest its authentic religious sense in a secondary expression of belief.[16] Even if wary souls do not give up believing in doctrine, they find themselves searching for a luminous teaching that will declare itself valid as if by magic. And of course, this does not occur.

In the classical formulations concerning assent to official ecclesial teaching, believers were expected to give external and internal assent to doctrines expressing revelation. These occurred extraordinarily when bishops met in council or the pope spoke solemnly as supreme teacher on matters of faith or morals. The ordinary papal magisterium and the nonuniversal episcopal magisterium bound individuals through internal religious assent. These positions were reformulated and reaffirmed at Vatican Council II in its "Dogmatic Constitution on the Church." Beyond that, ecclesiastical opinions should bind through a fair hearing.

Dissent was possible in relationship to fallible, that is, changeable teaching, but the line between official teaching and opinions about faith was not always clearly drawn. Doctrinal inflation occurred: what was custom could too easily appear as binding teaching. Yet, if believers (1) had reason to suspect that a teaching was incorrect; (2) thought that the teaching proposed was not really infallible; (3) did not understand what they were being asked to believe; or (4) found what was proposed as teaching to be incredible or absurd, it was possible to dissent.

Karl Rahner has pointed out that given the complex and ever-increasing character of human knowledge, it is no longer possible for our faith to be coincident with all that is known or taught. In effect, by reason of their own history, conversions, and secondary world views, believers automatically select what they believe. "The Church's teaching office is no longer the selfevident referencepoint of faith, the selfevident and unproblematic court of appeal to which a preacher can have recourse."[17] Freedom will make a decision for or against God by virtue of its very constitution, but at the level of explicit reflection and public adherence, believers may find it difficult even to know what is being asked of them. Should we say that they are lesser participants in the tradition?

The church's teaching authority finds its specific origins in the definitive character of the gospel's victory over falsehood and error. Its primary processes of developing a position are the genuine human elements of reason, consultation, and consensus. "I cannot escape the impression that attempts are still constantly made to conceal these genuinely human factors in the concrete process by which the Church's teaching office arrives at the truth."[18] Theologians can profitably spend their time demonstrating the historical, social background of ecclesiastical decisions. God works in and through human efforts to discover the truth. For example, conciliar argument and majority vote have always been both process and policy; they did not invalidate the binding force of decisions made.

Our faith is discovered in and through human procedures. The truths of faith are always institutionally formulated, but faith does not exist on the basis of the institution. We believe because of God's grace in Christ. To assent only because of the formal authority found in ecclesiastical officeholders is to misunderstand the basic movement of faith.[19] Formal authority is ultimately dependent upon faith in Christ; as a result, those holding authoritative teaching positions in an ecclesial community must indicate that the content of their decisions does not rest on office alone. If there is no intrinsic connection between faith, teaching, and the authority claimed for beliefs, then the gospel as transmitted to the contemporary world loses credibility. If all that can be mustered for the gospel is a weak ecclesiastical force, then the implicit assumption is that the message conveyed cannot be disclosed otherwise. The basic objective of the authoritative teaching office of the church is to render itself obsolete, to allow the gospel to stand for itself, to preserve its most basic meanings in a radically pluralist world.

For Rahner, as for us, an authoritative tradition of interpretation remains not only acceptable but helpful. No one has the ability to be an expert in everything. We do not wait to live our lives on the basis of absolute certainty concerning all issues. To have a guide through the thickets of contemporary medical-moral problems, on sexual mores, on confusing economic or military opinions, is an important asset. Moreover, we often are in danger of being dominated by our own narrow subjectivity, deciding to overhaul through private opinions any religious machine we think needs retooling. An ecclesial synthesis requires that we take account of opinions other than our own modest experience and understanding. The experience of dogma and of official doctrines reminds us, just as the genres of narrative, prophecy, hymns, and visions do, that salvation does not come from a gnostic self-analysis. We grant an antecedent credibility to the official teachings of the community because we ultimately believe that we do not save ourselves. Listening attentively to normative, noninfallible statements, assimilating their meaning, deciding for or against their intrinsic attachment to faith are important activities in the appropriation of the ordinary teaching in the church.

The Hierarchy of Truths

Trusting the tradition, giving the benefit of the doubt to the official teachings of the community, examining our own prejudices before presuming that the doctrines are incorrect — these attitudes do not exempt us from discerning which truths of our faith are central and which peripheral. The Second Vatican Council maintained,

> When comparing doctrines with one another, they should remember that in Catholic doctrine there exists an order or "hierarchy" of truths, since they vary in their relation to the foundation of the Christian faith.[20]

A distinct gradation exists, therefore, not just according to the subjective disposition of believers but according to the nature of doctrines themselves. Dogmas are not all equal. Most interpreters indicate that official teachings that focus the scriptural experience of God and Christ are at the center of doctrinal interpretations — but after that, the disagreement occurs. Avery Dulles argues that the Catholic Marian dogmas (immaculate conception, 1854; the assumption, 1950; and papal infallibility itself, 1870) are "too unclear in their meaning and too peripheral in importance to be of decisive moment for good standing in the Church."[21] Gerald O'Collins would include in the category of peripheral doctrines those dealing with the church, the sacraments according to the Council of Trent (1545–63), and the virgin Mary.[22]

Karl Rahner observed that not only was there an objective ordering of revelatory truth, such that the New Testament would always be its foundation, but Christians themselves establish a system by which they believe. As a result, some public teachings enter a limbo of noncomprehension or effective nondefinition.[23]

In the objective order of truths, there are two important questions: Is there already a priority of truths in the Scriptures themselves? and, What will be the final importance of certain doctrines when the kingdom ultimately arrives? At both the beginning of faith and its historical end, a certain ambiguity appears about the status of doctrinal statements. Dogmas as official reflections upon faith do not release the Christian church from faith into a secure "already out there now" set of maxims that if accepted in an unquestioning spirit will absolve believers of decision. Doctrines are meant to awaken faith within a given culture, not replace it.

In essence, the shift from a classicist notion of normativity in which a single cultural formulation of doctrinal statements is the sole legitimate expression of faith to an understanding of norms that includes history has just begun. Committed to the authoritative character of the Scriptures, their official interpretations, and the rightful role of the magisterium, theologians are now attempting to "think" the authoritative character of office, teaching, and text through the prism of historical change. The tentative nature of their conclusions is obvious, and as in all disciplines, until a theoretic paradigm emerges that includes the previous understanding and goes beyond it, the older classical formulas will be repeated and adjusted to "fit" the contemporary scene. Though not a total solution to the problems posed, such a stance is to be expected. Our modest attempts to express the older forms of normativity and to move beyond them must stand or fall with their ability to face both cultures.

Teaching and Preaching

The many doctrinal formulations of the Christian churches, such as Chalcedon, Trent, the Augsburg Confession (1530), the Heidelberg Catechism (1562), The Thirty-Nine Articles (1563–71), the Book of Concord (1580), Vatican Council I, Vatican Council II, and the various bilateral ecumenical agreements (e.g., Anglican Roman Catholic Dialogues, 1971 [Eucharist], 1973 [ministry], and 1976 [authority]), as well as many others, do not mean simply to articulate private witness. They are statements about the world and the significance of Christian faith within society, and contain an expectation that believers will adhere to the vision elaborated within them. They describe and prescribe certain beliefs for the communities of faithful.

Preachers and teachers, though they have different roles within the church, have a responsibility to attend to these normative documents. To ignore them is to forget the history of one's own community. As Milan Kundera notes in *The Book of Laughter and Forgetting*, to violate the past is to destroy the integrity of the present.[24] We are, at least partially, what our communities' traditions have made us. To take responsibility for that past requires authentic reinterpretation to present audiences; repetition without interpretation either automatically alienates or replaces invited integration with force.

Those who stand in pulpits and those who enter classrooms speak two related but distinct languages. Teachers aim for the ideals of science: complete retrieval of information concerning a topic, interpretations collateral to their own, subsequent histories generated by the text, an authentic decision for or against the subject matter, and a thematized position that can generate intelligent and coherent understanding. Their positions are hypothetical, probable, particular to the data at hand, investigative, at the edges of the discipline. The precision teachers offer is open to revision and correction. No matter how definite lecturers may seem, their opinions remain just that — opinions heuristically valid until proved otherwise. They hold pride of place until a more comprehensive theory can take their place.

Preachers, on the other hand, are engaged in the rhetoric of the marketplace. They hope that their audiences will commit themselves to the realities of which they speak. Rather than precision, they want effective and constitutive assimilation. The preached word uses poetic images, timely narratives, evocative symbols, and prescriptive questions to encourage participation in the events of revelation.[25] If the scientific speech of the theologian often uses the neuter (such and such is the case), and the passive and self-reflexive voice (the sacraments are accomplished in . . . ; the church finds itself . . .), the preacher speaks an inclusive first personal plural (we must listen to . . .) and a direct prescriptive claim (The gospel says you should . . .). If the scientific theologian wants to find a clarified language distinct from ordinary discourse, preachers season their speech with exemplary slang to "trick" the audience into attention. Preaching must become a reflected, artful common sense.

Because of the distinct linguistic forms, each speaker makes use of doctrinal or normative statements in a different fashion. Preachers, pastors, and priests have a publicly defined role in the community, a union with the explicit tradition that has formed the church. Part of their authority, whether in pastoral care or in worship, is constituted by authorities beyond themselves, whether congregational, episcopal, papal, or presbyteral. As catalysts within the communities in their charge, they have both the right and the duty to assist their congregations toward a fuller understanding of that tradition. This demands an ability not only to translate the faith of believers into its local cultural expressions but to mediate the doctrines of the past into the preaching and worship of the present. In the formation of consciences, they stand convicted of dreadful neglect if they do not attend to both the circumstances of believers and the faith they hope to continue. Capitulating to subjectivist biases no more assists the faith in coming into the present than does forced repetitive imposition of opaque doctrinal or ethical standards. Believers have an authoritative right to listen to the authentic Word of God spoken by their pastors. Ever conscious of their public roles, preachers must speak for the integrity of their own tradition, lest scandal ensue.

Though we might stress the differences between homiletic and academic discourse, we do not wish to divide them. Within the continuing rhetoric of the tradition, there exists an exigency for thoughtful reflection, for provocative questions and tantalizing insights that would need further elaboration. Such is the origin of doctrines from the languages of the Scriptures. And science always has an invisible ear cocked for its effective use in the marketplace, studying the rhetorical advantage of an idea. Nor does this interconnection compromise either discourse or the public for which each is intended. We are not only scientists, poets, or ordinary struggling believers, as though each were a prepackaged cargo container on the ship of life. Hence the delicacy with which preachers introduce intellectual information into their sermons and the hesitancy with which scientists look toward the practical applications that theological investigation might have on the faith of believers.

Catholics have been reminded of the interconnection of these two roles in the community with some force by Pope John Paul II and the various curial commissions under his guidance.[26] As he has expressed it, the priest has as one of his primary duties to obtain the personal knowledge necessary to distinguish between what is held by the community surely and what is open for free discussion. Clearly, solidly, and organically, the preaching and teaching pastor must offer authentic teaching, with pride of place given to the official doctrines of the church. Such instruction, offered objectively, positively, without irony or humor, must appear with an integrity that fits into the entire Christian tradition. Those who prepare preachers and pastors for their role in the Catholic church are expected to accomplish their task in the same way.

Other Christian traditions indicate varying degrees of interaction between pastors and theologians.[27] But in general, it can be said that preachers are required to adhere closely to doctrinal and confessional traditions; theologians can study the complex edges of linguistic difficulty and offer some dissent, as long as they are faithful to the common methods of theology. In lectures, conferences, various media presentations, and books, they might use the abstract jargon they have developed, largely unintelligible to the uninitiated. They must expend much time in interrelating various doctrines, clarifying their consistencies and confusions. And by the best lights they have available to them, they may certainly dissent, though they must expect a dialogue to ensue from their assumed positions. The pulpit, on the other hand, is in principle not the place for contradiction of ecclesial teachings nor for abstruse information or controversy. Concentrating on the central content of faith, preachers guide and vivify hearts and consciences, but just as they should not give scandal by heedlessly overturning the common understanding of faith, neither should they offend by ignorance or superstition. We may quote Saint Augustine: "Not even love itself, which is the end of the commandment and the fulfilling of the law, can be rightly exercised unless the objects of love are true and not false."[28]

The Drive Toward
Systematic/Constructive Theology

The differentiation between the languages of preaching and teaching, the problem of official doctrines and authoritative offices in the community, and the issue of the origination of these elements from the New Testament faith points to an emergent sense of systematic theology.[29] Since one can be only a single individual, one always hopes that the many languages of faith, from

Scripture through the most complicated theological jargon, can be integrated consistently. We are not interested in preaching and praying one thing and thinking or doing another.[30] Worship, sermons, doctrines, and ethics require coherence and aim toward an assimilable whole.

The principal function of systematic or constructive theology is to promote the understanding of the mysteries of faith we already know. Systematics does not so much provide new data as try to understand why the various religious facts of our lives got to be the way they are. Its goal is an interrelated network of terms and relations based upon the general notions that will be understood by all culturally educated men and women and upon the specific categories that appear from Christian witness and the gift of God's love to believers.

Systematic theology attempts some understanding of the mystery that is first faced by adoration and then expressed in symbols, stories, prophecies, and visions.[31] It asks how the content of each can be related to that of the other. It will tend to be speculative and exploratory but not fanciful; it will be based in the converted lives of believers, whether theologians or not. Systematics will appear to some as rather elitist, but that will be the case only as it is in contemporary mathematics, astrophysics, or biochemistry. In this discipline, one understands the interrelationships between one's interpretations of Christ and those about God, and the knowledge of the church about the sacraments and about the Bible. It permits taking any single central belief and trying to see the way other topics of faith connect. As an investigative tool, systematic theology provides a holistic though incomplete intellectual vision of Christian experience, believing that the knowledge of the consequences of one's beliefs is an intrinsically important part of faith itself.

MODES OF THEOLOGICAL NORMATIVE REFLECTION

The Nature of Models

In this context, we need only remind readers of our previous use of the notion of model.[32] Scale or picture models copy an object exactly, according to a measure that miniaturizes or enlarges the image, such as the architectural model of a building. Disclosure or analogue models do not provide exact details, but like the drawing for a sculpture, evoke the final product. They are a basic sketch, a guiding tool for inquiry, simplifying for the sake of identification. Their imaginative configuration approximates the result and invites understanding. In our investigation of models of ethical interpretation, and below in the description of general theological models of inquiry, we use the second notion. In idealized types, we can distinguish two poles: the subject investigating and the object or world disclosed by the study.

Five Models of Theological Inquiry[33]

Classical Model. In the mode of theology that reigned supreme for some eighteen hundred years, the theologian was a believer within a particular confessional tradition who used various philosophic tools (Platonic, Neoplatonic, Augustinian, Aristotelian, etc.) to investigate the beliefs within the church. His (during this time, the theologian was almost always male) task was to express a carefully formulated tradition to the world. The world's understanding of itself had no explicit "internal" relevance in theological reflection. As examples, we might think of Thomas Aquinas, Bonaventure, Martin Luther (1483–1546), and John Calvin (1509–64). Though it can be said quite justly that a theologian such as Aquinas included the intellectual concerns of Muslims and Jews, classical thinkers had as a goal the conversion of others. Their heirs during the later scholastic period (such as the Jesuit Francesco de Suarez, 1548–1617; and the Lutheran Johann Gerhard, 1582–1637) exemplified an often logically brilliant organization, together with strict confessional polemics.

Liberal Model. In reaction to the academic form of Christian theologies, the period from 1750 to 1840 experienced an explosion of religious devotion as well as radical cultural departures in painting, poetry, music, and other arts. Romanticism in theology hoped to overcome a dry intellectual assent to doctrines through a resurrection of affective attachment to worship, the Scriptures, and beliefs. Whether in France (with René Chateaubriand, 1768–1848), in England (with Samuel Taylor Coleridge, 1772–1834; or later, F. D. Maurice, 1805–72), in Germany (with Friedrich Schleiermacher), or somewhat later in America (with Horace Bushnell, 1802–76; and Walter Rauschenbusch, 1861–1918), the emphasis in theology shifted from the objective contents of faith to the subjective conditions of belief. The emerging sciences, developing political idealism, and artistic subjectivity had inner relevance to faith. Thus the subject in this theological model is committed to modernity as a personal enterprise and sees the object of theology to be the Christian tradition — but as reformulated for the sake of the claims of the modern world.

Neo-orthodox Model. There were strong responses to the nineteenth century's mode of theological investigation. In the early twentieth century, the Catholic community responded with a broad negative action against what were called modernists (esp. Alfred Loisy, 1857–1940; and George Tyrell, 1861–1909), condemning any "subjectivization" of Christian doctrines. After the devastating trench warfare of World War I, Karl Barth (1886–1968), especially in his *Commentary on the Epistle to the Romans* (1919) and his *Church Dogmatics* (1932–67), said a resounding no to the optimistic beliefs of liberal theology. Convinced (as the Catholic antimodernists were) that theological study had collapsed the dialectically critical character of the Christian proclamation into the scientific, cultural, and artistic biases of the age, he proposed a return to the prophetic immediacy of the Scriptures with the Reformers as the most authentic interpreters of the message. Because of the Fall, human beings are caught in a realm of sin such that only God's infinite qualitative difference, his radical otherness, can transform our existence.

Reinhold Niebuhr (1891–1971), in *The Nature and Destiny of Man* (1939–43), mediated the language of dialectical divine presence to the American scene. In a sense, neo-orthodoxy allowed modernity to define the questions of experience, its quest for the infinite, and its sense of sinful personal and social alienation, but it maintained that only the unique claims of Christianity could transform the problems into grace. The object pole of theology, therefore, is the wholly other God, a paradoxical mystery whose reality calls into question all our paltry reasonings and religious pretensions. The subject engaging in theology, called into existence by this God, is a human being dedicated to the quest forged by an authentic faith, trust, and love.

Radical Model. This theological endeavor looks at the development of postclassical thought and reminds us that modernity will not disappear. Is not the God who is wholly other busy overturning human expectations? Is not this God constantly competing with human projects? And hence, must not believers in this God conclude that our commitment to moral action is inconsequential at best, sinful at worst? Can language about such a divinity be in any sense truthful, let alone verified? In this type, the concerns of the modern world are paramount; they define both theologians and the world disclosed by their study. The subject is committed to contemporary science, transforming political endeavors and affective honesty; the object remains the Christian message, but this message concerns a person (Jesus) and doctrines (salvation) without any clearly defined or sharply argued transcendent reference. The theological questions asked use the tools of early linguistic analysis (esp. those of Ludwig Wittgenstein, 1889–1951; and A. J. Ayer) and cultural commentary to argue that (at least the old classical or neo-orthodox) God is dead. This primarily American phenomenon is associated with figures like Paul van Buren, Gabriel Vehanian, Thomas J. J. Altizer, and Joseph Fletcher.

Revisionist Model. A proposal that hopes to integrate the concerns of all these models has been recently suggested by David Tracy. It involves commitments at both poles of the model with a correlative process of interaction. The subject/theologian is committed both to an authentic public secularity (note: not secularism) and to an authentic Christian quest for truth, justice, and love. The object disclosed by theology is a critical reformulation of both secular concerns and the motifs of Christian doctrine. Because faith and the world are taken seriously, they involve a mutually corrective interpretation. Faith must listen to both the questions and the answers proposed by the world. The truthful character of the investigation is clarified by an examination of the ontological claims made for religious as well as worldly "objects." Subject and object are correlatively "revised."

PROBLEMS AND CONCLUSIONS

These models for theological reflection place the normative dimension in differing places, but the standards at stake are primarily intellectual values. The models then establish a relationship between the conceptualized norms.

In the classical formula, the norm is to be found in the confessional tradition and its doctrines; in the liberal model, the standard is modernity's teachings as they reformulate Christian experience; in the neo-orthodox model, God's otherness is the normative judgment upon humanity's reasoning powers; and in the radical model, modernity shapes both believer and beliefs. In the final model, there is a dialogical norm: beliefs and reason are mutually related, so that if we say that faith is primary, we must recognize that its expressions are always culturally shaped. Since both faith and the mystery of the Wholly Other exceed our ability to explicate them, we recognize that the subjective and objective poles of theological investigation, psychologically, socially, and culturally determined as they are, must be willing to "let go" of themselves when more adequate formulations appear.

The second important point is that we have carefully grounded the development of foundational theology in the experience of a critical Christian conversion. The models just described focus primarily upon the *theoretic* character of Christian theology. What can we say of the social and personal engagement of theological endeavor? In our model of foundations, theologians are converting believers within prayerful communities. Are these five models rooted in the ecclesial and societal praxis required by our examination of modernity? What would they look like if they also had to account for critical religious and moral experience?

The five theoretic correlations described here can be judged according to their engagement in *praxis*.[34] The classical model focuses on the primacy of theory. "Theory regards objective knowledge as the formulation and verification of intelligibilities; it primarily regards possible, probable, or certain constructs of reality."[35] It mediates doctrines in a particular cultural context, so that Christian activity implements good theory. Our religious and moral knowing is not intrinsically changed by doing.

In models in which only praxis is important, Christianity gains an internal relation to human activity, both religious and secular, but at the cost of losing theoretic criticism of itself. Christian service would always be paramount but without a doctrinal spine or theoretic warrants. Praxis should be understood as what we actually do, as involved and committed, the intersubjective home in which we establish ourselves as authentic or inauthentic subjects. A theology that stresses this dimension tends to think of doctrine as secondary, teaching as second-rate, and noncommitment to sociopolitical transformation as sinful. Many of the forms of liberal or radical theology fall within this category.

There is also a type of praxis theology that stresses the primacy of faith and love. Christianity stands in judgment on both the theoretic formulations and the commitments of human praxis. The primary focus is upon the wholly other God. The prototype remains Karl Barth, for whom theology was always dialectically related to human activity. His Catholic friend Hans Urs von Balthasar (b. 1905) can also be understood within this framework.

In the final two models for theology, there is an attempt to include both theory and praxis within religious discourse while maintaining the specific values Christianity has to offer to both. Where theory remains primary, the correlations between life, thought, and Christian conversion are mediated primarily through the extraordinarily tough demands of various contemporary sciences and theoretic disciplines. Matthew Lamb believes that Rudolf Bultmann, Paul Tillich (1886–1965), the Niebuhrs, Karl Rahner (1904–84), and the revisionist model we have sketched belong in this category. Here theoretic issues are mutually and critically correlated, but nonintellectualized praxis becomes largely the application of already constituted theories. Human praxis fails to be the true origin of Christian knowing and loving.

In our final correction of theoretic models, we must opt for the primacy of critical Christian praxis. It is not only the goal but the foundation of theory. As we have indicated, Christian transformation is the beginning of authentic theology. Theoretic and practical reflections are never "innocent," disinterested, or unrelated to the sociopolitical sphere; they always have a self-justifying function in relation to praxis. There remains an "unfinished" quality to thought, theological or otherwise.

Christian praxis, by its loyalty to the suffering and poor, by its commitment to the radically unloved, by its recognition of atonement within creation groaning to be completed, better informs both thought and action. Theologians such as Bernard Lonergan, John Baptist Metz, and various "liberation theologians" are committed to the implementation of an interdisciplinary praxis that aims at academic, ecclesial, and social transformation. Interdisciplinary investigation at all levels of normative theological activity is not, therefore, a luxury of the academy. It is the lifeblood of the human enterprise for theologians. Seeking to articulate the contradictions between past inadequacies of theory and the imperatives of action, thinkers hope to contribute to the liberation of noetic praxis, on the one hand, and provide a critical basis for continuing collaboration in society, on the other.

Our work, finally, indicates how a foundational theology of both ethics and doctrine can contribute to a theoretic understanding of the critical praxis that supports all theology. How does it sort out the complementarities and contradictions between present and past theories? Can an authentic stance be assumed such that Christians can not only comment on their own experience but assist in the transformation of social and political realities for the future? In giving up the dying ideals of an old Christendom, Christian theologians do not thereby forgo the possibility of living their faith in a public world.

NOTES

1. On Melchior Cano, see Eberhard Haible, "Loci Theologici," in *Sacramentum Mundi*, ed. Karl Rahner et al. (New York: Herder & Herder, 1970), 6:224–26; Wolfhart Pannenberg, *Theology and the Philosophy of Science*, trans. Francis McDonagh (Philadelphia: Westminster Press, 1976), 243ff.; Walter Kasper, *The Methods of Dogmatic Theology*, trans. John Drury (New York: Paulist Press, 1969); Bernard J. F. Lonergan, *Philosophy of God, and Theology* (Philadelphia: Westminster Press, 1973), 21–44; and idem, *Method in Theology* (London: Darton, Longman & Todd, 1972), 278–81.

2. See Avery Dulles, *The Survival of Dogma: Faith, Authority, and Dogma in a Changing World* (Garden City, N.Y.: Doubleday & Co., 1973), 79–95; and Gerald O'Collins, *Has Dogma a Future?* (London: Darton, Longman & Todd, 1975), 9–22.

3. See Karl Rahner, "Observations on the Situation of Faith Today," in *Problems and Perspectives of Fundamental Theology*, ed. René Latourelle and Gerald O'Collins, trans. Matthew J. O'Connell (New York: Paulist Press, 1982), esp. 280–86.

4. For a defense of this principle, see Francis Schüssler Fiorenza, *Foundational

Theology: Jesus and the Church (New York: Crossroad, 1984), 5–55; Giuseppe Ghiberti, "Contemporary Discussion of the Resurrection of Jesus," in *Problems*, ed. Latourelle and O'Collins, 223–55; and David Tracy, *Analogical Imagination: Christian Theology and the Culture of Pluralism* (New York: Seabury Press, 1981), 248–338.

5. Gerald O'Collins, *Fundamental Theology* (New York: Paulist Press, 1981), 161–91; and Dulles, *Survival*, 155–75.

6. Yves Congar, "Pour une histoire semantique du terme 'magisterium,' " *Revue des sciences philosophiques et théologiques* 60 (1976): 85–98; T. Howland Sanks, "Cooperation, Cooptation, Condemnation: Theologians and the Magisterium, 1870–1978," *Chicago Studies* 17 (1978): 242–63. This entire issue of *Chicago Studies* is pertinent.

7. Philip Wheelwright, *Metaphor and Reality* (Bloomington: Ind. Univ. Press, 1962), 45–69; and Paul Ricoeur's use of Wheelwright in *The Rule of Metaphor: Multidisciplinary Studies of the Creation of Meaning in Language*, trans. Robert Czerny with Kathleen McLaughlin and John Costello (Toronto: Univ. of Toronto Press, 1977), 247–51.

8. See Hans Robert Jauss, *Toward an Aesthetic of Reception*, trans. Timothy Bahti (Minneapolis: Univ. of Minn. Press, 1982), and Wolfgang Iser, *The Act of Reading: A Theory of Aesthetic Response* (Baltimore: Johns Hopkins Univ. Press, 1978).

9. Most standard works have this schema; for ready reference and interpretation, see O'Collins, *Fundamental Theology*, 186–91.

10. Vincenz Gasser on papal infallibility, as quoted in Avery Dulles, "Moderate Infallibilism: An Ecumenical Approach," in his *A Church to Believe In: Discipleship and the Dynamics of Freedom* (New York: Crossroad, 1982), 136.

11. Karl Rahner, "On the Concept of Infallibility in Catholic Theology," in his *Theological Investigations*, vol. 14, trans. David Bourke (New York: Crossroad, 1976), 68.

12. See the "early" understanding of this principle in Edward Schillebeeckx, "Towards a Catholic Use of Hermeneutics," in his *God the Future of Man*, trans. N. D. Smith (New York: Sheed & Ward, 1968), 1–49; and Karl Rahner, "Basic Observations on the Subject of Changeable and Unchangeable Factors in the Church," in his *Theological Investigations* 14:3–23.

13. "Now according to Catholic doctrine there is in fact no authority in this world constituting an absolute norm for the individual without the personal decision of his own conscience" (Karl Rahner, "The Dispute Concerning the Church's Teaching Office," in his *Theological Investigations* 14:95).

14. A summary of classical positions concerning dissent in doctrinal matters can be found in Charles E. Curran and Robert L. Hunt, eds., *Dissent in and for the Church: Theologians and Humanae Vitae* (New York: Sheed & Ward, 1969), 40–54; Karl Rahner, "Opposition in the Church," in his *Theological Investigations*, vol. 17, trans. Margaret Kohl (New York: Crossroad, 1981), 127–38; and Avery Dulles, "Doctrinal Authority for a Pilgrim Church," in his *The Resilient Church: The Necessity and Limits of Adaptation* (Garden City, N.Y.: Doubleday & Co., 1977), esp. 107–12; see idem, "Authority: The Divided Legacy," *Commonweal* (12 July 1985): 400–403.

15. Lists of changed teachings may be found in Curran and Hunt, eds., *Dissent*, 66–80; and Karl Rahner, "Teaching Office," in his *Theological Investigations* 14:92.

16. Karl Rahner, "Concerning Our Assent to the Church as She Exists in the Con-

crete," in his *Theological Investigations*, vol. 12, trans. David Bourke (London: Darton, Longman & Todd, 1974), 142–60.

17. Rahner, "Faith Today," 280.

18. Rahner, "Teaching Office," in his *Theological Investigations* 12:12.

19. Rahner, "Concerning Our Assent," 148–56.

20. "Unitatis Redintegratio," par. 11 (1964), in *Vatican Council II: The Conciliar and Post-Conciliar Documents*, ed. Austin Flannery (Northport, N.Y.: Costello Pub. House, 1975), 462.

21. Dulles, "Moderate Infallibilism," 147–48.

22. O'Collins, *Dogma*, 46.

23. Rahner, "Faith Today," 274–91.

24. Milan Kundera, *The Book of Laughter and Forgetting*, trans. Michael Henry Heim (New York: Alfred A. Knopf, 1980).

25. See Chaim S. Perelman, *The Realm of Rhetoric*, trans. William Kluback (Notre Dame, Ind.: Univ. of Notre Dame Press, 1982), 35–36.

26. To the International Theological Commission, *Origins* 9.24 (29 November 1979): 392–95; To the Cardinals, *Origins* 10.11 (28 August 1980): 172; To the American Bishops, *Origins* 9.18 (October 1979): 290, 292; To the Bishops of Central France, *Origins* 12.14 (16 September 1982): 215, 216; To Seminarians, Priests, and Deacons of Paris, *Acta apostolicae sedis* (1980): 695–702.

27. See, e.g., Edward Farley and Peter C. Hodgson, "Scripture and Tradition," in *Christian Theology: An Introduction to Its Traditions and Tasks*, rev. ed., ed. Peter C. Hodgson and Robert H. King (Philadelphia: Fortress Press, 1985), 82; and in the evangelical tradition, Kenneth F. W. Prior, "The Minister as Teacher," in *The Necessity of Systematic Theology*, rev. ed., ed. John Jefferson Davis (Grand Rapids: Baker Book House, 1980), 49–59.

28. *On Christian Doctrine* 4.28.61, in *The Nicene and Post-Nicene Fathers*, ed. Philip Schaff (New York: Charles Scribner's Sons, 1903), 596.

29. Lonergan, *Method*, 335–53.

30. See David Friedrich Strauss's paradigm on the hypocrisy of many liberal preachers who were caught between their historical-critical sense and their pastoral need for communicating the gospel, in Horton Harris, *David Friedrich Strauss and His Theology* (New York and Cambridge: Cambridge Univ. Press, 1973), 56–57.

31. Systematics, like all theological disciplines, functions as a "partial understanding" of mystery, as called for by Vatican Council I in its decree on faith and reason. See the "Dogmatic Constitution on the Catholic Faith" (1870), in *The Teaching of the Catholic Church*, ed. Karl Rahner, trans. Geoffrey Stevens (Staten Island, N.Y.: Alba House, 1967), 36.

32. David Tracy, *Blessed Rage for Order: The New Pluralism in Theology* (New York: Seabury Press, 1975), 22–23. See also above, 163.

33. These models are based upon Tracy, *Blessed Rage*, 24–63, though we have shifted them to gain a historical dimension.

34. See Matthew Lamb, *Solidarity with Victims: Toward a Theology of Social Transformation* (New York: Crossroad, 1982), 61–99; also see Schüssler Fiorenza, *Foundational Theology*, 282–321.

35. Lamb, *Solidarity*, 62.

FURTHER READINGS

James Barr. *Beyond Fundamentalism: Biblical Foundations for Evangelical Christianity*. Philadelphia: Westminster Press, 1984.

Peter Chirico. *Infallibility: The Crossroads of Doctrine*. Mission, Kans.: Sheed Andrews & McMeel, 1977.

Edward Farley. *Ecclesial Reflection*. Philadelphia: Fortress Press, 1982.

Robert M. Grant with David Tracy. *A Short History of the Interpretation of the Bible*, 2d ed. Philadelphia: Fortress Press, 1984.

Nicholas Lobkowicz. *Theory and Practice: History of a Concept from Aristotle to Marx*. Notre Dame, Ind.: Univ. of Notre Dame Press, 1967.

T. Howland Sanks. *Authority in the Church: A Study in Changing Paradigms*. Missoula, Mont.: Scholars Press, 1974.

PART 4

DIALOGICAL STRUCTURES
OF CONVERSION:
A CONSTRUCTIVE FUTURE

CHAPTER 10

A DIALOGICAL NORMATIVE
HORIZON IN CATHOLICISM

Foundations once destroyed, what can the just do?
Psalm 11:3, Grail trans.

There has been a single thread that has run through this entire volume: a method for the exercise of contemporary theology. We have uncovered the nodal issues that construct a modern foundational theology attentive to the experiences and questions of our culture, on the one hand, and the experiences, symbols, texts, and actions of the Christian community, on the other. One final issue remains to be discussed, though, and our proposal for its solution is more suggestive and anticipatory than settled and confirmed. Before the reader turns his or her attention to specialized analyses of ethical issues (e.g., abortion) and specific doctrines (e.g., Christology), we must state briefly what a normative stance in ethics and doctrine will look like if the previous terms and relations have been assimilated. In it lie the foundations of both the ethical and the doctrinal imperative.

THE ETHICAL IMPERATIVE

The search for the "imperative," whether in moral or religious experience, is one of the human desires for meaning. In the moral life the "ought" is part of the very process of self-transcendence through which we seek to conform our decisions and lives to judgments of value. Since judgments are not guesses but probable truths, normative judgments of value are concerned with the way the world and human relations probably ought to be. Yet the discernment of particular imperatives is not enough; there is also the need for a coherence among all the normative judgments we make. Stated more concretely, it is not sufficient for us to arrive at distinct normative decisions on the issues of the value of human life and economic policies affecting Third World countries. There must be some congruence and coherence between these two sorts of normative judgments. The desires for coherence and congruence result in what is called a stance. Simply defined, an ethical stance is a coherent combination of value judgments about the world, God, and self.

An ethical stance is formed through the interaction between a subject pole (existential questions about our commitments, lived values, actions, etc.) and an object pole (the range of data or "world" that comes into view for us to interpret, judge, and act on). The interaction between these two referents fashions the ways in which we look on reality and structure our understandings and judgments about the world. For example, we have seen the classical theologian's subject pole comprise a commitment to a particular religious-moral tradition, and the furthest range of the object pole include the beliefs of that tradition. The ethical stance of such a theologian, then, represented an almost monolithic way of viewing and structuring the moral life. Specific imperatives, values, and actions were understood and judged according to the established moral principles of the tradition, and alternative ways of understanding and judging were thought erroneous or were beyond the boundaries of the theologian's consciousness.

When we seek to thematize the contents of a stance, we attempt to make explicit the foundations of the ethical imperative. In other words, the ethical imperative arises from within the context of a normative stance, and so the stance is actually the ground of the ethical imperative itself. Once again, for most classical theologians the ethical imperative arose only from within the confines of their particular religious-moral traditions.

If a theologian was committed to Roman Catholicism, then all ethical imperatives found their ground from within that tradition. For example, until the middle of this century almost all Roman Catholic theologians argued the primary purpose of marital sexual relations was procreation. They were committed to preserving their longstanding understanding of sexuality that can be traced back to Augustine and Thomas Aquinas. This tradition had understood sexual relations between spouses as acts of nature (and not primarily as acts of love) having a moral intentionality or finality (procreation) built into them by God. To act against this moral finality by some form of artificial contraception was tantamount to acting directly against God. We can see, then, that how we discern, argue, and justify the ethical imperative is a function of how we intend and understand the human world.

Correct judgments of value, that is, value judgments that are probably true, rest on the conversion of the individual making the judgments. It is necessary, then, that the stance itself, as a coherent combination of value judgments, be founded on the four conversions. The ethical imperative will be authentic only to the extent that it arises from converted consciousness. An ethical imperative that arises in the absence of all four conversions is no imperative at all, and the imperative that arises from severe deficiencies in one or more of the conversions in the individual is at least biased. This is why we argue that the disciples' normative stance must be interpreted by reference to the four conversions.

There have been several normative stances proposed within the Christian traditions.[1] In classical Protestantism, for example, in Martin Luther's writings, faith was considered the stance for the moral life. *Sola fide* (by faith alone) was the fundamental viewpoint from which the ethical imperative was discerned, argued, and justified. Second, in some forms of Protestant liberalism of this century, love (*agape*) became an alternative stance to faith. For example, Adolf von Harnack (1851–1930) thought that the entire gospel of Jesus could be embraced under the rubric of love without depreciating the gospel message itself.[2] Thus, von Harnack considered the entire moral life to be founded on the single commandment to love in the New Testament.

Some neo-orthodox Protestant theologians proposed a third stance based on Jesus Christ. For example, in reaction to Protestant liberalism, Karl Barth argued that it is only through Jesus Christ that the Christian is enabled to know and do the good. Thus, his ethics are a form of christological monism in that the ethical imperative must always be founded on Jesus Christ alone and can be authentically discovered only through belief in him.[3]

Against all three stances, James Sellers has recently proposed the stance of promise and fulfillment as the normative horizon of the Judeo-Christian moral life. For him, salvation is best understood as "wholeness," but humanity has not yet possessed this wholeness fully and therefore must search for it. Humanity is moving toward the plenitude of salvation (wholeness) that has been promised, and so the best stance from which to discover the ethical imperative is within the horizon of promise and fulfillment.[4]

We argue that all the proposed normative stances are far too content-oriented and doctrinaire in their intent and far too narrow in their scope. In other words, these stances are interpreted through content categories alone, for example, Jesus Christ or love (*agape*), and the content is too indigenous to a specific confessional tradition (doctrinaire). We are aware that the content categories of the disciple's stance can be specifically Christian, particularly when explicit reference is made to Jesus and his teachings of the kingdom, but we argue that the proper category by which we should understand a stance should be formal or structural in nature. Furthermore, an ethical stance must be as comprehensive as possible to take into view as many elements of moral experience as possible. All the stances discussed above lack this comprehensive scope. For example, Barth's stance (Jesus Christ) fails to appreciate that in fact nonreligious people do experience an authentic ethical imperative although they have no reflective experience of God or of Jesus Christ. Finally, none of the proposals grounds its stance in the necessity for the four conversions (structural categories) as the central criteria for the discernment of the ethical imperative.

THE CRITICAL-DIALOGICAL CHARACTER
OF THE ETHICAL STANCE

We propose a critical-dialogical stance as the most appropriate horizon from which to discover the human and Christian ethical imperative. The stance is dialogical in that the ethical imperative is discerned by correlating the praxis claims that arise from both contemporary human experience and the Christian traditions. We mean by praxis claims the values formulated from all fields of human doing and performance, whether symbolic, affective, cognitive, moral, economic, political, social, cultural, or religious.[5] For example, we can formulate various demands from what we are doing in celebrating the Eucharist (that we ought to give thanks for what Jesus has done for us) or from what we are doing by setting up welfare programs for the poor (that the neighbor in need deserves our care). These claims emerge from praxis because they find their origin in what we do.

The stance is "critical" in that the criteria that guide and ultimately judge the dialogue between the praxis claims of human experience and those of the Christian traditions are the four conversions of the human person. Not all human doing or performance is converted, and so not all lived values, ethical principles, and moral norms are valid praxis claims. Conflicts of interpretation about what is normatively good and conflicts between the various evaluative resources for normative-decision making partially arise because of a lack of conversion. For example, some say that the normative good is pleasure; others say it is union with God. Similarly, some ecclesial authorities assert certain proposals for the nature of human sexuality, and specialists in the empirical and human sciences maintain others. Resolution of these conflicts of interpretation and of value judgments must take place. We argue that at least a partial solution is possible by discerning the ethical imperative within a dialogic stance that is at once open and critical.

The dialogue is made possible because the praxis claims of secular society and those of the Christian traditions have a certain autonomy relative to each other. This is so because the resources and specific methods of the empirical and human sciences enjoy a rightful independence from those used in the Christian theological sciences.[6] In addition, the results produced by secular experience and science possess a relative cognitive independence from those produced by faith/moral experience and religious science in the Christian community. For example, the religious sciences do not take over the secular sciences and attempt to generate conclusions about the nature of the atom or the psychic makeup of persons who are engaged in psychoanalysis. Conversely, the secular sciences cannot take over the religious sciences and generate judgments about the nature of the triune God or the validity of revelation.

To speak of a "rightful autonomy" must mean in principle that the conclusions of the secular sciences can contain valid insights into the way the world probably is. In other words, the empirical and human sciences, which are produced from experience, can generate valid judgments of fact about human beings and their needs that are important for discerning the ethical imperative. In chapter 5, we argued that moral interpretations of value and obligation rest in part on the truthfulness of the judgments of fact. The ethical imperative, then, can be valid and binding only to the extent that it is informed by adequate beliefs about the true nature of persons.

The religious sciences do not just take over these conclusions and treat them as "gospel truth." The cognitive praxis claims that originate from the secular sciences must be critically correlated with the conclusions arrived at by the religious sciences. For example, in the area of human sexuality the secular sciences of biology, psychology, and sociology, on the one hand, and the religious sciences of systematic and moral theology, on the other hand, use their own respective sources and methods of interpretation. From them, each science generates its own set of conclusions on the nature of human sexual relations. These conclusions or cognitive praxis claims must be correlated to discover the full meaning of sexual relations. The criteria used to discern the truthfulness of the correlated meanings are the four conversions of the individuals making the claims.

In a similar way, there is the need to correlate the *moral* praxis claims that arise from both secular and religious experience. Reflection on contemporary secular experience in the political, social, and economic realms can result in lived values and actions that may or may not be the result of conversion. Likewise, the lived values and actions emanating from the faith/moral experience in the Christian community may or may not be the result of converted consciousness. The moral praxis claims of both secular experience and the Christian traditions must be critically correlated to discover the normatively good value to be pursued in actions that will transform not only the individuals performing the actions but also the structures of society. Once again, the correlated moral claims are judged for their truthfulness according to the transformative power of the conversions. For example, the political and economic experiences of those who live in countries disadvantaged by direct or indirect actions of the First World nations have resulted in moral praxis claims for liberation and justice. These claims must be critically correlated with the moral praxis claims for liberation and justice that have arisen from the faith and moral experience of the Christian traditions.

At times, we might find that the praxis of the Christian community lags behind that of secular society, or vice versa. Here, the claims of the one can become a principle of mediation for the transformation of the other. For example, before Vatican II the political experience of some modern democratic societies resulted in moral claims for the religious liberty to believe and practice openly what one judged to be the truth. The Roman Catholic church at this period of history continued to deny the validity of this moral claim, and therefore it refused to accept religious liberty as a general principle for all. However, at Vatican II the *Declaration on Religious Liberty* was issued.[7] No doubt, secular political experience became a principle of mediation for the transformation of the church's position.[8] By critically correlating the moral praxis claims of the two "societies," it was discerned that the ecclesial claim needed to give way to the secular.

On the other hand, in the western world at least the Christian traditions have been, and continue to be, a principle of mediation for the preservation and advancement of secular society. The Christian emphasis on the abiding sacredness of the individual has had some transformative influence on western legal systems, marriage practices, and claims to human rights. We need think only of the recent attempts to preserve the rights of the poor by Christian missionaries in Central and South America to see how the Christian traditions can be a transformative power in secular society. Although the evangelical ideals represented in the Sermon on the Mount are far from realized in contemporary society, they continue to be points of reference from which Christians can correlate all proposals for social change. In other words, Christians need to correlate the moral praxis claims for social change with the moral praxis claims that are part of their religious tradition and experience.

COMPARISON OF THE CRITICAL-DIALOGICAL
STANCE WITH LUTHER'S STANCE

We might be able to make the critical-dialogical stance more concrete if we compared it with another proposed stance. We choose Luther's stance of faith (*sola fide*) for two reasons: it is a classical stance within Christianity that continues in revised forms in postclassical Lutheran Protestantism,[9] and it is a fairly coherent position.[10]

Moral Praxis

Luther's central viewpoint from which all moral praxis was judged was justification by grace through faith. Justification was both the presupposition and the source of the Christian's moral experience and interpretations. For Luther, justification by faith determined the Christian ethos because it governed the believer's self-understanding in two ways: negatively, it drove home to the believer that salvation is given and cannot be attained by human activity; and positively, it gave the Christian a good conscience about his or her works. Luther's position on justification led him to adopt a paradoxical stance on the moral life, through the development of what is called the "two realm" theory.[11]

Luther's reading of Scripture and Augustine's *City of God* brought him to realize that there are two kingdoms: the kingdom of God and the kingdom of the world over which Satan rules. Within God's kingdom there are two distinct but paradoxically related realms: the secular realm and the spiritual realm. The realms are distinguished according to the manner in which God rules over and acts toward humanity as a manifestation of his love. In one way, God rules over humanity through his creative "hand," by which the world and humanity are created and preserved. After the Fall, however, God rules this realm now by wrath and justice. In the other way, God rules through his redeeming "hand," by which humanity is granted mercy, forgiveness, and redemption.

As figure 1 illustrates, Luther maintained that God issues moral commands to the Christian through both realms, and thus the Christian is subject to two different, although paradoxically related, moral obligations. In the Christian's public life within the secular realm God commands one thing, and in the private life within the spiritual realm God commands something else. So, for example, Luther would have argued that if a Christian held a public office such as magistrate's, he or she would be commanded to apply the law as just punishment for a crime committed. In this way the magistrate would be representing God's preserving activity toward humanity. Yet the strict application of the law inflicting severe punishment on the criminal might very well seem paradoxical to the Christian magistrate in his or her private life, when the command to offer mercy and forgiveness would be demanded by the gospel.

In addition, because Christ rules over the spiritual realm but does not as yet rule over the secular realm of public life, the Christian is subject to two authorities in daily moral life, namely, Christ in the private realm and the civil authorities who are God's representatives in the public realm. The gospel applies as a principle of action only in the private realm of the spiritual life; in the secular realm, the Christian relies on reason, which must be conformed to the command of God.[12]

FIGURE 1

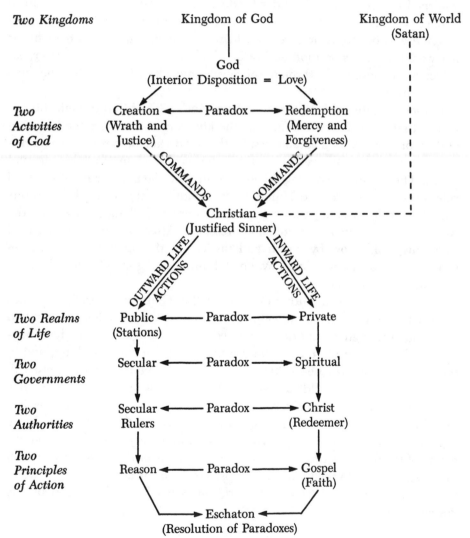

Two Kingdoms	Kingdom of God	Kingdom of World (Satan)
	God (Interior Disposition = Love)	
Two Activities of God	Creation (Wrath and Justice) ←— Paradox —→ Redemption (Mercy and Forgiveness)	
	COMMANDS COMMANDS	
	Christian ← – – – – – – – – – – – (Justified Sinner)	
	OUTWARD LIFE ACTIONS INWARD LIFE ACTIONS	
Two Realms of Life	Public (Stations) ←— Paradox —→ Private	
Two Governments	Secular ←— Paradox —→ Spiritual	
Two Authorities	Secular Rulers ←— Paradox —→ Christ (Redeemer)	
Two Principles of Action	Reason ←— Paradox —→ Gospel (Faith)	
	Eschaton (Resolution of Paradoxes)	

Luther created a normative stance of the moral life in which there was little or no room to correlate the moral praxis claims of the secular and spiritual realms. Each realm is distinct from the other, and each generates a moral praxis that in principle cannot be applied to the other realm. Luther's refusal to support the Peasants' War (1524–26) with the gospel message of love (spiritual realm) indicates how seriously he believed in the distinction between the two realms. In effect, the moral experience of the Christian is imbued with paradox, since he or she must be the subject of two kinds of commands, two realms of life (public and private), two forms of government (secular and spiritual), two kinds of authorities (civil authorities and Christ), and two principles of action (reason and the gospel). There is no principle that can mediate these two realms, so the Christian can only hope for the coming of the eschaton, when all the paradoxes will be resolved.

In one way, Luther's position on the two realms in the moral life is analogous to his theological position on the nature of humanity as justified and sinner at the same time (*simul justus et peccator*). In both positions, Luther did not see that authentic faith/moral praxis, achieved through the conversion processes, could truly transform the individual in all realms of life, as well as the structures of society.

In a critical-dialogical stance the ethical imperative is discovered, argued, and justified in the critical reciprocity of contemporary human experience and the Christian traditions. Only after the process of critical correlation of the cognitive and moral praxis claims (judgments of fact and of value) by reference to the conversions has been completed, do we authentically experience the obligation to conform our decisions and life to judgments of value. Finally, it is only after our judgments of fact and of value have been discerned, after the process of critical correlation has taken place, and after our decisions have been made that we can engage in a transformative action that truly changes both human hearts and human social and cultural institutions.[13]

Doctrinal Praxis

Luther contributed two important notes to contemporary theology with his stress on Christian conversion and the Scriptures.[14] Heavily influenced by Augustine, Luther dramatically inserted the intrinsic value of subjective attachment into faith and theology. For him, assent can never be a primarily intellectual exercise; Christian praxis is encompassing. "Theological knowledge is won by experiencing it."[15] Echoing his monastic ancestors, Luther maintained, "I experience that God's word is powerful over me and that . . . it so convinces and grasps me that it takes me captive and does not let me go."[16]

Justification,[17] as we have argued, is a primary personal and social symbol for Lutheran theology. The justifying grace of God comes through the proclaimed word that frees us from any attempts to save ourselves. External commands tell us what to do but do not give us the power to do it. Only God's grace, working interiorly, can resurrect human ability. Our own subjective efforts are flawed, caught in sinful self-destruction. God frees us from within, clothing us with the love he sees in Christ.

Christ's obedient love is prior to ours,[18] the sole way we know God's attitude toward us. The scriptural stories, healing our radically bent willfulness, allow us to hear the authentic call to inward conversion and external witness. Though the proclaimed word is the effective divine voice, without the inner call the Scriptures would remain only letters, a challenge that convicts us of sin. "For the Spirit is necessary to understand all of Scripture as well as every part of it."[19]

Paradoxical antitheses emerge from Luther's position. The dialectical character of the relationship between outer and inner, between world and church, sin and grace, works and the Spirit, promise and fulfillment, and reason and the Bible can, of course, become a principle of criticism against evils within the church (as in Luther himself) or against the sins of the world (as, e.g., in the theology of Karl Barth). Yet even though the first side of the polarities contains its own internal structure operative without grace, when it is confronted by the gospel it is seen for what it "really" is—sickly and weak.[20]

The role of reason in relation to faith is always a bit suspect.[21] Though Luther adhered to creedal and doctrinal formulas, they were always to be subservient to the Word of God, the fundamental apostolic authority.[22] Philosophy could know almost nothing about God or human existence, except vaguely, opaquely. It could never tell us God's attitude toward us nor convince us of how we should act toward God.[23] Rational activity is limited to the affairs of this world and most often functions with sinful vanity. Only in faith does the substance of reason remain, illuminated by the spirit, its pride destroyed.

In this respect, Luther can grant "some" cognitive dimension to creedal and dogmatic formulas, especially those of the early councils. As with any classical theologian, he can affirm the substance while arguing that the terms change.[24] But at no time can the symbolic language of the Scriptures be superseded; they always judge any human forms.

The priority of the scriptural Word, justification by faith, and insistence upon the fundamental distinction between the divine and the human give the sacramental life of the community a particular shape. Not only did Luther limit the explicit acts of ecclesial life to those defined by institution in the New

Testament (Baptism and the Lord's Supper), but he concentrated upon the "Word" character of the sacraments.[25] "We baptize with the Word."[26] The signs are combined with a word of divine promise that constitutes them as sacraments.[27] There is the one grace of God in Christ, the forgiveness of sins, that is granted to those who hear the Word.[28] Luther always opposed the theological position that anyone who did not place an obstacle to God's grace in the sacrament would receive it. He emphasized the interpersonal nature of divine interaction with us, and he held that without trusting faith, we could not hear the word of promise.[29] Without the inner word, the outer sign cannot be seen for what it is.

As a result, one might dispense with the externals. Faith, not baptism, saves. In 1522, Luther argued, "You can believe even though you are not baptized, for baptism is nothing more than an external sign which reminds us of the divine promise."[30] In his arguments with the radical wing of the Reform, Luther felt that his emphasis on faith had been used to devalue the sacraments. In this context, he stressed the command of God to make use of these external signs. God has chosen to bind himself through his Word to these external signs, so that grace can be perceived by our sense. Without the Word, the material gestures were ordinary; through the commanded word, they become a pledge and a promise.

Paralleling his discussion of the Lord's Supper on that of baptism, Luther focused upon the word of promise, the testament that was given by Christ through the signs of bread and wine. Luther rejected the traditional (since 1215) doctrine of the transubstantiation of elements as a metaphysical explanation substituted for faith. In its place, he later (1527–28) maintained, particularly in his arguments with Zwingli (1484–1531), that Christ's word "brings with it everything of which it speaks, namely, Christ with his flesh and blood and everything that he is and has."[31] But what remains paramount is the offer of grace in the Word, not in the physical elements. The literal, nontropological meaning of the scriptural text "This is my body" commands us toward faith in what we could not see with our eyes; to speculate beyond this adherence is stupid, even sinful.[32]

Through his refusal of "natural" mediations, Luther's paradoxes make theological argumentation difficult. In effect, there is a single source of theological and religious "work"—the Scriptures, which evoke faith. Because the concerns of reason, society, and their nonreligious techniques do not have an even relatively autonomous, let alone rightful, role to play in theology, they become at best that matter upon which Christians "work," ideologically reshaping it or replacing its personal and social concerns with their own Christian replicas. Rather than imaginatively creating or embodying Christian concerns in an authentic matrix of social beliefs and actions, the believer's stance requires primarily paradoxical judgment of error and substitution with specifically biblical content. Where Catholic thinkers stress the sacramental realization of God in both church and society, Lutheran theologians must focus upon the prophetic demands of the Word taming the world. Since there is no true dialogical conversion, the alternative can only be to divide the world and faith such that we are left with a publicly available culture and a privately operative piety.

It is not surprising, therefore, that during the controversies of the sixteenth century, Catholic insistence upon sacramental realism and ecclesial structure met Luther's anxiety for the unfinished and beleaguered character of the material world and human society.[33] It was not too difficult to see that neither had been an authentically expressive moment of divine presence.

However, the Catholic stance, classically enshrined at the Council of Trent, was determined to grant material gestures and institutional offices, as blessings of creation, a partial voice in the discussion. In essence, Luther had theologically parallel but extrinsically related poles. By external assumption, God commanded the material world to be the vehicle of his promise; between inner and outer, world and gospel, there seemed to be no intrinsic mediation.

THE CRITICAL-DIALOGICAL CHARACTER
OF THE DOCTRINAL STANCE

We have described Luther's positions at some length because of their value and their inner coherence. But we have a controversial intent as well. Throughout this text, we have stressed the importance of conversion, discipleship, and the consequent cognitive, normative dimensions that emerge from experience. We have argued that in both moral and doctrinal matters, there exist mediations through which the world and the gospel carry on a respectable, sometimes transformative, conversation. In this same discussion, however, when Luther's notion of "promise" is brought to a reflective refinement as an understanding of the permanent claim God has on reality by grace, Luther himself begins to grant an inner human effect. In the doctrinal stance that follows, it will be clear that at foundational levels, there nonetheless remain problems for us with the theological positions typologically illustrated by Luther.

The Doctrinal Imperative

When we speak of imperatives in the human spirit, we mean that eros which is the desire for meaning, for answering a question. What does it mean? Why is this the way that it is? What is it for? The "doctrinal" desire is for intellectual clarity, for sharply refined judgments about oneself, the world, and God. Doctrines are products of this desire—the judgments of fact (the ways things are) and of value (the way decisions encounter what is good) that return upon the world and self and maintain that this is the way the world "ought" to be. When doctrines become social as well as individual, they are called dogmas, the officially defined statements of the believing community.

Our multiple reflections upon Christian behavior in the world cry out for coherent, consistent systems. Beyond the particular events, persons, and ideas that modify the incidental activities of our lives, there is a desire for a shaped foundation upon which we can stand. A stance brings to the surface the ethical and doctrinal skeleton undergirding the individual cognitive and moral moments. Since models provide primarily an intellectual correlation, a stance is not simply an analogue in disguise. We aim for something more—a position that takes seriously the critical praxis of believers.

Stance includes judgments of value as a guide for the particular decisions that focus our ongoing conversions. Stances are not neutral descriptions of data; they register a direction that is dependent upon the participant and the objective intention of value. To "understand" a stance even incipiently, one must "try it," as Coleridge said of the validation of Christianity.[34] The interconnection of mental and moral bones, made visible by intellectual x-ray, permits us to locate the genus and species of our Christian character. Moreover, we can also anticipate something of the world we would build were we to assume responsibility for the imperatives operative in our hearts and minds.

The Sources of a Doctrinal Stance

Our doctrinal stance, like that for morality, includes in the subject and object the relatively autonomous sources of the world's praxis and of Christianity's praxis. Each has a rightful and partial independence in that each realm can contribute something true, if limited, to the whole. Secular thoughts and actions have regularly prompted Christian behavior and reflection (as in the case of religious liberty), and doctrinal judgments have challenged local cultures to reexamine their bases (e.g., in advocacy for the poor in South America).

The sources of information that interpret the doctrinal imperative require their native tools to clarify nature, functions, and values. Such hermeneutical patterns will involve analyses that recover meanings of the past as well as propose partisan positions for the future. They will coherently interrelate the various levels of cognitive and affective expression, from symbols, through

concepts and judgments of fact and value, to ideas and decisions. Secular behavior has its own interpretive tools, such as economic, political, and social
theory that understands individuals' and communities' performances. Christian action and thought, both as subjectively operative and as objectively
thematized, have their own interpretive techniques to clarify the sui generis
nature of their experience (the death and resurrection of Jesus) and to embody
it within the world.

A Mutually Critical Conversation

Theologians are engaged in a noetic praxis that demands thematization of
the inner claims of both secular and Christian thought and action as they interpret and change the praxis of the world.[35] The complexities of this conversation are manifold. Christian thought can meet the past as a historical-
critical recovery as well as a product of contemporary questions. Theology
can focus on the literary genres in the subject matter, noting their anthropological, sociological, and pragmatic consequences. Existential questions of society (e.g., feminism) can require a rereading of Christian history and
religious paradigms. Medieval patterns of monastic life and ordination contributed to the formation of feudal society. Notions of satisfaction for sin
decreased the frequency of tribal vendettas. Answers given by either the
world's praxis or Christian behavior can promote further conversation.

If, however, the possibility of interaction between all these elements is to
be more than idealistically and abstractly realized, each side must be willing
to enter a conversation. (1) Each must risk its own preunderstanding of the
subject matter, because each believes that it can only be freed from bias by
another with authentically differing perspectives. Believing that the other has
some autonomous unique knowledge and action to impart, Christians listen.
(2) The claim of the other must then hold weight *within* one's personal position. We allow the truth claims in the praxis of the other to draw us toward
a better practical understanding of the subject matter. (3) In dialogue, we respond appropriately to the questions and positions formulated by the other.
(4) In turn, the partners in dialogue return to their own wider communities
of discourse for confirmation and contrast. (5) Each then takes an appropriate action consistent with the responses discovered. (6) In time, collaboration
focuses common conversation.

What if the partners in dialogue are unwilling to risk their personal, social,
historical, and communal understandings?[36] There is the possibility, indeed,
the probability, of systematic distortion within the praxis of both past and
present. There are mistakes and blind alleys not only in intellectual journeys;
there are equally many failures in the experience of trial and error toward

pragmatic achievement of individual and social goods. Moreover, there are fears generated by even the most humble invitation by an authentic other over whom we have no control. We must be willing to suspend our congenital suspicious instincts that we are about to be "taken over" by our correspondent.[37] Besides the various biases (affective, intellectual, and social) that fog our conversations, there is the malice of sin, the refusal to listen, the decision to cheat, and the desire to lie. Existing dialogue is already riddled with negative as well as positive influences. To presume otherwise assumes a unidirectional innocent rationality, an ideal community of intelligent speakers. Praxis, especially noetic praxis, is never disinterested or so naive.

Part of what the Christian doctrinal position has thematized is the experience of grace, the existential knowledge that the only way the interdependent variables in the human conversation can function honestly will be through the liberation from sin that God alone gives. This claim maintains that in form and in content Christian subjects and thematizations embody a unique operator exceeding finite activity and explanation.

The gracious Actor who converses with us discloses divinity within changing human beings. Hence the criteria for determining authentic correlation among the various elements of Christian discussion are the transformation of the subject through what we have called four conversions and the incarnated change in objective thematizations (individually and socially embodied truth, justice, love, and self-emptying service). The dissymmetry between the goal of an unlimited, openhearted, and open-minded conversation and our innate limits or the intrinsic biases that poison it require both personal and social conversions.[38]

Christian Imagination

Critical Christian praxis is neither doctrinal propaganda nor self-interested moralism dictating to others their questions as well as their answers. Rather, our stance on the cognitive dimensions of faith requires a steady collaboration with all those willing to carry on a dialogue about the common human project. Because Christian praxis, as operative in the subject or thematized in the object, has the cultural baggage of its previous incarnations, it can only hope to use past particulars and the formal authenticity of its conversions as the subject matter for discussion. As believers listen to the secular, often postreligious, sometimes anti-Christian queries and responses of their dialogue partners, they must forge from the material a new shape for selves in society.

In such a complex conversation, the relative autonomy of the many partners will not build the uniform European Christendom of the past, and it will demand new multicultural, polyfocal cultural syntheses. Christians cannot retreat from societal transformation simply because the stakes have now become global instead of national or continental. The yearning restlessness and the recognition of sinful self-nihilism and oppression that propel Christians into continued conversion of self and of the worlds in which they live require ongoing commitment to the discovery of, and to the development of, effective words and gestures for the churches.

Christians create effective preaching and authentic sacraments through the incarnating imagination.[39] Imagination is the operative intentionality within human experience which discloses the real historical transformation within possible and alternative futures. The "real" of imaginative experience is dependent upon the "alternative," the willingness to suspend one's disbelief enough (to have faith) to enter into the creative artifact with the factual event of being changed. Imaginative cognition knows the truth by becoming part of the world disclosed by the object. Shocked into discovery by tumbling into symbols, stories, paintings, or melodies, participants become what they see and hear—however incipiently. For every human transformation is partial, incomplete, awakening in us a thirst for a greater horizon that defines itself in the particular art of the foreground.

The force behind the doctrinal or moral imperative and its stance in our world is the Christian imagination. Evangelical vision believes that eventually its critically imaginative praxis will liberate all realities to be at once authentically themselves and to point beyond themselves, disclosive of their origin. Christian imagination expresses authentically ecstatic believers operating in liberating patterns of experience in the world. Everyone will become words of the one Word and gestures of the one Sacrament—the Christ who belongs to God. "Yet you belong to Christ, and Christ to God" (1 Corinthians 3:23, NEB).

Sacrament: The Focus of a Catholic Stance

The doctrinal stance we have articulated centers on commitment to authentic gestures and words that transform both the subject and societies. Christian sacraments are traditionally described as symbolic disclosures of God's effective love during critical moments in human experience.[40] As affective, they negotiate the simultaneous awe and dread we feel in the presence of the divine. As effective, they counsel, persuade, and enact God's love, healing us in the progressive embodiment of our own mutual care. As cognitive, they tell us about the world God accomplishes in and for those who love. As constitutive, they establish a shared, ecclesial experience, founding communitarian potential as well as action. They communicate a traditional history that is passed down to our children through prayers, ritual gestures, and songs. As norms, the sacraments challenge us toward greater disposition to converted life in the world.

The typically Catholic focus for a doctrinal stance is therefore ecclesial and sacramental: social sign and cause of God's praxis of redeeming love in our world. Understood as sacrament, the doctrinal component of the Catholic stance is a church that is institutional but not reduced to its instrumental administrative techniques. The church is a community of believers and lovers rather than a clan with religious decorations, an easy sectarian nest for the socially frustrated, a department store for holiness where people can buy moral strength for desires they have and reject the products they don't like. Christian communities by their aggressive partisan involvement on the side of truth, justice, and love look for and create those progressive formulations that will transform social systems. Through the sacraments, they do not take out an insurance policy against their fears of themselves or of their world.

The sacraments are what the church is and wants to become. The sacramentalizing imagination of believers transforms Christians modestly but surely into the criterion that can discern the authentic from the inauthentic formulations of life in our world. As sacramental, the church supports and elicits truth and love; it contradicts error and incarnates the true and the good, however slowly, in itself as a mediating sign to and for the local environment and within the world.

CONCLUSION

Christian theology must take a stand in relationship to both its own past and the culture in which it exists. As a noetic praxis, it intends to clarify the confused meanings that occupy both Christians and non-Christians and to liberate them from the religious, social, and economic oppressions that paralyze their creative embrace of the world. Both reflection and change are at stake.

The stance we have proposed involves an imaginative rearticulation of both culture and faith. Each has an authentic role to play with its rightful methodological tools. The conversation can be engaged on the basis of truthful willingness to listen to one another. The biases or systematic distortions within human existence, however, make it clear that some active transformation of conversing speakers is required. Looking to articulate those transformative criteria, we have called for four conversions, through which it becomes possible to know with some certainty when the conversation is awry.

In other words, the experience of faith in Christ is prior to all formulations, including ecclesiastical ones, though it is only known through them. The origin of all expressions, faith, is overheard simultaneously in the words and gestures. Taking on the incarnate subjectivity of Christ changes us and the worlds in which we live in such a way that we cannot imagine doing anything but working for the realm of knowledge and love he makes real within us. The collaborative efforts in theology for building a new earth are dependent upon that foundational Word that initiates the conversation by which we exist and through which we are healed.

NOTES

1. For a more complete discussion of the stances that have been proposed within the Christian traditions, see James Sellers, *Theological Ethics* (New York: Macmillan Co., 1966), 31–68.

2. Adolf von Harnack, *What Is Christianity?* trans. T. B. Saunders (New York: Harper & Brothers, 1957), 70–74.

3. Karl Barth, *Church Dogmatics* II/2, trans. G. W. Bromiley et al. (Edinburgh: T. & T. Clark, 1957), 509–49.

4. Sellers, *Theological Ethics*, 55–65. For a critique of and an alternative to these stances already discussed, see Charles E. Curran, *New Perspectives in Moral Theology* (Notre Dame, Ind.: Fides Pubs., 1974), 47–86.

5. Matthew L. Lamb, *Solidarity with Victims: Toward a Theology of Social Transformation* (New York: Crossroad, 1982), 95. n. 75.

6. "Pastoral Constitution on the Church in the Modern World (*Gaudium et Spes*)," no. 36, in *The Documents of Vatican II*, ed. Walter M. Abbott (New York: American Press, 1966).

7. "Declaration on Religious Freedom (*Dignitatis Humanae*)," in *The Documents of Vatican II*, ed. Abbott.

8. John Courtney Murray, S.J., "The Issue of Church and State at Vatican Council II," *Theological Studies* 27 (1966): 509–606.

9. E.g., see Helmut Thielicke, *Theological Ethics*, vol. 1, *Foundations*, ed. William H. Lazareth (Grand Rapids: Wm. B. Eerdmans, 1979).

10. John Calvin, or several of his Protestant Reformed followers in this century, could also have been chosen for comparison with our stance, but the issues are clearer with Luther. For a comparison of the critical-dialogical stance with that of some advocates of the Reformed tradition (e.g., Karl Barth), see James J. Walter, "The Relation Between Faith and Morality: Sources for Christian Ethics," *Horizons* 9 (1982): 251–70.

11. Paul Althaus, *The Ethics of Martin Luther*, trans. Robert C. Schultz (Philadelphia: Fortress Press, 1972), 3–24.

12. Ibid., 43–82.

13. Lamb, *Solidarity with Victims*, 129.

14. For a standard introduction to these themes, see Paul Althaus, *The Theology of Martin Luther*, trans. Robert C. Schultz (Philadelphia: Fortress Press, 1966), 3–8, 43–63.

15. Ibid., 8.
16. Ibid., 60.
17. Ibid., 224–50.
18. Ibid., 179–223.
19. Ibid., 78.
20. Ibid., 18.
21. Ibid., 64–71.
22. Ibid., 6.
23. Ibid., 17–18.
24. Ibid., 8.
25. Ibid., 345 nn. 2–3.
26. Ibid., 346 n. 7.
27. Ibid., 345 n. 3.
28. Ibid., 346.
29. Ibid., 347–48 n. 17.
30. Ibid., 349 n. 20.
31. Ibid., 380 n. 16.
32. Ibid., 390 n. 40.
33. Ibid., 345–403.

34. Samuel Taylor Coleridge, *Aids to Reflection* (Port Washington, N.Y.: Kennikat Press, 1971), 201. The moving experiential character of this book comes partly from the possibility that readers may learn to appropriate "along the road" the goals of the journey.

35. For the emphasis upon praxis as originative of knowledge and action, see pages 107, 198–99. On the way that retroductive warrants in argumentation can become a hypothesis that generates illuminative inferences, see Francis Schüssler Fiorenza, *Foundational Theology: Jesus and the Church* (New York: Crossroad, 1984), 306–11. See also David Tracy's use of H. G. Gadamer (*Truth and Method*, trans. Garrett Barden and John Cumming [New York: Crossroad-Seabury Press, 1975], 235–447) in *The Analogical Imagination: Christian Theology and the Culture of Pluralism* (New York: Crossroad, 1981), 101ff.

36. See Helmut Peukert, *Science, Action, and Fundamental Theology: Towards a Theology of Communicative Action*, trans. James Bohman (Cambridge: M.I.T. Press, 1984), 164–93, 214–45.

37. See the description of the development of a social ontology in Michael Theunissen, *The Other: Studies in The Social Ontology of Husserl, Heidegger, Sartre, and Buber*, trans. Christopher Macann (Cambridge: M.I.T. Press, 1984), esp. the discussion of J.-P. Sartre, 199–243.

38. Lamb, *Solidarity with Victims*, 1–60, 109–15.

39. For a historical introduction to the development of the "productive imagination," see James Engell, *The Creative Imagination: Enlightenment to Romanticism* (Cambridge: Harvard Univ. Press, 1981).

40. For a description of this central Catholic theme, see Avery Dulles, "The Church: Sacrament and Ground of Faith," in *Problems and Perspectives of Fundamental Theology*, ed. René Latourelle and Gerald O'Collins, trans. Matthew J. O'Connell (New York: Paulist Press, 1982), 259–73; Stephen Happel, "The

Sacraments—Symbols That Redirect Our Desires," in *Desires of the Human Spirit: An Introduction to Bernard Lonergan*, ed. Vernon Gregson (New York: Paulist Press, forthcoming); and Fiorenza, *Foundational Theology*, 60–245.

FURTHER READINGS

Charles E. Curran. *Catholic Moral Theology in Dialogue*. Notre Dame, Ind.: Fides Pub., 1972.

James M. Gustafson. *Can Ethics Be Christian?* Chicago: Univ. of Chicago Press, 1975.

Stanley Hauerwas. *A Community of Character: Toward a Constructive Christian Social Ethic*. Notre Dame, Ind.: Univ. of Notre Dame Press, 1981.

Knud Løgstrup. *The Ethical Demand*, trans. Theodor I. Jensen. Philadelphia: Fortress Press, 1971.

H. Richard Niebuhr. *Christ and Culture*. New York: Harper & Brothers, 1951.

Reinhold Niebuhr. *Moral Man and Immoral Society: A Study in Ethics and Politics*. New York: Charles Scribner's Sons, 1960.

Paul Ramsey. *Basic Christian Ethics*. New York: Charles Scribner's Sons, 1950.

Gibson Winter. *Elements for a Social Ethic: The Role of Social Science in Public Policy*. New York: Macmillan Co., 1966.

John Howard Yoder. *The Politics of Jesus*. Grand Rapids: Wm. B. Eerdmans, 1972.

INDEX